Sunset

BEST HOME PLANS

One-Story Living

Contemporary plantation-style home packs plenty of style and flexibility
into modest square footage. See plan EOF-25 on page 151.

Sunset Publishing Corporation ■ Menlo Park, California

Photographers: Mark Englund: 4 bottom, 5 bottom; **Philip Harvey:** 10 top, back cover; **Stephen Marley:** 11 top left and right; **Kevin Robinson:** 5 top left and right; **Russ Widstrand:** 10 bottom; **Tom Wyatt:** 11 bottom.

Cover: Pictured is plan E-2302 on page 217. Cover design by Susan Bryant and Naganuma Design & Direction. Photography by Gil Ford.

Editor, Sunset Books: Elizabeth L. Hogan

Second printing April 1994

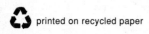 printed on recycled paper

A Dream Come True

Planning and building a house is one of life's most creative and rewarding challenges. Whether you're seriously considering building a new home or you're just dreaming about it, this book offers a wealth of inspiration and information to help you get started.

On the following pages, you'll learn how to plan and manage a home-building project—and how to ensure its success. Then you'll discover more than 200 proven home plans, designed for families just like yours by architects and professional designers. Peruse the pages and study the floor plans; you're sure to find a home that's just right for you. When you're ready to order blueprints, you can simply call or mail in your order, and you'll receive the plans within days.

Enjoy the adventure!

Contents

Featuring a distinctive exterior of brick and wood, this budget-minded single-story home offers three bedrooms and two full baths. See plan E-1212 on page 36.

Single-Story Living

Are you thinking or dreaming about building a custom home? One of your first decisions will be whether to build a one-story or a multi-level house, a choice based on the building site you have in mind and your family's needs and preferences.

What are the benefits of a single-story house? Young families often prefer a home where bedrooms and bathrooms are in convenient proximity, where the master bedroom is within easy earshot of the nursery, and where the dangers posed by staircases are avoided. For older people, the ease of getting around a one-story home is primary.

Moreover, a low-profile, one-story house won't overwhelm a neighborhood with its bulk, as a two-story house can. Single-story homes are also easier to build, simpler to maintain, and have more flexible interiors—living spaces without floors overhead allow for dramatic vaulted ceilings, clerestory windows, and generous use of skylights.

The two keys to success in building are capable project management and good design. The next few pages will walk you through some of the most important aspects of project management: you'll find an overview of the building process, directions for selecting the right plan and getting the most from it, and methods for successfully working with a builder and other professionals.

The balance of the book presents professionally designed plans for single-level houses in a wide range of styles and configurations. Once you find a plan that will work for you—perhaps with a few modifications made later to personalize it for your family—you can order construction blueprints for a fraction of the cost of a custom design, a savings of many thousands of dollars (see pages 12–15 for information on how to order).

Gracefully arching windows accent this expansive, single-story family home. See plan DD-2802 on page 218.

Behind the traditional façade of this French-style home lies an open floor plan with generous entertaining areas that open to a covered porch. See plan E-2004 on page 224.

Designed for a hillside, this contemporary home features a vaulted ceiling in the living/dining area and a two-car garage below. See plan H-2045-5 on page 222.

Single-story brick home, relatively modest from the curb, surprises with its angular rooms. Optional plan includes a daylight basement. See plans P-7661-3A and -3D on page 149.

The Art of Building

As you embark on your home-building project, think of it as a trip—clearly not a vacation but rather an interesting, adventurous, at times difficult expedition. Meticulous planning will make your journey not only far more enjoyable but also much more successful. By careful planning, you can avoid—or at least minimize—some of the pitfalls along the way.

Start with realistic expectations of the road ahead. To do this, you'll want to gain an understanding of the basic house-building process, settle on a design that will work for you and your family, and make sure your project is actually doable. By taking those initial steps, you can gain a clear idea of how much time, money, and energy you'll need to invest to make your dream come true.

The Building Process

Your role in planning and managing a house-building project can be divided into two parts: prebuilding preparation and construction management.

■ **Prebuilding preparation.** This is where you should focus most of your attention. In the hands of a qualified contractor whose expertise you can rely on, the actual building process should go fairly smoothly. But during most of the prebuilding stage, you're generally on your own. Your job will be to launch the project and develop a talented team that can help you bring your new home to fruition.

When you work with stock plans, the prebuilding process usually goes as follows:

First, you research the general area where you want to live, selecting one or more possible home sites (unless you already own a suitable lot). Then you choose a basic house design, with the idea that it may require some modification. Finally, you analyze the site, the design, and your budget to determine if the project is actually attainable.

If you decide that it is, you purchase the land and order blueprints. If you want to modify them, you consult an architect, designer, or contractor. Once the plans are finalized, you request bids from contractors and arrange any necessary construction financing.

After selecting a builder and signing a contract, you (or your contractor) then file the plans with the building department. When the plans are approved, often several weeks—or even months—later, you're ready to begin construction.

■ **Construction management.** Unless you intend to act as your own contractor, your role during the building process is mostly one of quality control and time management. Even so, it's important to know the sequence of events and something about construction methods so you can discuss progress with your builder and prepare for any important decisions you may need to make along the way.

Decision-making is critical. Once construction begins, the builder must usually plunge ahead, keeping his carpenters and subcontractors progressing steadily. If you haven't made a key decision—which model bathtub or sink to install, for example—it can bring construction to a frustrating and expensive halt.

Usually, you'll make such decisions before the onset of building, but, inevitably, some issue or another will arise during construction. Being knowledgeable about the building process will help you anticipate and circumvent potential logjams.

Selecting a House Plan

Searching for the right plan can be a fun, interactive family experience—one of the most exciting parts of a house-building project. Gather the family around as you peruse the home plans in this book. Study the size, location, and configuration of each room; traffic patterns both inside the house and to the outdoors; exterior style; and how you'll use the available space. Discuss the pros and cons of the various plans.

Browse through pictures of homes in magazines to stimulate ideas. Clip the photos you like so you can think about your favorite options. When you visit the homes of friends, note special features that appeal to you. Also, look carefully at the homes in your neighborhood, noting their style and how they fit the site.

Mark those plans that most closely suit your ideals. Then, to narrow down your choices, critique each plan, using the following information as a guide.

■ **Overall size and budget.** How large a house do you want? Will the house you're considering fit your family's requirements? Look at the overall square footage and room sizes. If you have a hard time visualizing room sizes, measure some of the rooms in your present home and compare.

It's often better for the house to be a little too big than a little too small, but remember that every extra square foot will cost more money to build and maintain.

■ **Number and type of rooms.** Beyond thinking about the number of bedrooms and baths you want, consider your family's life-style and how you use space. Do you want both a family room and a living room? Do you need a formal dining space? Will you require some extra rooms, or "swing spaces," that can serve multiple purposes, such as a home office–guest room combination?

■ **Room placement and traffic patterns.** What are your preferences for locations of formal living areas, master bedroom, and children's rooms? Do you prefer a kitchen that's open to family areas or one that's private and out of the way? How much do you use exterior spaces and how should they relate to the interior?

Once you make those determinations, look carefully at the floor plan of the house you're considering to see if it meets your needs and if the traffic flow will be convenient for your family.

Architectural style. Have you always wanted to live in a Victorian farmhouse? Now is your chance to create a house that matches your idea of "home" (taking into account, of course, styles in your neighborhood). But don't let your preference for one particular architectural style dictate your home's floor plan. If the floor plan doesn't work for your family, keep looking.

Site considerations. Most people choose a site before selecting a plan—or at least they've zeroed in on the basic type of land where they'll situate their house. It sounds elementary, but choose a house that will fit the site.

When figuring the "footprint" of a house, you must know about any restrictions that will affect your home's height or proximity to the property lines. Call the local building department (look under city or county listings in the phone book) and get a very clear description of any restrictions, such as setbacks, height limits, and lot coverage, that will affect what you can build on the site (see "Working with City Hall," at right).

When you visit potential sites, note trees, rock outcroppings, slopes, views, winds, sun, neighboring homes, and other factors. All will impact on how your house works on a particular site.

Once you've narrowed down the choice of sites, consult an architect or building designer (see page 8) to help you evaluate how some potential houses will work on the sites you have in mind.

Is Your Project Doable?

Before you purchase land, make sure your project is doable. Although it's too early at this stage to pinpoint costs, making a few phone calls will help you determine whether your project is realistic. You'll be able to learn if you can afford to build the house, how long it will take, and what obstacles may stand in your way.

To get a ballpark estimate of cost, multiply a house's total square footage (of livable space) by the local average cost per square foot for new construction. (To obtain local averages, call a contractor, an architect, a realtor, or the local chapter of the National Association of Home Builders.) Some contractors may even be willing to give you a preliminary bid. Once you know approximate costs, speak to your lender to explore financing.

Working with City Hall

For any building project, even a minor one, it's essential to be familiar with building codes and other restrictions that can affect your project.

Building codes, generally implemented by the city or county building department, set the standards for safe, lasting construction. Codes specify minimum construction techniques and materials for foundations, framing, electrical wiring, plumbing, insulation, and all other aspects of a building. Although codes are adopted and enforced locally, most regional codes conform to the standards set by the national Uniform Building Code, Standard Building Code, or Basic Building Code. In some cases, local codes set more restrictive standards than national ones.

Building permits are required for home-building projects nearly everywhere. If you work with a contractor, the builder's firm should handle all necessary permits.

More than one permit may be needed; for example, one will cover the foundation, another the electrical wiring, and still another the heating equipment installation. Each will probably involve a fee and require inspections by building officials before work can proceed. (Inspections benefit *you*, as they ensure that the job is being done satisfactorily.) Permit fees are generally a percentage (1 to 1.5 percent) of the project's estimated value, often calculated on square footage.

It's important to file for the necessary permits. Failure to do so can result in fines or legal action against you. You can even be forced to undo the work performed. At the very least, your negligence may come back to haunt you later when you're ready to sell your house.

Zoning ordinances, particular to your community, restrict setbacks (how near to property lines you may build), your house's allowable height, lot coverage factors (how much of your property you can cover with structures), and other factors that impact design and building. If your plans don't conform to zoning ordinances, you can try to obtain a variance, an exception to the rules. But this legal work can be expensive and time-consuming. Even if you prove that your project won't negatively affect your neighbors, the building department can still refuse to grant the variance.

Deeds and covenants attach to the lot. Deeds set out property lines and easements; covenants may establish architectural standards in a neighborhood. Since both can seriously impact your project, make sure you have complete information on any deeds or covenants before you turn over a spadeful of soil.

It's a good idea to discuss your project with several contractors (see page 8). They may be aware of problems in your area that could limit your options—bedrock that makes digging basements difficult, for example. These conversations are actually the first step in developing a list of contractors from which you'll choose the one who will build your home.

Recruiting Your Home Team

A home-building project will inter-ject you and your family into the building business, an area that may be unfamiliar territory. Among the people you'll be working with are architects, designers, landscapers, contractors, and subcontractors.

Design Help

A qualified architect or designer can help you modify and personal-ize your home plan, taking into account your family's needs and budget and the house's style. In fact, you may want to consider consulting such a person while you're selecting a plan to help you articulate your needs.

Design professionals are capable of handling any or all aspects of the design process. For example, they can review your house plans, suggest options, and then provide rough sketches of the options on tracing paper. Many architects will even secure needed permits and negotiate with contractors or sub-contractors, as well as oversee the quality of the work.

Of course, you don't necessarily need an architect or designer to implement minor changes in a plan; although most contractors aren't trained in design, some can help you with modifications.

An open-ended, hourly-fee arrangement that you work out with your architect or designer allows for flexibility, but it often turns out to be more costly than working on a flat-fee basis. On a flat fee, you agree to pay a specific amount of money for a certain amount of work.

To find architects and designers, contact such trade associations as the American Institute of Architects (AIA), American Institute of Build-ing Designers (AIBD), American Society of Landscape Architects (ASLA), and American Society of Interior Designers (ASID). Although many professionals choose not to belong to trade associations, those who do have met the standards of their respective associations. For phone numbers of local branches, check the Yellow Pages.

■ **Architects** are licensed by the state and have degrees. They're trained in all facets of building design and construction. Although some can handle interior design and structural engineering, others hire specialists for those tasks.

■ **Building designers** are generally unlicensed but may be accredited by the American Institute of Building Designers. Their back-grounds are varied: some may be unlicensed architects in apprentice-ship; others are interior designers or contractors with design skills.

■ **Draftspersons** offer an economi-cal route to making simple changes on your drawings. Like building designers, these people may be unlicensed architect apprentices, engineers, or members of related trades. Most are accomplished at drawing up plans.

■ **Interior designers,** as their job title suggests, design interiors. They work with you to choose room fin-ishes, furnishings, appliances, and decorative elements. Part of their expertise is in arranging furnishings to create a workable space plan. Some interior designers are em-ployed by architectural firms; others work independently. Financial arrangements vary, depending on the designer's preference.

Related professionals are kitchen and bathroom designers, who con-centrate on fixtures, cabinetry, appliances, materials, and space planning for the kitchen and bath.

■ **Landscape architects, design-ers, and contractors** design out-door areas. Landscape architects are state-licensed to practice landscape design. A landscape designer usual-ly has a landscape architect's educa-tion and training but does not have a state license. Licensed landscape contractors specialize in garden construction, though some also have design skills and experience.

■ **Soils specialists and structural engineers** may be needed for proj-ects where unstable soils or uncom-mon wind loads or seismic forces must be taken into account. Any

structural changes to a house re-quire the expertise of a structural engineer to verify that the house won't fall down.

Services of these specialists can be expensive, but they're impera-tive in certain conditions to ensure a safe, sturdy structure. Your build-ing department will probably let you know if their services are re-quired.

General Contractors

To build your house, hire a licensed general contractor. Most states re-quire a contractor to be licensed and insured for worker's compensa-tion in order to contract a building project and hire other subcontrac-tors. State licensing ensures that contractors have met minimum training standards and have a spec-ified level of experience. Licensing does not guarantee, however, that they're good at what they do.

When contractors hire subcon-tractors, they're responsible for overseeing the quality of work and materials of the subcontractors and for paying them.

■ **Finding a contractor.** How do you find a good contractor? Start by getting referrals from people you know who have built or remodeled their home. Nothing beats a personal recommendation. The best contractors are usually busily moving from one satisfied client to another prospect, adver-tised only by word of mouth.

You can also ask local real estate brokers and lenders or even your building inspector for names of qualified builders. Experienced lumber dealers are another good source of names.

In the Yellow Pages, look under "Contractors–Building, General"; or call the local chapter of the National Association of Home Builders.

■ **Choosing a contractor.** Once you have a list of names of pro-spective builders, call several of them. On the telephone, ask first whether they handle your type of job and can work within your schedule. If they can, arrange a meeting with each one and ask them to be prepared with references of former clients and photos of previous jobs. Better still, meet them at one of their current work sites so you can get a glimpse of the quality of their work and how organized and thorough they are.

Take your plan to the meeting and discuss it enough to request a rough estimate (some builders will comply, while others will be reluctant to offer a ballpark estimate, preferring to give you a hard bid based on complete drawings). Don't hesitate to probe for advice or suggestions that might make building your house less expensive.

Be especially aware of each contractor's personality and how well you communicate. Good chemistry between you and your builder is a key ingredient for success.

Narrow down the candidates to three or four. Ask each for a firm bid, based on the exact same set of plans and specifications. For the bids to be accurate, your plans need to be complete and the specifications as precise as possible, call-

ing out particular appliances, fixtures, floorings, roofing material, and so forth. (Some of these are specified in a stock-plan set; others are not.)

Call the contractors' references and ask about the quality of their work, their relationship with their clients, their promptness, and their readiness to follow up on problems. Visit former clients to check the contractor's work firsthand.

Be sure your final candidates are licensed, bonded, and insured for worker's compensation, public liability, and property damage. Also, try to determine how financially solvent they are (you can call their bank and credit references). Avoid contractors who are operating hand-to-mouth.

Don't automatically hire the contractor with the lowest bid if you don't think you'll get along well or if you have any doubts about the quality of the person's work. Instead, look for both the most reasonable bid and the contractor with the best credentials, references, terms, and compatibility with your family.

A word about bonds: You can request a performance bond that guarantees that your job will be finished by your contractor. If the job isn't completed, the bonding company will cover the cost of hiring another contractor to finish it. Bonds cost from 2 to 6 percent of the value of the project.

Your Building Contract

A building contract (see below) binds and protects both you and your contractor. It isn't just a legal document. It's also a list of the expectations of both parties. The best way to minimize the possibility of misunderstandings and costly changes later on is to write down every possible detail. Whether the contract is a standard form or one composed by you, have an attorney look it over before both you and the contractor sign it.

The contract should clearly specify all the work that needs to be done, including particular materials and work descriptions, the time schedule, and method of payment. It should be keyed to the working drawings.

A Sample Building Contract

Project and participants. Give a general description of the project, its address, and the names and addresses of both you and the builder.

Construction materials. Identify all construction materials by brand name, quality markings (species, grades, etc.), and model numbers where applicable. Avoid the clause "or equal," which allows the builder to substitute other materials for your choices. For materials you can't specify now, set down a budget figure.

Time schedule. Include both start and completion dates and specify that work will be "continuous." Although a contractor cannot be responsible for delays caused by strikes and material shortages, your builder should assume responsibility for completing the project within a reasonable period of time.

Work to be performed. State all work you expect the contractor to perform, from initial grading to finished painting.

Method and schedule of payment. Specify how and when payments are to be made. Typical agreements specify installment payments as particular phases of work are completed. Final payment is withheld until the job receives its final inspection and is cleared of all liens.

Waiver of liens. Protect yourself with a waiver of liens signed by the general contractor, the subcontractors, and all major suppliers. That way, subcontractors who are not paid for materials or services cannot place a lien on your property.

Personalizing Stock Plans

The beauty of buying stock plans for your new home is that they offer tested, well-conceived design at an affordable price. And stock plans dramatically reduce the time it takes to design a house, since the plans are ready when you are.

Because they were not created specifically for your family, stock plans may not reflect your personal taste. But it's not difficult to make revisions in stock plans that will turn your home into an expression of your family's personality. You'll surely want to add personal touches and choose your own finishes.

Ideally, the modifications you implement will be fairly minor. The more extensive the changes, the more expensive the plans. Major changes take valuable design time, and those that affect a house's structure may require a structural engineer's approval.

If you anticipate wholesale changes, such as moving a number of bearing walls or changing the roofline significantly, you may be better off selecting another plan. On the other hand, reconfiguring or changing the sizes of some rooms can probably be handled fairly easily.

Some structural changes may even be necessary to comply with local codes. Your area may have specific requirements for snow loads, energy codes, seismic or wind resistance, and so forth. Those types of modifications are likely to require the services of an architect or structural engineer.

Plan Modifications

Before you pencil in any changes, live with your plans for a while. Study them carefully—at your building site, if possible. Try to picture the finished house: how rooms will interrelate, where the sun will enter and at what angle, what the view will be from each window. Think about traffic patterns, access to rooms, room sizes, window and door locations, natural light, and kitchen and bathroom layouts.

Typical changes might involve adding windows or skylights to bring in natural light or capture a view. Or you may want to widen a hallway or doorway for roomier access, extend a room, eliminate doors, or change window and door sizes. Perhaps you'd like to shorten a room, stealing the gained space for a large closet. Look closely at the kitchen; it's not difficult to reconfigure the layout if it makes the space more convenient for you.

Above all, take your time—this is your home and it should reflect your taste and needs. Make your changes now, during the planning stage. Once construction begins, it will take crowbars, hammers, saws, new materials, and, most significantly, time to alter the plans. Because changes are not part of your building contract, you can count on them being expensive extras once construction begins.

Specifying Finishes

One way to personalize a house without changing its structure is to substitute your favorite finishes for those specified on the plan.

Would you prefer a stuccoed exterior rather than the wood siding shown on the plan? In most cases, this is a relatively easy change. Do you like the look of a wood shingle roof rather than the composition shingles shown on the plan? This, too, is easy. Perhaps you would like to change the windows from sliders to casements, or upgrade to high-efficiency glazing. No problem. Many of those kinds of changes can be worked out with your contractor.

Inside, you may want hardwood where vinyl flooring is shown. In fact, you can—and should—choose types, colors, and styles of floorings, wall coverings, tile, plumbing fixtures, door hardware, cabinetry, appliances, lighting fixtures, and other interior details, for it's these materials that will personalize your home. For help in making selections, consult an architect or interior designer (see page 8).

Each material you select should be spelled out clearly and precisely in your building contract.

Finishing touches can transform a house built from stock plans into an expression of your family's taste and style. Clockwise, from far left: Colorful tilework and custom cabinetry enliven a bathroom (Design: Osburn Design); highly organized closet system maximizes storage space (Architect: David Jeremiah Hurley); low-level deck expands living space to outdoor areas (Landscape architects: The Runa Group, Inc.); built-ins convert the corner of a guest room into a home office (Design: Lynn Williams of The French Connection); French country cabinetry lends style and old-world charm to a kitchen (Design: Garry Bishop/Showcase Kitchens).

What the Plans Include

Complete construction blueprints are available for every house shown in this book. Clear and concise, these detailed blueprints are designed by licensed architects or members of the American Institute of Building Designers (AIBD). Each plan is designed to meet standards set down by nationally recognized building codes (the Uniform Building Code, Standard Building Code, or Basic Building Code) at the time and for the area where they were drawn.

Remember, however, that every state, county, and municipality has its own codes, zoning requirements, ordinances, and building regulations. Modifications may be necessary to comply with such local requirements as snow loads, energy codes, seismic zones, and flood areas.

Although blueprint sets vary depending on the size and complexity of the house and on the individual designer's style, each set may include the elements described below and shown at right.

■ **Exterior elevations** show the front, rear, and sides of the house, including exterior materials, details, and measurements.

■ **Foundation plans** include drawings for a full, partial, or daylight basement, crawlspace, pole, pier, or slab foundation. All necessary notations and dimensions are included. (Foundation options will vary for each plan. If the plan you choose doesn't have the type of foundation you desire, a generic conversion diagram is available.)

■ **Detailed floor plans** show the placement of interior walls and the dimensions of rooms, doors, windows, stairways, and similar elements for each level of the house.

■ **Cross sections** show details of the house as though it were cut in slices from the roof to the foundation. The cross sections give the home's construction, insulation, flooring, and roofing details.

■ **Interior elevations** show the specific details of cabinets (kitchen, bathroom, and utility room), fireplaces, built-in units, and other special interior features.

■ **Roof details** give the layout of rafters, dormers, gables, and other roof elements, including clerestory windows and skylights. These details may be shown on the elevation sheet or on a separate diagram.

■ **Schematic electrical layouts** show the suggested locations for switches, fixtures, and outlets. These details may be shown on the floor plan or on a separate diagram.

■ **General specifications** provide instructions and information regarding excavation and grading, masonry and concrete work, carpentry and woodwork, thermal and moisture protection, drywall, tile, flooring, glazing, and caulking and sealants.

Other Helpful Building Aids

In addition to the construction information on every set of plans, you can buy the following guides.

■ **Reproducible blueprints** are helpful if you'll be making changes to the stock plan you've chosen. These blueprints are original line drawings produced on erasable, reproducible paper for the purpose of modification. When alterations are complete, working copies can be made.

■ **Itemized materials list** details the quantity, type, and size of materials needed to build your home. (This list is extremely helpful in obtaining an accurate construction bid. It's not intended for use to order materials.)

■ **Mirror-reverse plans** are useful if you want to build your home in the reverse of the plan that's shown. Because the lettering and dimensions read backwards, be sure to buy at least one regular-reading set of blueprints.

■ **Description of materials** gives the type and quality of materials suggested for the home. This form may be required for obtaining FHA or VA financing.

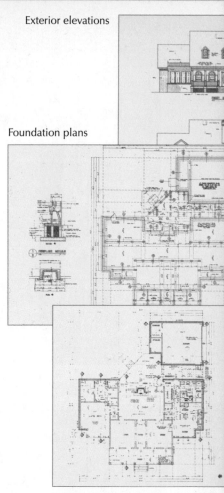

Exterior elevations

Foundation plans

Detailed floor plans

■ **How-to diagrams** for plumbing, wiring, solar heating, framing and foundation conversions show how to plumb, wire, install a solar heating system, convert plans with 2 by 4 exterior walls to 2 by 6 construction (or vice versa), and adapt a plan for a basement, crawlspace, or slab foundation. These diagrams are not specific to any one plan.

NOTE: Due to regional variations, local availability of materials, local codes, methods of installation, and individual preferences, detailed heating, plumbing, and electrical specifications are not included on plans. The duct work, venting, and other details will vary, depending on the heating and cooling system you use and the type of energy that operates it. These details and specifications are easily obtained from your builder or local supplier.

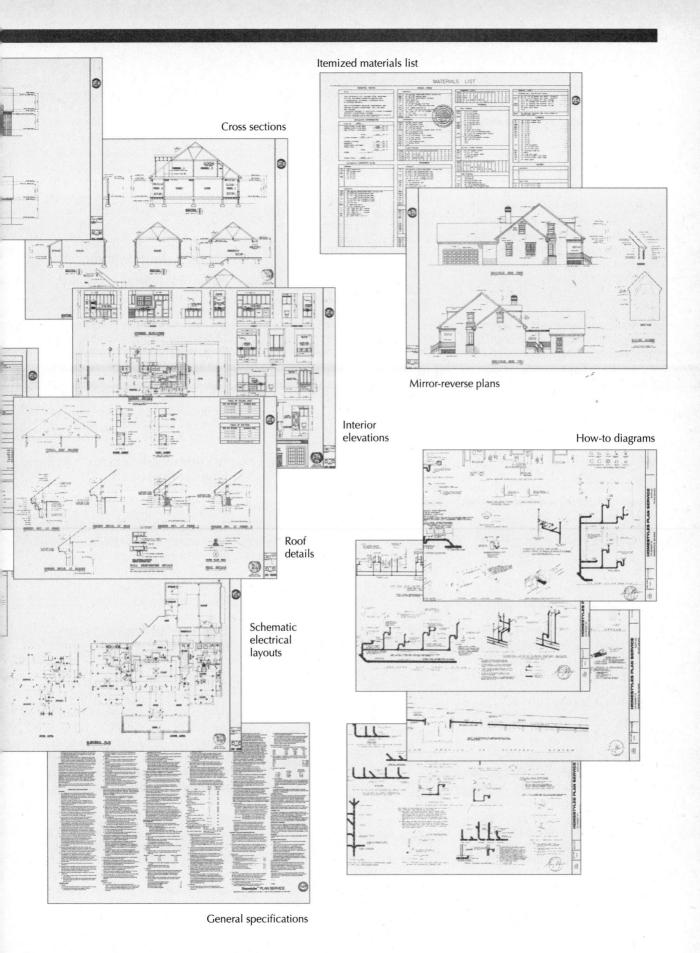

Itemized materials list

Cross sections

Mirror-reverse plans

Interior elevations

How-to diagrams

Roof details

Schematic electrical layouts

General specifications

Before You Order

Once you've chosen the one or two house plans that work best for you, you're ready to order blueprints. Before filling in the form on the facing page, note the information that follows.

How Many Blueprints Will You Need?

A single set of blueprints will allow you to study a home design in detail. You'll need more for obtaining bids and permits, as well as some to use as reference at the building site. If you'll be modifying your home plan, order a reproducible set (see page 12).

Figure you'll need at least one set each for yourself, your builder, the building department, and your lender. In addition, some subcontractors—foundation, plumber, electrician, and HVAC—may also need at least partial sets. If they do, ask them to return the sets when they're finished. The chart below can help you calculate how many sets you're likely to need.

Blueprint Checklist

____ Owner's set(s)

____ **Builder usually requires at least three sets: one for legal documentation, one for inspections, and a minimum of one set for subcontractors.**

____ **Building department requires at least one set. Check with your local department before ordering.**

____ **Lending institution usually needs one set for a conventional mortgage, three sets for FHA or VA loans.**

____ **TOTAL SETS NEEDED**

Blueprint Prices

The cost of having an architect design a new custom home typically runs from 5 to 15 percent of the building cost, or from $5,000 to $15,000 for a $100,000 home. A single set of blueprints for the plans in this book ranges from $265 to $550, depending on the house's size. Working with these drawings, you can save enough on design fees to add a deck, a swimming pool, or a luxurious kitchen.

Pricing is based on "total finished living space." Garages, porches, decks, and unfinished basements are not included.

Price Code (Size)	1 Set	4 Sets	7 Sets	Reproducible Set
A (under 1,500 sq. ft.)	$265	$310	$340	$440
B (1,500-1,999 sq. ft.)	$300	$345	$375	$475
C (2,000-2,499 sq. ft.)	$335	$380	$410	$510
D (2,500-2,999 sq. ft.)	$370	$415	$445	$545
E (3,000-3,499 sq. ft.)	$405	$450	$480	$580
F (3,500-3,999 sq. ft.)	$440	$485	$515	$615
G (4,000 sq. ft. and up)	$475	$520	$550	$650

Building Costs

Building costs vary widely, depending on a number of factors, including local material and labor costs and the finishing materials you select. For help estimating costs, see "Is Your Project Doable?" on page 7.

Foundation Options & Exterior Construction

Depending on your site and climate, your home will be built with a slab, pier, pole, crawlspace, or basement foundation. Exterior walls will be framed with either 2 by 4s or 2 by 6s, determined by structural and insulation standards in your area. Most contractors can easily adapt a home to meet the foundation and/or wall requirements for your area. Or ask for a conversion how-to diagram (see page 12).

Service & Blueprint Delivery

Service representatives are available to answer questions and assist you in placing your order. Every effort is made to process and ship orders within 48 hours.

Returns & Exchanges

Each set of blueprints is specially printed and shipped to you in response to your specific order; consequently, requests for refunds cannot be honored. However, if the prints you order cannot be used, you may exchange them for another plan from any Sunset home plan book. For an exchange, you must return all sets of plans within 30 days. A nonrefundable service charge will be assessed for all exchanges; for more information, call the toll-free number on the facing page. Note: Reproducible sets cannot be exchanged or returned.

Compliance with Local Codes & Regulations

Because of climatic, geographic, and political variations, building codes and regulations vary from one area to another. These plans are authorized for your use expressly conditioned on your obligation and agreement to comply strictly with all local building codes, ordinances, regulations, and requirements, including permits and inspections at time of construction.

Architectural & Engineering Seals

With increased concern about energy costs and safety, many cities and states now require that an architect or engineer review and "seal" a blueprint prior to construction. To find out whether this is a requirement in your area, contact your local building department.

License Agreement, Copy Restrictions & Copyright

When you purchase your blueprints, you are granted the right to use those documents to construct a single unit. All the plans in this publication are protected under the Federal Copyright Act, Title XVII of the United States Code and Chapter 37 of the Code of Federal Regulations. Each designer retains title and ownership of the original documents. The blueprints licensed to you cannot be used by or resold to any other person, copied, or reproduced by any means. The copying restrictions do not apply to reproducible blueprints. When you buy a reproducible set, you may modify and reproduce it for your own use.

Blueprint Order Form

Complete this order form in just three easy steps. Then mail in your order or, for faster service, call toll-free.

1. Blueprints & Accessories

BLUEPRINT CHART

Price Code	1 Set	4 Sets	7 Sets	Reproducible Set*
A	$265	$310	$340	$440
B	$300	$345	$375	$475
C	$335	$380	$410	$510
D	$370	$415	$445	$545
E	$405	$450	$480	$580
F	$440	$485	$515	$615
G	$475	$520	$550	$650

Prices subject to change

*A reproducible set is produced on erasable paper for the purpose of modification. It is only available for plans with prefixes AG, AGH, AH, AHP, APS, AX, B, BOD, C, CPS, DD, DW, E, EOF, FB, GL, GML, GSA, H, HDS, HFL, J, K, KLF, LMB, LRD, M, NW, OH, PH, PI, PM, S, SDG, THD, U, UDG, V.

Mirror-Reverse Sets: $40 surcharge. From the total number of sets you ordered above, choose the number you want to be reversed. *Note: All writing on mirror-reverse plans is backwards. Order at least one regular-reading set.*

Itemized Materials List: One set $40; each additional set $10. Details the quantity, type, and size of materials needed to build your home.

Description of Materials: Sold in a set of two for $40 (for use in obtaining FHA or VA financing).

Typical How-To Diagrams: One set $12.50; two sets $23; three sets $30; four sets $35. General guides on plumbing, wiring, and solar heating, plus information on how to convert from one foundation or exterior framing to another. *Note: These diagrams are not specific to any one plan.*

2. Sales Tax & Shipping

Determine your subtotal and add appropriate local state sales tax, plus shipping and handling (see chart below).

SHIPPING & HANDLING

	1–3 Sets	4–6 Sets/ Reproducible Set	7 or More Sets
U.S. Regular (4–6 working days)	$12.50	$15.00	$17.50
U.S. Express (2 working days)	$25.00	$27.50	$30.00
Canada Regular (2–3 weeks)	$12.50	$15.00	$17.50
Canada Express (4–6 working days)	$25.00	$30.00	$35.00
Overseas/Airmail (7–10 working days)	$50.00	$60.00	$70.00

3. Customer Information

Choose the method of payment you prefer. Include check, money order, or credit card information, complete name and address portion, and mail to:

Sunset/HomeStyles Plan Service
P.O. Box 50670
Minneapolis, MN 55405

FOR FASTER SERVICE CALL 1-800-547-5570

SS04

COMPLETE THIS FORM

Plan Number _____ Price Code _____

Foundation_____
(Review your plan carefully for foundation options—basement, pole, pier, crawlspace, or slab. Many plans offer several options; others offer only one.)

Number of Sets: $_____
- ☐ One Set   (See chart at left)
- ☐ Four Sets
- ☐ Seven Sets
- ☐ One Reproducible Set

Additional Sets _____ $_____
                                                ($35 each)

Mirror-Reverse Sets _____ $_____
                                                ($40 surcharge)

Itemized Materials List $_____
Only available for plans with prefixes AH, AHP, APS*, AX, B*, C, CAR, CDG*, CPS, DD*, DW, E, FB, GSA, H, HFL, I, J, K, LMB*, LRD, N, NW*, P, PH, R, S, THD, U, UDG, VL. *Not available on all plans. Please call before ordering.

Description of Materials $_____
Only available for plans with prefixes AHP, C, DW, H, HFL, J, K, LMB, N, P, PH, VL.

Typical How-To Diagrams $_____
- ☐ Plumbing ☐ Wiring ☐ Solar Heating ☐ Foundation & Framing Conversion

SUBTOTAL	$_____
SALES TAX	$_____
SHIPPING & HANDLING	$_____
GRAND TOTAL	$_____

☐ Check/money order enclosed (in U.S. funds)
☐ VISA ☐ MasterCard ☐ AmEx ☐ Discover

Credit
Card # _____ Exp. Date _____

Signature _____

Name _____

Address _____

City _____ State _____ Country _____

Zip _____ Daytime Phone (_____)_____
☐ Please check if you are a contractor.

Mail form to: Sunset/HomeStyles Plan Service
P.O. Box 50670
Minneapolis, MN 55405

Or Fax to: (612) 338-1626

FOR FASTER SERVICE CALL 1-800-547-5570

SS04

Angles Open Rear of Home to More Sunshine

PATIO

PORCH
12' x 6'

DINING
12' x 12'

MASTER SUITE
16' x 12'

BED RM.
14' x 12'

BAR

DW SINK

KITCHEN

LIVING
18' x 16'

HALL

BATH

REF.

RANGE

BATH

CLO.

PANT
BRM
STOR

UTIL
9' x 6'

STORAGE
10' x 6'

CLO.

ENTRY

CLO.

BED RM.
14' x 12'

50'

ATTIC STAIRS

PORCH
8' x 4'

GARAGE
22' x 22'

AREAS

Living	1415 sq. ft.
Porches	114 sq. ft.
Garage, Storage Equip.	565 sq. ft.
Total	2094 sq. ft.

Exterior walls are 2x6 construction.
Specify crawlspace or slab foundation.

56'

Blueprint Price Code A
Plan E-1424

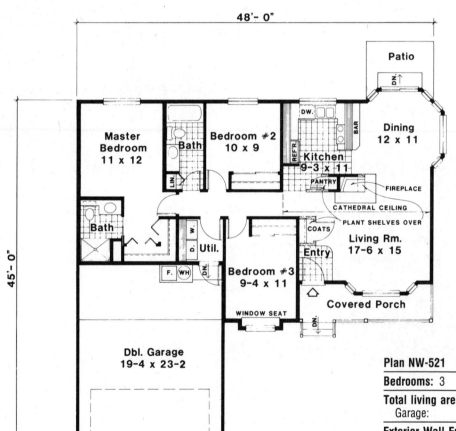

48'- 0"

Patio

DN.

DW.

Dining
12 x 11

REF'R.

BAR

Master
Bedroom
11 x 12

Bath

Bedroom #2
10 x 9

Kitchen
9-3 x 11

LIN.

PANTRY

FIREPLACE

CATHEDRAL CEILING

Bath

D. W.

Util.

COATS

PLANT SHELVES OVER

Living Rm.
17-6 x 15

F.

WH

DN.

Bedroom #3
9-4 x 11

Entry

45'- 0"

WINDOW SEAT

DN.

Covered Porch

Dbl. Garage
19-4 x 23-2

Classic One-Story Farmhouse

- This classic farmhouse design features a shady and inviting front porch.
- Inside, vaulted ceilings in the living and dining rooms make the home seem larger than it really is.
- An abundance of windows brightens up the living room and dining area.
- The functional kitchen includes a pantry and plenty of cabinet space.
- The master bedroom boasts a mirrored dressing area, private bath and abundant closet space.
- Bedroom 3 includes a cozy window seat.

Plan NW-521

Bedrooms: 3	Baths: 2
Total living area:	1,187 sq. ft.
Garage:	448 sq. ft.
Exterior Wall Framing:	2x6

Foundation options:
Crawlspace only.
(Foundation & framing conversion diagram available — see order form.)

Blueprint Price Code:	A

Plan NW-521

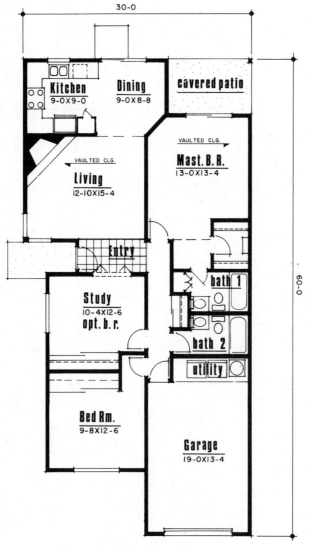

Vaulted Ceilings in Long, Low Plan

- Both the living room and master suite feature vaulted ceilings.
- Living room focuses on distinctive corner fireplace.
- Living and dining rooms flow together to make big space for entertaining.
- Master suite includes private bath and large walk-in closet.
- Study off the entry could be an office, if not needed as a third bedroom.
- Kitchen opens to the dining area to eliminate the confined feeling often experienced in many kitchens.

Plan Q-1190-1A

Bedrooms: 2-3	Baths: 2
Total living area:	1,190 sq. ft.
Garage:	253 sq. ft.
Exterior Wall Framing:	2x4

Foundation options:
Slab only.
(Foundation & framing conversion diagram available — see order form.)

Blueprint Price Code:	A

Plan Q-1190-1A

Rustic Look for Compact Home

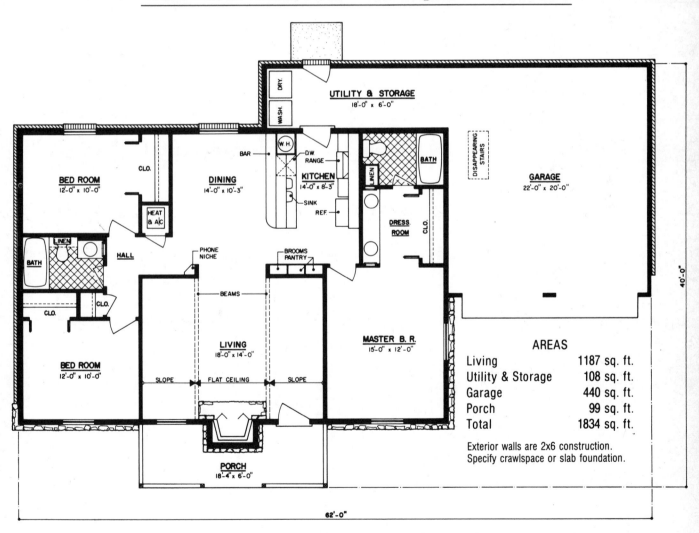

UTILITY & STORAGE
18'-0" x 6'-0"

DRY.

WASH.

BAR

W. H.

D.W.

RANGE

KITCHEN
14'-0" x 8'-3"

SINK

REF.

LINEN

BATH

DISAPPEARING STAIRS

GARAGE
22'-0" x 20'-0"

BED ROOM
12'-0" x 10'-0"

CLO.

DINING
14'-0" x 10'-3"

HEAT & A/C

LINEN

DRESS. ROOM

CLO.

BATH

HALL

CLO.

PHONE NICHE

BROOMS PANTRY

BEAMS

LIVING
18'-0" x 14'-0"

MASTER B. R.
15'-0" x 12'-0"

BED ROOM
12'-0" x 10'-0"

SLOPE   FLAT CEILING   SLOPE

PORCH
18'-4" x 6'-0"

40'-0"

62'-0"

AREAS

Living	1187 sq. ft.
Utility & Storage	108 sq. ft.
Garage	440 sq. ft.
Porch	99 sq. ft.
Total	1834 sq. ft.

Exterior walls are 2x6 construction.
Specify crawlspace or slab foundation.

Blueprint Price Code A

Plan E-1106

TO ORDER THIS BLUEPRINT,
CALL TOLL-FREE 1-800-547-5570
(prices and details on pp. 12-15.)

Great Use of Modest Space

- Open planning provides feeling of spaciousness in combined living/dining area.
- Both bedrooms have their own baths.
- Sheltered entry area adds extra touch of class.

Plan Q-980-1A

Bedrooms: 2	Baths: 2
Total living area:	980 sq. ft.
Garage:	432 sq. ft.
Exterior Wall Framing:	2x4

Foundation options:
Slab only.
(Foundation & framing conversion diagram available — see order form.)

Blueprint Price Code:	A

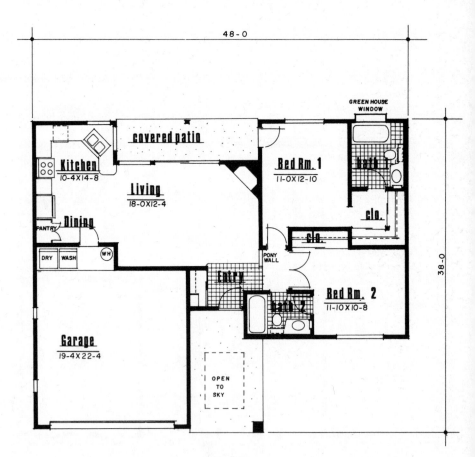

Plan Q-980-1A

Efficient Side-Entry Design

- Side entry eliminates need for space-wasting hallway to take visitors from the front to the rear.
- Living and dining areas are put together to produce a respectable space for gatherings of family and friends.
- Master bedroom suite includes a private bath and ample closet space.
- Optional third bedroom could be convenient home office.
- Living/dining area sports an impressive cathedral ceiling.

Plan Q-1125-1A

Bedrooms: 2-3	Baths: 2

Space:

Total living area:	1,125 sq. ft.
Garage:	314 sq. ft.

Exterior Wall Framing:	2x4

Foundation options:
   Slab only.
(Foundation & framing conversion diagram available — see order form.)

Blueprint Price Code:	A

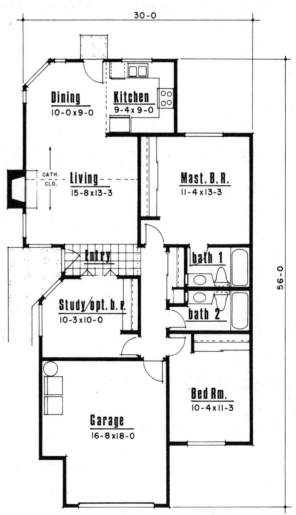

Plan Q-1125-1A

Compact Impact

- There's no doubt that this is a compact home designed for a small lot, yet the plan makes use of every possible square foot of space to create a truly livable design.
- The Great Room, already generous in size, is made to seem even larger by adding a vaulted ceiling.
- The dining area flows into the Great Room to create an even larger space.
- The kitchen boasts an efficient design and ample counter space.
- Two bedrooms share a bath, and the laundry area is in the most convenient place possible.
- Where not vaulted, ceilings are 9' high to create a more spacious feeling.

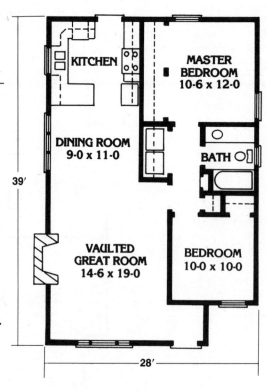

Plan V-984

Bedrooms: 2		Baths:	1
Total living area:			984 sq. ft.
Exterior Wall Framing:			2x6
Ceiling Height:			9'

Foundation options:
Crawlspace only.
(Foundation & framing conversion diagram available — see order form.)

Blueprint Price Code: A

Plan V-984

Floating Sunspace

Designed to take advantage of narrow and sometimes "left-over" lots, whether urban or rural, this compact dwelling is intended to attract the economy-minded small family. Though it boasts a private, traffic-directing entry hall, all other rooms, especially baths and kitchen, are scaled down to suit the more modest pocketbook. An exception is the beautiful passive sun room (every home should have at least one unique feature). Besides the practical advantage of collecting and storing the free heat of the sun, the room will act as a solarium, for relaxation, or a greenhouse for botanical buffs. In any case it will allow full enjoyment of nature's gifts in an otherwise limited location.

First floor:	1,075 sq. ft.
Sun room:	100 sq. ft.
Total living area:	1,175 sq. ft.
(Not counting basement or garage)	

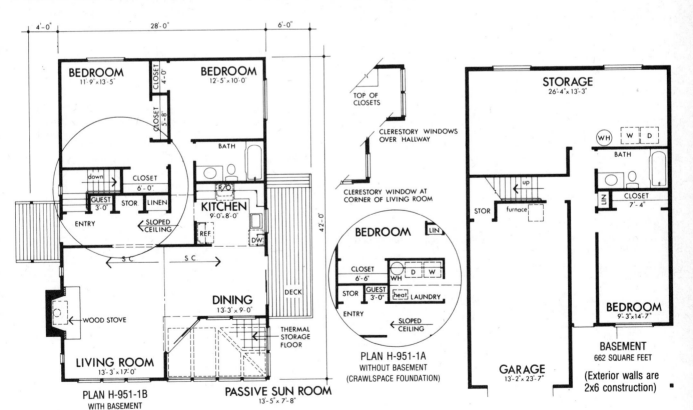

PLAN H-951-1B
WITH BASEMENT

PASSIVE SUN ROOM
13'-5" x 7'-8"

PLAN H-951-1A
WITHOUT BASEMENT
(CRAWLSPACE FOUNDATION)

BASEMENT
662 SQUARE FEET

(Exterior walls are 2x6 construction)

Blueprint Price Code A

Plans H-951-1A & H-951-1B

Design for Today's Lifestyle

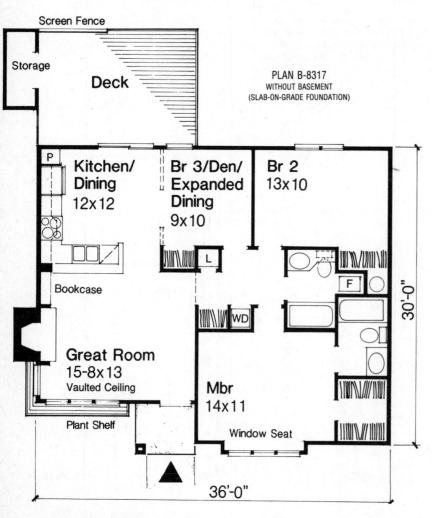

Screen Fence

Storage

Deck

PLAN B-8317
WITHOUT BASEMENT
(SLAB-ON-GRADE FOUNDATION)

P

Kitchen/ Dining 12x12

Br 3/Den/ Expanded Dining 9x10

Br 2 13x10

L

Bookcase

WD

F

30'-0"

Great Room 15-8x13
Vaulted Ceiling

Mbr 14x11

Plant Shelf

Window Seat

36'-0"

- Compact and affordable, this home is designed for today's young families.
- The kitchen/dining room combination offers space for two people to share food preparation and clean-up chores.
- The master suite is impressive for a home of this size, and includes a cozy window seat, large walk-in closet and a private bath.
- The Great Room features an impressive fireplace and vaulted ceiling.
- The optional third bedroom could be used as a den or an expanded dining area.

Plan B-8317

Bedrooms: 2-3	Baths: 2
Total living area:	1,016 sq. ft.
Exterior Wall Framing:	2x4

Foundation options:
Slab only.
(Foundation & framing conversion diagram available — see order form.)

Blueprint Price Code:	A

TO ORDER THIS BLUEPRINT,
CALL TOLL-FREE 1-800-547-5570

(prices and details on pp. 12-15.)

Plan B-8317

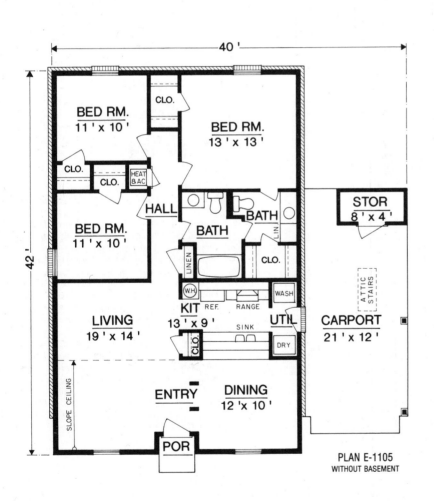

Simple, Economical to Build

AREAS

Living	1168 sq. ft.
Carport, Storage, Stoops	316 sq. ft.
Total	1484 sq. ft.

Exterior walls are 2x6 construction.
Specify crawlspace or slab foundation.

PLAN E-1105
WITHOUT BASEMENT

Blueprint Price Code A

Plan E-1105

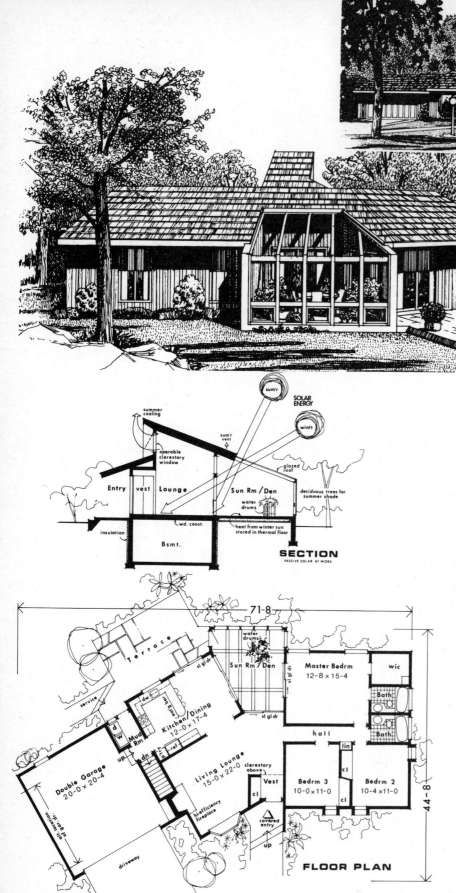

Dramatic Angles

Dramatically angled to maximize the benefits of passive solar technology, this compact one-story home can be adapted to many sites and orientations. South-facing rooms, including sun room/den, absorb and store heat energy in thermal floors for night time radiation. Heavy insulation in exterior walls and ceilings, plus double glazing in windows, keep heat loss to a minimum. During the summer, heat is expelled through an operable clerestory window and through an automatic vent in the sun room.

Inside, entrance vestibule overlooks a breathtaking view of the sun room and the outdoors beyond; kitchen/dining area opens to a large rear terrace. Three bedrooms are isolated for total privacy. Living area, excluding sun room, is 1,223 sq. ft.; garage, mud room, etc. 504 sq. ft.; partial basement, 1,030 sq. ft.

Living Area:	1,223 sq. ft.
Garage and Mud Room:	504 sq. ft.
Basement (Opt.):	1,030 sq. ft.

(Alternate slab-on-grade foundation plan included.)

Blueprint Price Code A
Plan K-505-R

Vaulted Ceilings Create More Space

● Vaulted ceilings in both the living room and master suite create a feeling of spaciousness in this compact home.

● Efficient U-shaped kitchen opens to the dining area, to reduce the closed-in feeling found in many kitchens.

● Master suite includes a private bath, large walk-in closet and access to a covered patio.

● Second bedroom would make a great home office if not needed for a sleeping room.

Plan Q-1034-1A

Bedrooms: 1-2	Baths: 2

Space:

Total living area:	1,034 sq. ft.
Garage:	387 sq. ft.

Exterior Wall Framing:	2x4

Foundation options:
Slab.
(Foundation & framing conversion diagram available — see order form.)

Blueprint Price Code:	A

Plan Q-1034-1A

Build It on Weekends

- The basic design and use of truss roof framing promote easy and speedy erection.
- See-through kitchen allows a look into the living or dining rooms.
- Living room reveals the outdoors and surrounding deck through sliding glass doors.
- Separate bedroom/bathroom area eliminates cross-room traffic and wasted hall space.
- Plan H-921-2A utilizes the sealed crawlspace as an air distribution chamber for a Plen-Wood heating system.
- Plan H-921-1A has a standard crawlspace foundation and optional solar heating system.

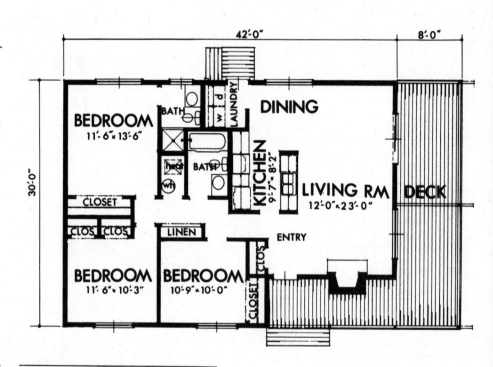

Plans H-921-1A & -2A

Bedrooms: 3	Baths: 2
Space:	
Main floor:	1,164 sq. ft.
Total living area:	1,164 sq. ft.
Exterior Wall Framing:	2x6

Foundation options:
Plen-Wood crawlspace system (Plan H-921-2A).
Standard crawlspace (Plan H-921-1A).
(Foundation & framing conversion diagram available — see order form.)

Blueprint Price Code: A

TO ORDER THIS BLUEPRINT,
CALL TOLL-FREE 1-800-547-5570

Plans H-921-1A & -2A

Living With Sunpower

Angled wood siding accentuates the architectural geometry of this flexible leisure home. The house is designed to exploit sun power and conserve energy. Focal point of the plan is an outsized living lounge that has pitched ceiling and overall dimensions of 18'-8" by 26'-0". Note the glass wall that leads to the spacious sun deck. A roomy kitchen is accessible from another sun deck and serves two eating bars as well as the dining room. The three bedrooms are well isolated from noise and traffic. Adjacent to the kitchen is the utility-storage room that can accommodate laundry facilities.

As an option, two solar collectors can be installed on the roof, either over the living lounge, or on the opposite roof, depending on the southern exposure. Solar equipment may be installed now or in the future.

Total living area: 1,077 sq. ft.
(Not counting garage)

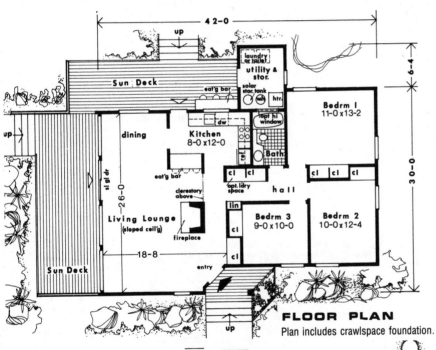

FLOOR PLAN
Plan includes crawlspace foundation.

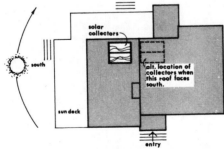

ORIENTATION FEASIBILITY
mirror plan also possible
home may be built without solar system

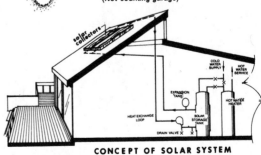

**CONCEPT OF SOLAR SYSTEM
FOR DOMESTIC HOT WATER**

Blueprint Price Code A

Plan K-166-T

Basic, Economical Design

- Partial brick front adds touch of warmth.
- Basic rectangle shape means easy construction.
- Great Room with fireplace lends itself to easy entertaining.

Plan Q-1196-1A	
Bedrooms: 3	Baths: 2
Total living area:	1,196 sq. ft.
Exterior Wall Framing:	2x4
Foundation options: Slab only. (Foundation & framing conversion diagram available — see order form.)	
Blueprint Price Code:	A

46-0

26-0

Dining
8-8X11-4

Kitchen
11-10 X 8-7

bath 1

bath 2

Mast. B. R.
11-4X12-10

Carport

Great Rm.
16-8X14-0

Entry

Bed Rm.
9-4X13-1

Bed Rm.
12-4X9-10

Plan Q-1196-1A

Affordable Country Charm

- A covered front porch, attached garage, and bay window add appeal to this efficient, affordable home.
- A spacious living room with fireplace and window seat offer plenty of family living space.
- The kitchen/dining room opens to a rear patio for indoor/outdoor living.
- The attached garage incorporates stairs for the optional basement.
- The plan includes three bedrooms and two baths on the same level, a plus for young families.

Plan AX-98602

Bedrooms: 3	Baths: 2

Space:	
Total living area:	1,253 sq. ft.
Basement:	1,253 sq. ft.
Garage:	368 sq. ft.

Exterior Wall Framing:	2x4

Foundation options:
Standard basement.
Slab.
(Foundation & framing conversion diagram available — see order form.)

Blueprint Price Code:	A

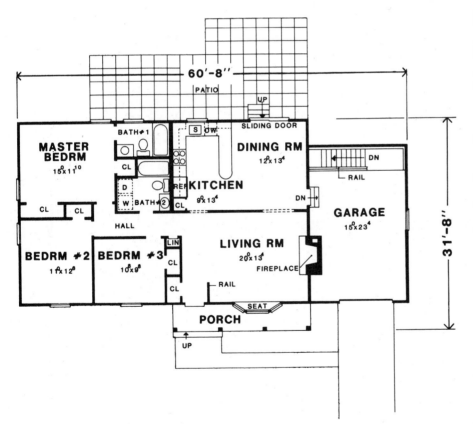

Plan AX-98602

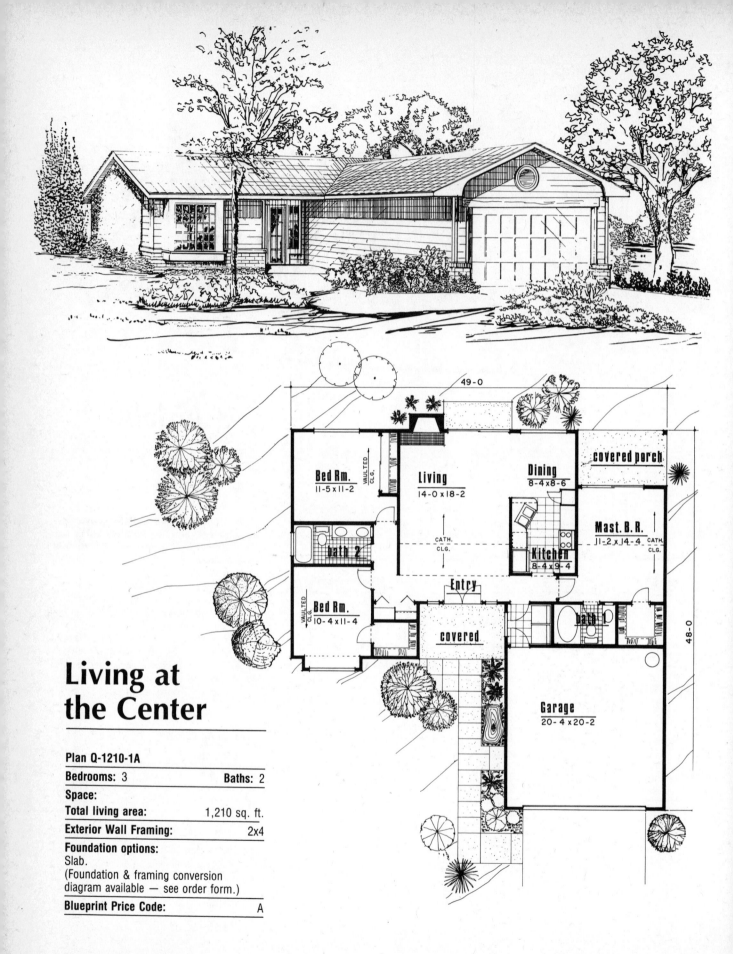

Living at the Center

Plan Q-1210-1A

Bedrooms: 3	**Baths:** 2

Space:

Total living area:	1,210 sq. ft.
Exterior Wall Framing:	2x4

Foundation options:
Slab.
(Foundation & framing conversion diagram available — see order form.)

Blueprint Price Code:	A

Floor plan labels:

- Bed Rm. 11-5 x 11-2 VAULTED CLG.
- Living 14-0 x 18-2 CATH. CLG.
- Dining 8-4 x 8-6
- covered porch
- Mast. B.R. 11-2 x 14-4 CATH. CLG.
- Kitchen 8-4 x 9-4
- Bath 2
- Bed Rm. 10-4 x 11-4 VAULTED CLG.
- Entry
- covered
- bath 1
- Garage 20-4 x 20-2
- 49-0
- 48-0

TO ORDER THIS BLUEPRINT,
CALL TOLL-FREE 1-800-547-5570

Plan Q-1210-1A

Economical One-Level Design

● Great Room design concept creates large open area for living, dining rooms and kitchen.
● Large covered patio in rear extends entertaining area.
● Master bedroom includes walk-in closet and private bath.

Plan Q-1248-1A

Bedrooms: 3	Baths: 2

Total living area:	1,248 sq. ft.
Garage:	400 sq. ft.

Exterior Wall Framing:	2x4

Foundation options:
Slab only.
(Foundation & framing conversion diagram available — see order form.)

Blueprint Price Code:	A

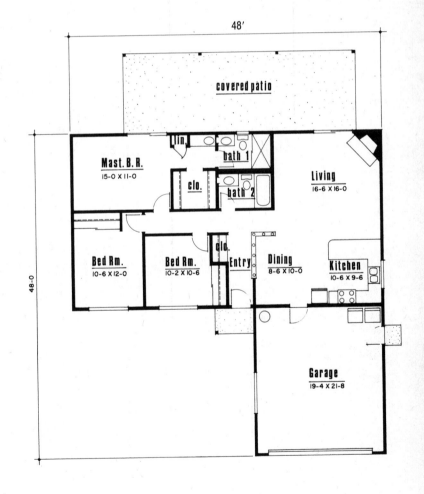

Plan Q-1248-1A

Unique Design for Narrow Corner Lot

- Interesting and different design inside and out.
- Unique dining area angles off the living room.
- Living room provides fireplace and easy access to a covered porch.
- Note that the living room and master suite also include vaulted ceilings.
- The master suite is unusually large for a home of this size and includes a luxurious master bath and large walk-in closet.
- Stucco finish provides a low-maintenance exterior in any climate.

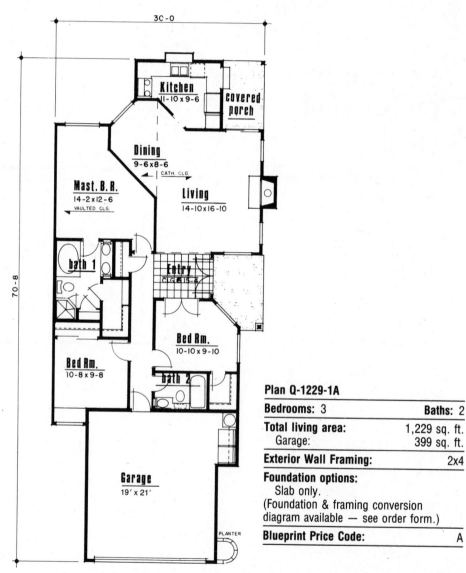

Plan Q-1229-1A

Plan Q-1229-1A	
Bedrooms: 3	Baths: 2
Total living area:	1,229 sq. ft.
Garage:	399 sq. ft.
Exterior Wall Framing:	2x4

Foundation options:
Slab only.
(Foundation & framing conversion diagram available — see order form.)

Blueprint Price Code:	A

Plan Q-1229-1A

Packed with Conveniences

Simply stated and economically structured, this handsome clapboard ranch is ideal for privacy and casual indoor-outdoor living. A reception hall, at the core of the house, leads to a sloped-ceilinged living room and dining room, highlighted by a brick fireplace and sliding glass doors overlooking the back terrace.

The cozy family room/kitchen, with a large bay window, is planned for family togetherness. The U-shaped cooking area includes a window above the sink and an eating bar, convenient for informal meals.

Sequestered in one wing, away from the activity area, are three bedrooms and two full baths. Master bedroom has a private terrace, ample closets and a personal bath that features a whirlpool tub. Total living area is 1,220 sq. ft.; optional basement is 1,247 sq. ft.; garage, mud room, etc., 635 sq. ft.

Total living area: 1,220 sq. ft.
(Not counting basement or garage)

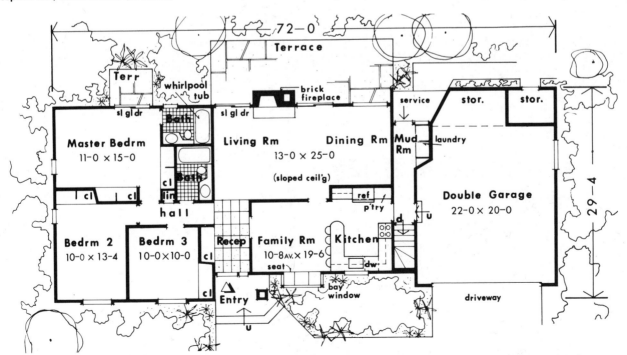

Blueprint Price Code A

Plan K-518-A

TO ORDER THIS BLUEPRINT, CALL TOLL-FREE 1-800-547-5570

(prices and details on pp. 12-15.)

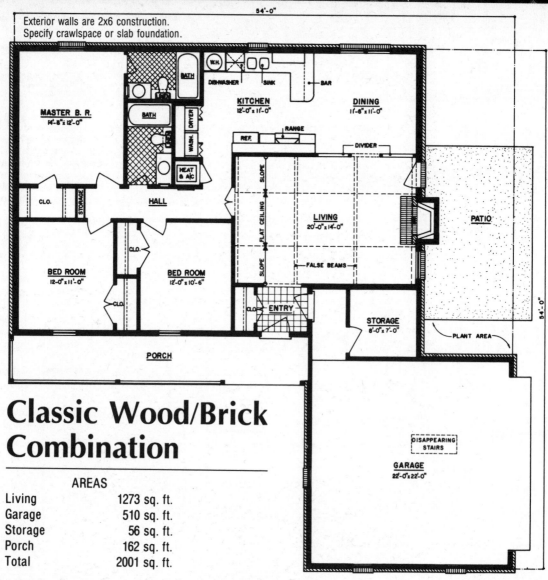

Exterior walls are 2x6 construction.
Specify crawlspace or slab foundation.

54'-0"

54'-0"

MASTER B. R.
14'-8" x 12'-0"

BATH

BATH

W.H.

DISHWASHER   SINK   BAR

DRYER

WASH.

HEAT & A/C

KITCHEN
12'-0" x 11'-0"

DINING
11'-6" x 11'-0"

REF.   RANGE

DIVIDER

CLO.   STORAGE

HALL

SLOPE   FLAT CEILING   SLOPE

LIVING
20'-0" x 14'-0"

PATIO

BED ROOM
12'-0" x 11'-0"

CLO.

BED ROOM
12'-0" x 10'-6"

CLO.

FALSE BEAMS

PLANT AREA

CLO.   **ENTRY**

STORAGE
8'-0" x 7'-0"

PORCH

Classic Wood/Brick Combination

AREAS
Living	1273 sq. ft.
Garage	510 sq. ft.
Storage	56 sq. ft.
Porch	162 sq. ft.
Total	2001 sq. ft.

DISAPPEARING STAIRS

GARAGE
22'-0" x 22'-0"

TO ORDER THIS BLUEPRINT,
CALL TOLL-FREE 1-800-547-5570

(prices and details on pp. 12-15.)

Blueprint Price Code A
Plan E-1212

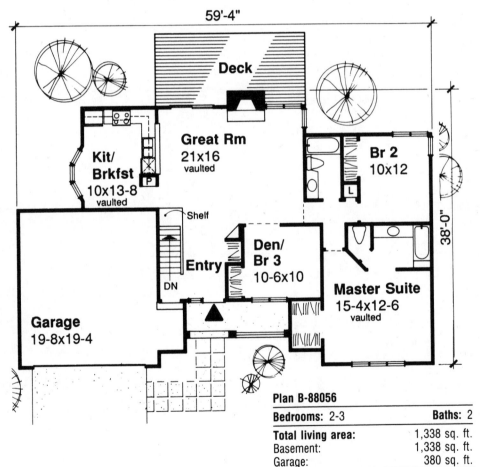

Deck

Great Rm
21x16
vaulted

Kit/ Brkfst
10x13-8
vaulted

Br 2
10x12

Shelf

Entry

Den/ Br 3
10-6x10

DN

Master Suite
15-4x12-6
vaulted

Garage
19-8x19-4

59'-4"

38'-0"

Spacious Great Room Featured

- A spacious Great Room takes this modest-sized home out of the ordinary.
- Great Room includes an impressive fireplace and easy access — both physically and visually — to a large deck.
- The kitchen/breakfast area includes sunny bay windows and a vaulted ceiling.
- The master suite also features a vaulted ceiling, and has a private, compartmentalized bath and large walk-in closet.
- The optional third bedroom would make an attractive and convenient home office.
- Basement stairs are convenient to both the front entry and garage door.

Plan B-88056

Bedrooms: 2-3	Baths: 2
Total living area:	1,338 sq. ft.
Basement:	1,338 sq. ft.
Garage:	380 sq. ft.
Exterior Wall Framing:	2x4

Foundation options:
Standard basement only.
(Foundation & framing conversion diagram available — see order form.)

Blueprint Price Code: A

Plan B-88056

Cozy Home
for Retirees or
New Families

Total living area: 1,283 sq. ft.
(Not counting basement or garage)

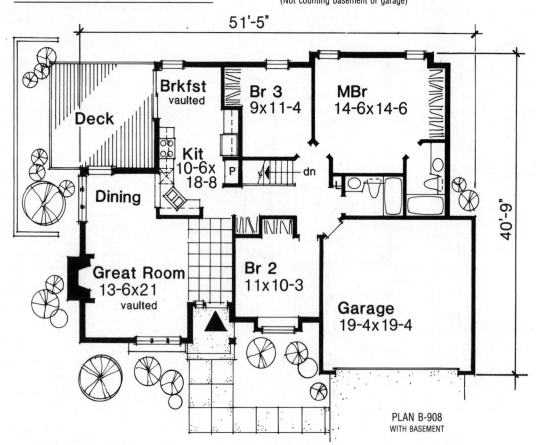

51'-5"

40'-9"

Deck

Brkfst vaulted

Br 3 9x11-4

MBr 14-6x14-6

Kit 10-6x 18-8

P

dn

Dining

Great Room 13-6x21 vaulted

Br 2 11x10-3

Garage 19-4x19-4

PLAN B-908
WITH BASEMENT

Blueprint Price Code A
Plan B-908

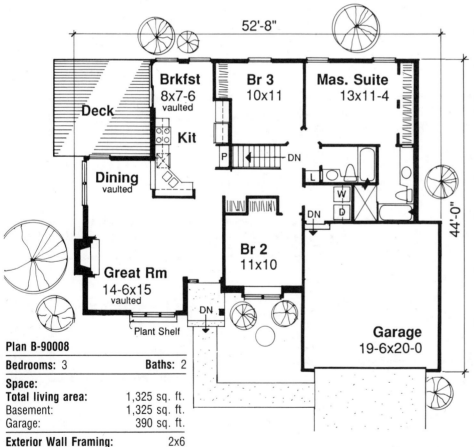

52'-8"

Deck

Brkfst
8x7-6
vaulted

Kit

Dining
vaulted

Br 3
10x11

Mas. Suite
13x11-4

P

DN

Great Rm
14-6x15
vaulted

Br 2
11x10

Plant Shelf

L

W
D

DN

DN

44'-0"

Garage
19-6x20-0

Plan B-90008

Bedrooms: 3	Baths: 2

Space:

Total living area:	1,325 sq. ft.
Basement:	1,325 sq. ft.
Garage:	390 sq. ft.

Exterior Wall Framing:	2x6

Foundation options:
Standard basement.
(Foundation & framing conversion
diagram available — see order form.)

Blueprint Price Code:	A

Window Wonderland

- The focal point of this open, efficient plan is a dramatic window in the Great Room with square transom windows plus half round glass above and plant shelf below.
- The resulting window-wall dramatizes the exterior and the interior as well.
- The Great Room also features an attractive fireplace and vaulted ceiling, and flows into the dining room.
- The vaulted kitchen incorporates a breakfast room with sliders to a deck. The kitchen also has a handy pass-thru to the dining room.
- The three bedrooms include a master suite with private bath which offers a separate tub and shower.

Plan B-90008

Economical Three-Bedroom Home

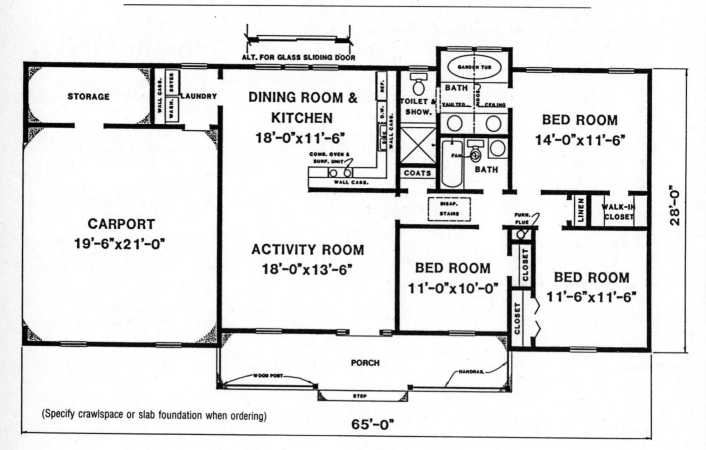

ALT. FOR GLASS SLIDING DOOR

STORAGE

WALL CABS.

WARM. DRYER

LAUNDRY

DINING ROOM & KITCHEN
18'-0"x11'-6"

REF.

D.W.

WALL CABS.

COMB. OVEN & SURF. UNIT

WALL CABS.

TOILET & SHOW.

BATH
VAULTED CEILING

GARDEN TUB

NOOK

COATS

FAN.

BATH

BED ROOM
14'-0"x11'-6"

DISAP. STAIRS

FURN. FLUE

LINEN

WALK-IN CLOSET

CARPORT
19'-6"x21'-0"

ACTIVITY ROOM
18'-0"x13'-6"

BED ROOM
11'-0"x10'-0"

CLOSET

CLOSET

BED ROOM
11'-6"x11'-6"

PORCH

WOOD POST

HANDRAIL

STEP

28'-0"

(Specify crawlspace or slab foundation when ordering)

65'-0"

PLAN W-289
WITHOUT BASEMENT

House: 1,285 sq. ft.
Carport & Storage: 515 sq. ft.
Porch: 168 sq. ft.

TO ORDER THIS BLUEPRINT,
CALL TOLL-FREE 1-800-547-5570
(prices and details on pp. 12-15.)

Blueprint Price Code A
Plan W-289

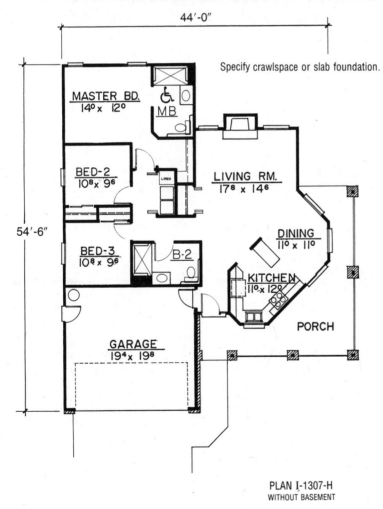

Specify crawlspace or slab foundation.

44'-0"

54'-6"

MASTER BD.
14⁰ x 12⁰

MB

BED-2
10⁸ x 9⁶

LINEN

BED-3
10⁸ x 9⁶

B-2

LIVING RM.
17⁸ x 14⁶

DINING
11⁰ x 11⁰

KITCHEN
11⁰ x 12⁸

PORCH

GARAGE
19⁴ x 19⁸

**Compact
Design
Features
Innovative
Floor Plan**

PLAN I-1307-H
WITHOUT BASEMENT

Total living area: 1,307 sq. ft.
(Not counting garage)

Blueprint Price Code A

Plan I-1307-H

**TO ORDER THIS BLUEPRINT,
CALL TOLL-FREE 1-800-547-5570**
(prices and details on pp. 12-15.)

Clean-Lined Design for Narrow Lot

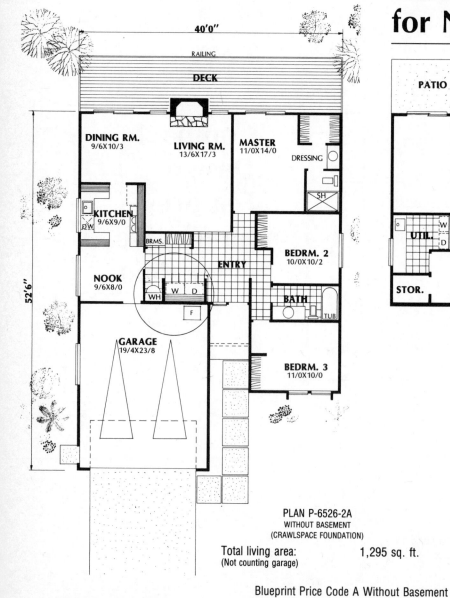

40'0"

RAILING

DECK

DINING RM.
9/6X10/3

LIVING RM.
13/6X17/3

MASTER
11/0X14/0

DRESSING

KITCHEN
9/6X9/0

SH

BRMS.

ENTRY

BEDRM. 2
10/0X10/2

NOOK
9/6X8/0

WH W D

F

BATH

TUB

52'6"

GARAGE
19/4X23/8

BEDRM. 3
11/0X10/0

PLAN P-6526-2A
WITHOUT BASEMENT
(CRAWLSPACE FOUNDATION)

Total living area: 1,295 sq. ft.
(Not counting garage)

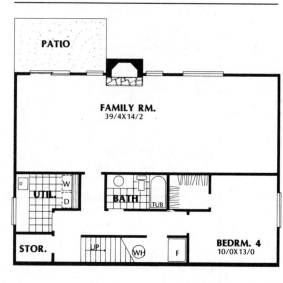

PATIO

FAMILY RM.
39/4X14/2

UTIL.

W
D

BATH

TUB

STOR.

UP

WH

F

BEDRM. 4
10/0X13/0

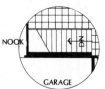

NOOK

GARAGE

PLAN P-6526-2D
WITH DAYLIGHT BASEMENT

Main floor: 1,295 sq. ft.
(Not counting garage)

Basement level: 1,120 sq. ft.

Total living area
with daylight basement: 2,415 sq. ft.

Blueprint Price Code A Without Basement
Blueprint Price Code C With Daylight Basement

Plans P-6526-2A & -2D

Cozy and Energy-Efficient

Planned for year-round comfort and energy efficiency, this passive solar design boasts a highly livable floor plan. Vertical wood siding and deep overhang give the exterior a natural appeal. Inside, the open plan is carefully designed to provide ample natural light with a minimum heat loss; windows and sliding doors are double-paned; heavy insulation is specified. In summer, operable clerestory windows aid in air circulation, cooling the house by convection.

The high-ceilinged reception hall neatly channels traffic. To the right is the family room/kitchen, equipped with an eating bar. Straight ahead are the living and dining rooms, dramatically accented by a sloped ceiling, a wood-burning fireplace and a light-filled sunroom. Sliding glass doors lead to a rear terrace.

Isolated on the left side are the quiet sleeping quarters, with three bedrooms. Master bedroom has a private terrace, a walk-in closet and a personal bath that features a whirlpool tub.

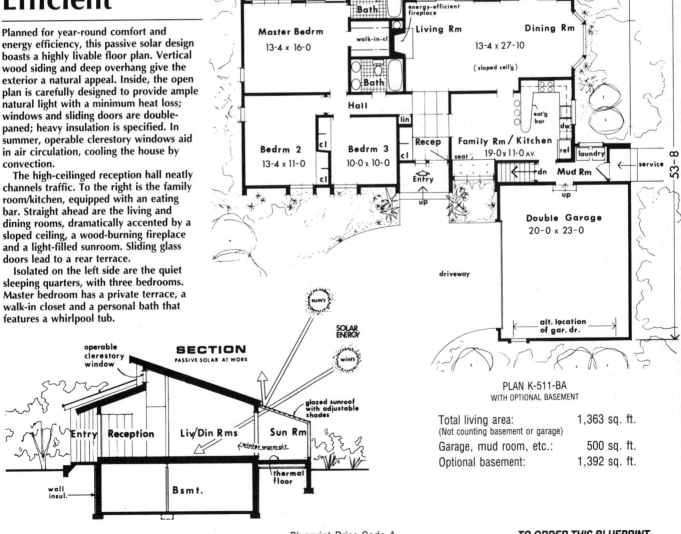

PLAN K-511-BA
WITH OPTIONAL BASEMENT

Total living area:	1,363 sq. ft.
(Not counting basement or garage)	
Garage, mud room, etc.:	500 sq. ft.
Optional basement:	1,392 sq. ft.

Blueprint Price Code A

Plan K-511-BA

***TO ORDER THIS BLUEPRINT,
CALL TOLL-FREE 1-800-547-5570***
(prices and details on pp. 12-15.)

43

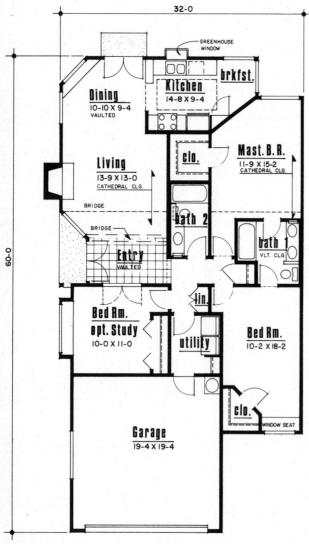

Space for Gracious Entertaining

● Although relatively modest in size, this plan contains abundant space for a fair-sized party or family gathering.
● Combined living/dining area creates a large open space, made to seem even larger by the vaulted ceiling.
● The entry area is also impressive for a home of this size.
● The large master suite includes a big walk-in closet and vaulted ceiling, as does the second bedroom.
● The third bedroom makes a nice home office if not needed for a sleeping room.
● The utility area is conveniently tucked away in the garage entry passage.
● The kitchen includes a cozy, sunny breakfast nook.

Plan Q-1300-1A

Bedrooms: 2-3	Baths: 2
Total living area:	1,300 sq. ft.
Garage:	374 sq. ft.
Exterior Wall Framing:	2x4

Foundation options:
  Slab only.
(Foundation & framing conversion diagram available — see order form.)

Blueprint Price Code:	A

Plan Q-1300-1A

Stately Columns Introduce Economical Home

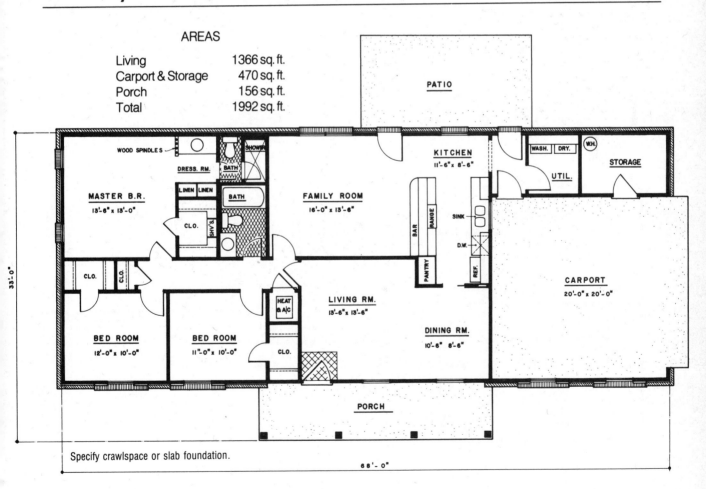

AREAS

Living	1366 sq. ft.
Carport & Storage	470 sq. ft.
Porch	156 sq. ft.
Total	1992 sq. ft.

PATIO

WOOD SPINDLES

DRESS. RM.

BATH

SHOWER

LINEN LINEN

KITCHEN
11'-6" x 8'-6"

WASH. DRY. W.H.

STORAGE

UTIL.

MASTER B.R.
13'-6" x 13'-0"

BATH

CLO.

SH'VS

FAMILY ROOM
16'-0" x 13'-6"

BAR

RANGE

SINK

D.W.

CLO. CLO.

PANTRY

REF.

CARPORT
20'-0" x 20'-0"

HEAT & A/C

LIVING RM.
13'-6" x 13'-6"

BED ROOM
12'-0" x 10'-0"

BED ROOM
11'-0" x 10'-0"

CLO.

DINING RM.
10'-6" 8'-6"

33'-0"

Specify crawlspace or slab foundation.

PORCH

68'-0"

Blueprint Price Code A

Plan E-1300

TO ORDER THIS BLUEPRINT,
CALL TOLL-FREE 1-800-547-5570
(prices and details on pp. 12-15.) **45**

Full-Width Veranda Welcomes Visitors

- A veranda invites you into this lovely traditionally styled ranch home.
- Inside, the entry allows a view through the dining room railing and straight back to the huge, central living room and backyard beyond.
- A massive stone fireplace, wood box and built-in bookshelves, plus exposed beams in the ceiling, highlight this main living area.
- The formal dining room and kitchen combine for easy meal service, with a counter bar separating the two.
- The main hallway ends at the sleeping wing, which offers a large master bedroom and private bath, two extra bedrooms and a convenient, concealed washer/dryer.

Plan E-1304	
Bedrooms: 3	**Baths: 2**
Space:	
Main floor	1,395 sq. ft.
Total Living Area	**1,395 sq. ft.**
Garage and Storage	481 sq. ft.
Exterior Wall Framing	2x4
Foundation options:	
Crawlspace	
Slab	
(Foundation & framing conversion diagram available—see order form.)	
Blueprint Price Code	**A**

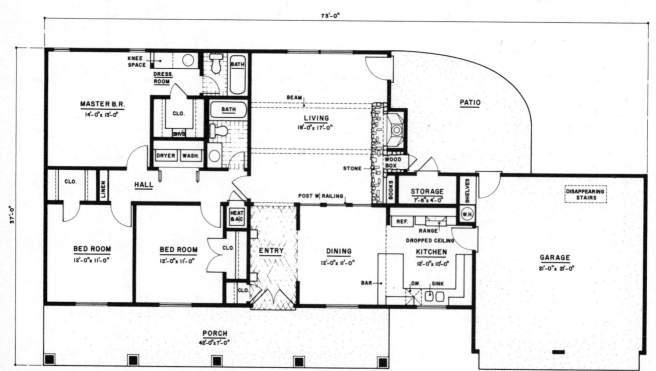

Plan E-1304

Warm Porch Welcomes Guests

- This cozy home provides adequate space for family life and for entertaining guests as well.
- Living and dining rooms are separate, yet flow together when the need for entertaining large gatherings arises.
- The large master suite includes a private bath and large closet.
- Kitchen is good sized and offers abundant counter space.
- A handy utility room is located in the entry area, and a large storage area is also positioned off the carport (there is optional storage space above the garage, also).

Plan E-1308

Bedrooms: 3	Baths: 2
Total living area:	1,375 sq. ft.
Porch:	102 sq. ft.
Carport:	430 sq. ft.
Storage:	95 sq. ft.
Exterior Wall Framing:	2x4

Foundation options:
  Crawlspace.
  Slab.
(Foundation & framing conversion diagram available — see order form.)

Blueprint Price Code: A

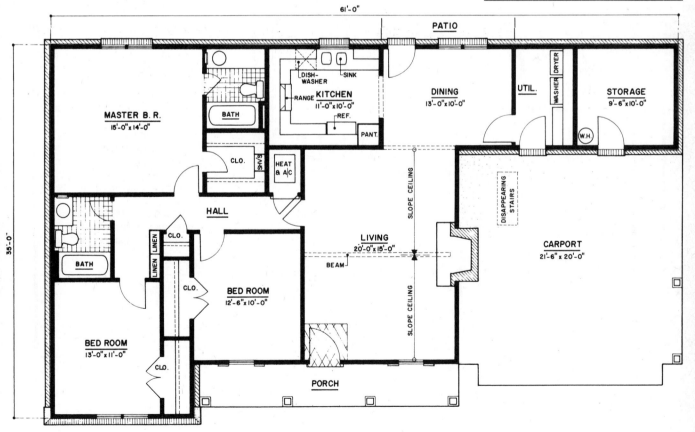

Plan E-1308

Designed for Quiet, Private Sleeping Area

- This moderate sized plan presents an impressive facade, with its large and interesting front window arrangement.
- An unusual Great Room plan allows for some separation of the kitchen/breakfast area from the dining/living section, but still makes them all part of one unit.
- The master bedroom includes a private bath with separate tub and shower, and another full bath serves the rest of the home.
- The third bedroom could serve as a den, study, or office if not needed for sleeping.
- The breakfast area offers easy access to an outdoor patio.
- Take special note of the unusual fireplace positioning in the Great Room.
- This plan comes with a full basement, which effectively doubles the space available.

Plan B-902

Bedrooms: 2-3	Baths: 2
Total living area:	1,368 sq. ft.
Basement:	1,368 sq. ft.
Garage:	412 sq. ft.
Exterior Wall Framing:	2x4

Foundation options:
Standard basement only.
(Foundation & framing conversion diagram available — see order form.)

Blueprint Price Code: A

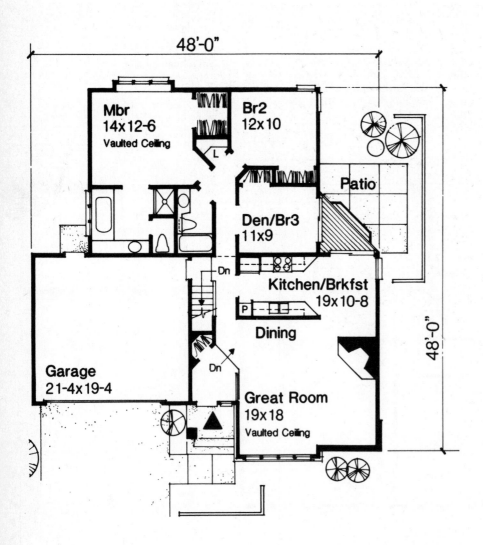

48'-0"

48'-0"

Mbr
14x12-6
Vaulted Ceiling

Br2
12x10

Patio

Den/Br3
11x9

Kitchen/Brkfst
19x10-8

Dining

Garage
21-4x19-4

Dn

Dn

Great Room
19x18
Vaulted Ceiling

Plan B-902

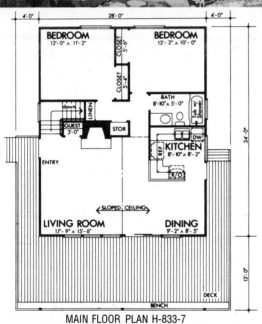

MAIN FLOOR PLAN H-833-7
WITH DAYLIGHT BASEMENT

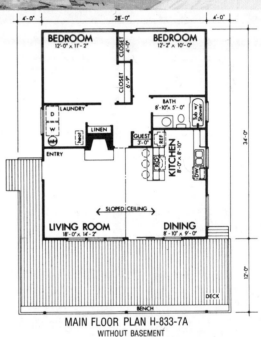

MAIN FLOOR PLAN H-833-7A
WITHOUT BASEMENT

An Owner-Builder Special

- Everything you need for a leisure or retirement retreat is neatly packaged in just 952 square feet.
- Basic rectangular design features unique wrap-around deck entirely covered by the projecting roof line.
- Vaulted ceilings and central fireplace visually enhance the cozy living-dining room.
- Daylight basement option is suitable for building on a sloping lot.

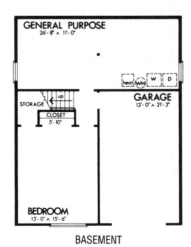

BASEMENT

Plans H-833-7 & -7A

Bedrooms: 2-3	Baths: 1

Space:	
Main floor:	952 sq. ft.

Total living area:	952 sq. ft.
Basement:	approx. 952 sq. ft.
Garage: (included in basement)	276 sq. ft.

Exterior Wall Framing:	2x6

Foundation options:
Daylight basement (Plan H-833-7).
Crawlspace (Plan H-833-7A).
(Foundation & framing conversion diagram available — see order form.)

Blueprint Price Code:

Without basement	A
With basement	B

Cozy, Rustic Country Home

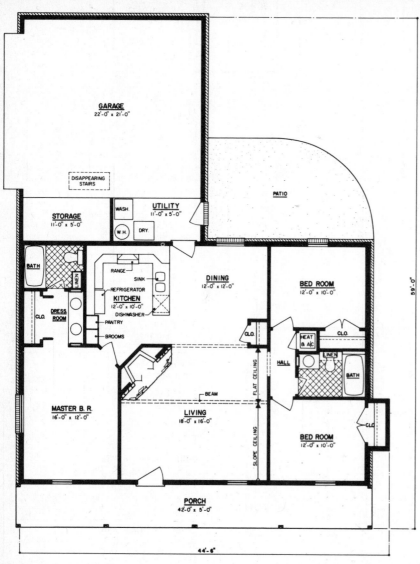

- This cozy, rustic home offers a modern, open interior that makes it look much larger than it really is.
- Note the large, beamed living room with its massive fireplace, which flows into the dining area.
- The efficient U-shaped kitchen includes a handy pantry as well as a convenient broom closet.
- The master suite and master bath are especially roomy for a home of this compact size.
- Two other bedrooms share a full bath and offer good closet space.
- Also note the handy utility space in the garage entry area, and the storage space in the garage.

Plan E-1109

Bedrooms: 3	Baths: 2

Space:	
Total living area:	1,191 sq. ft.
Garage:	462 sq. ft.
Storage & utility:	55 sq. ft.
Porch:	214 sq. ft.

Exterior Wall Framing:	2x6

Foundation options:
Crawlspace.
Slab.
(Foundation & framing conversion diagram available — see order form.)

Blueprint Price Code:	A

Plan E-1109

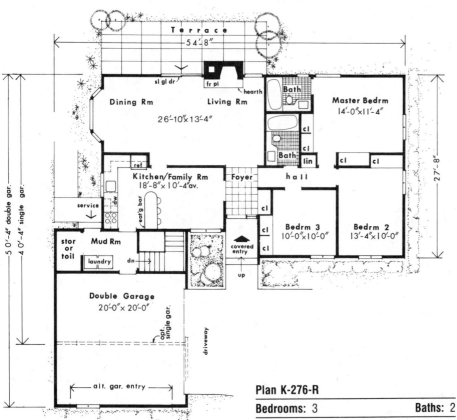

Compact, Economical to Build

- This economically-structured L-shaped ranch puts a great many desirable features into a mere 1,193 sq. ft. of living space. A wood-burning fireplace highlights the living area. Sliding glass doors open to the backyard terrace.
- The kitchen/family room features an eating bar.
- Covered entry welcomes you to the central foyer for easy channeling to any part of the house.
- Located in a wing of their own are three bedrooms and two baths.
- For a narrow lot, the garage door could face the front.

Plan K-276-R

Bedrooms: 3	Baths: 2

Space:

Total living area:	1,193 sq. ft.
Basement:	1,193 sq. ft.
Garage, mud room, etc.:	551 sq. ft.

Exterior Wall Framing:	2x4 or 2x6

Foundation options:
Standard basement.
Crawlspace.
Slab.
(Foundation & framing conversion diagram available — see order form)

Blueprint Price Code:	A

Plan K-276-R

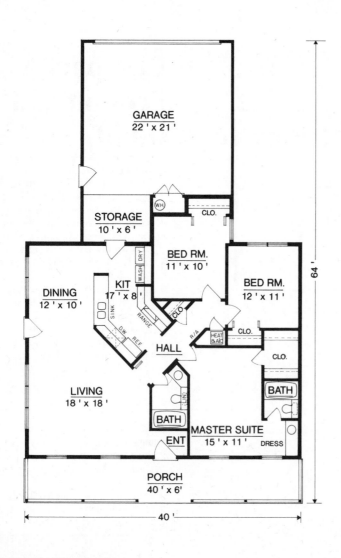

GARAGE
22' x 21'

STORAGE
10' x 6'

WH

CLO.

BED RM.
11' x 10'

DRY

WASH

KIT
17' x 8'

DINING
12' x 10'

SINK

RANGE

D.W.

REF

BED RM.
12' x 11'

R/A

CLO.

HEAT
& A/C

CLO.

CLO.

HALL

LIVING
18' x 18'

LIN.

BATH

BATH

ENT

MASTER SUITE
15' x 11'

DRESS

PORCH
40' x 6'

40'

64'

Cozy Veranda Invites Visitors

- Large covered front porch has detailed columns and railings.
- Compact size fits small lots, yet facade gives illusion of larger home.
- Space-saving angular design minimizes hallway space.
- Master suite features walk-in closet, private bath, and separate dressing and sink area.

Plan E-1217

Bedrooms: 3	Baths: 2

Space:	
Total living area:	1,266 sq. ft.
Garage and storage:	550 sq. ft.

Exterior Wall Framing:	2x6

Foundation options:
Crawlspace.
Slab.
(Foundation & framing conversion diagram available — see order form.)

Blueprint Price Code:	A

TO ORDER THIS BLUEPRINT,
CALL TOLL-FREE 1-800-547-5570

Plan E-1217

Angled Windows and Flowing Space

Photo courtesy of Barclay Home Designs

- This highly popular compact home proves that even smaller homes can be big on style and convenience.
- The bay-windowed living room and dining room combine to create a large space for entertaining.
- A sunny nook adjoins the kitchen, which includes a pantry.
- The master suite includes a private bath, roomy wardrobe closet and a double-door entry.
- The sheltered entry invites guests and family alike, and a convenient utility area is situated in the garage entry area.
- An optional third bedroom can be used for a den or TV room, open to the nook if desired.

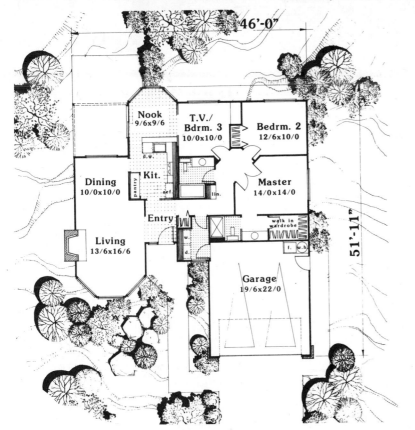

**NOTE:
The above photographed home may have been modified by the homeowner. Please refer to floor plan and/or drawn elevation shown for actual blueprint details.

Plan R-1028

Bedrooms: 2-3	**Baths:** 2
Total livng area:	1,305 sq. ft.
Garage:	429 sq. ft.
Exterior Wall Framing:	2x4

Foundation options:
Crawlspace only.
(Foundation & framing conversion diagram available — see order form.)

Blueprint Price Code:	A

Plan R-1028

Just Your Size

- This country-style cottage will fit anywhere, even on a small, in-town lot. Its charming character and 35-ft. width make it an ideal choice for those who value vintage styling along with plenty of yard space. The large covered front porch further extends living space and contributes to the attractive facade.
- Vaulted ceilings in the dining room and living room lend a spacious feel to the home. The living room features a fireplace framed by windows, and bay windows brighten the dining room. A galley-style kitchen leads to the utility and storage rooms placed near the back entrance.
- The master bedroom has French doors opening onto a backyard patio, a private bath with lots of storage space, plus a walk-in closet. Another full bath is centrally located, just across the hall from the remaining two bedrooms.

Plan J-86119

Bedrooms: 3	Baths: 2
Space:	
Main floor	1,346 sq. ft.
Total Living Area	**1,346 sq. ft.**
Basement	1,346 sq. ft.
Carport	400 sq. ft.
Exterior Wall Framing	2x4

Foundation options:
Standard Basement
Crawlspace
Slab
(Foundation & framing conversion diagram available—see order form.)

Blueprint Price Code	**A**

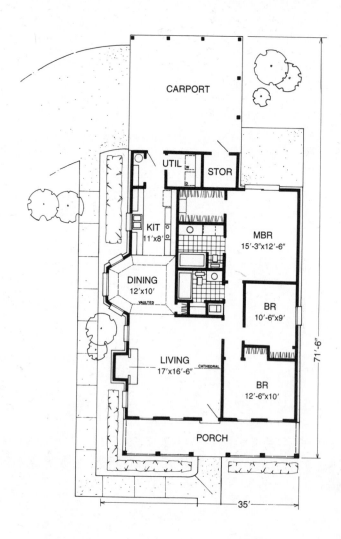

TO ORDER THIS BLUEPRINT,
CALL TOLL-FREE 1-800-547-5570
(prices and details on pp. 12-15.)

Plan J-86119

Vaulted Master Suite

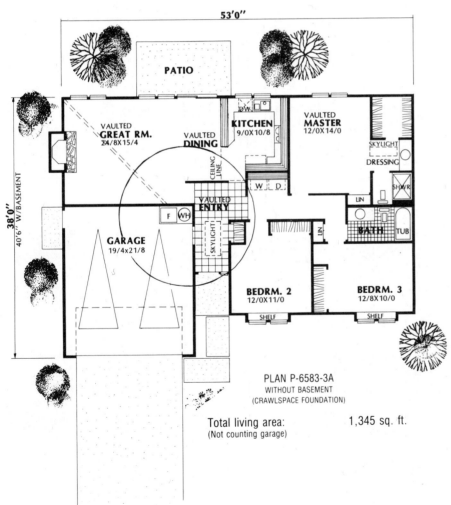

PLAN P-6583-3A
WITHOUT BASEMENT
(CRAWLSPACE FOUNDATION)

Total living area: 1,345 sq. ft.
(Not counting garage)

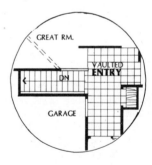

PLAN P-6583-3D
WITH DAYLIGHT BASEMENT

Main floor: 1,380 sq. ft.
(Not counting garage)
Basement level: 1,380 sq. ft.

Economical and Stylish

- A distinctive roof and window treatment on the front-facing kitchen extension lend a traditional look to this otherwise contemporary home.
- Well-suited to narrow lots, this efficient plan is only 40 feet wide, but still offers plenty of space for today's living.
- The Great Room and dining area flow together into one large space, made to look even more roomy by the vaulted ceilings.
- The Master Suite includes a sitting room as well as a private bath and walk-in closet.
- Two secondary bedrooms share another full bath, and offer a nice view into the side yard.
- The distinctive kitchen projects into a front courtyard and includes a bay window along with abundant counter space.
- An optional daylight basement nearly doubles the space.

Plans P-6588-2A & -2D

Bedrooms: 3	Baths: 2

Space:

Main floor (w/o basement):	1,362 sq. ft.
Main floor (with basement):	1,403 sq. ft.
Daylight basement:	1,303 sq. ft.
Garage:	427 sq. ft.

Exterior Wall Framing:	2x4

Foundation options:
Daylight basement (P-6588-2D).
Crawlspace (P-6588-2A).
(Foundation & framing conversion diagram available — see order form.)

Blueprint Price Code:	A

TO ORDER THIS BLUEPRINT, CALL TOLL-FREE 1-800-547-5570
(prices and details on pp. 12-15.)

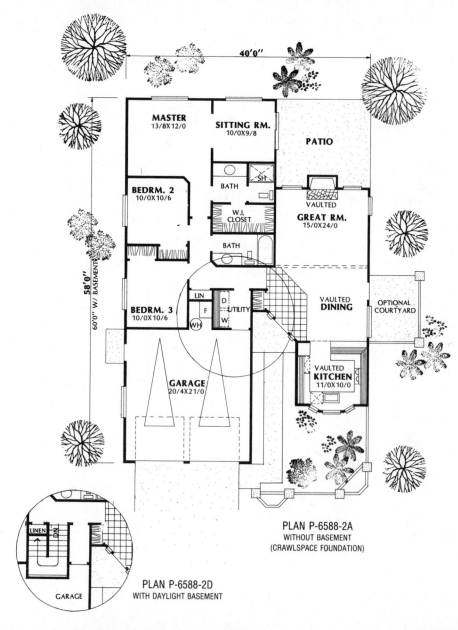

PLAN P-6588-2A
WITHOUT BASEMENT
(CRAWLSPACE FOUNDATION)

PLAN P-6588-2D
WITH DAYLIGHT BASEMENT

Plans P-6588-2A & -2D

L-Shaped Country-Style Home

- The classic L-shape and covered front poch with decorative railings and columns make this home reminiscent of the early 20th century farmhouse.
- The dormer windows give the home the look of a two-story, even though it is designed for convenient single-level living.
- The huge living room features ceilings that slope up to 13 feet. The beamed area of the ceiling is 8 feet high and creates a cozy atmosphere. A corner fireplace radiates warmth to both the living room and the dining room.
- The dining room overlooks the backyard patio and is open to the kitchen. Just off the kitchen is a large utility room.
- The master bedroom has a compartmentalized bath. The two smaller bedrooms at the other end of the home share a full bath.

Plan E-1412

Bedrooms: 3	Baths: 2
Space:	
Main floor	1,484 sq. ft.
Total Living Area	**1,484 sq. ft.**
Exterior Wall Framing	2x6

Foundation options:

Crawlspace

Slab

(Foundation & framing conversion diagram available—see order form.)

Blueprint Price Code	**A**

Plan E-1412

Charming Traditional Design

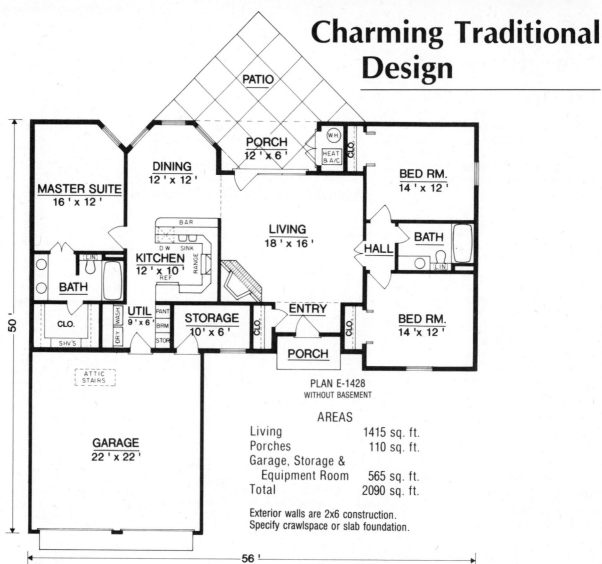

PATIO

PORCH
12' x 6'

DINING
12' x 12'

MASTER SUITE
16' x 12'

BED RM.
14' x 12'

BATH

LIVING
18' x 16'

BAR

KITCHEN
12' x 10'

HALL

50'

BATH

CLO.

SHV'S

UTIL
9' x 6'

STORAGE
10' x 6'

ENTRY

BED RM.
14' x 12'

PORCH

ATTIC STAIRS

GARAGE
22' x 22'

PLAN E-1428
WITHOUT BASEMENT

AREAS

Living	1415 sq. ft.
Porches	110 sq. ft.
Garage, Storage & Equipment Room	565 sq. ft.
Total	2090 sq. ft.

Exterior walls are 2x6 construction.
Specify crawlspace or slab foundation.

56'

Blueprint Price Code A

Plan E-1428

Deluxe Master Bath In Modest-Sized Plan

6' HIGH WOOD PRIVACY FENCE

BATH
LINEN
CLO.
SHV
VANITY
M.C.

LIN

MASTER SUITE
15' x 14'

BED RM.
13' x 12'
CLO.
CLO.
CLO.

PORCH
10' x 10'

DINING
12' x 10'

LIN

BATH
HALL
CLO.

LIVING
18' x 16'

BAR
SINK
D.W.
KITCHEN
12' x 10'
RANGE   REF

CLO.

WASH
UTIL
8' x 6'
DRY

STOR
12' x 5'

56'

BED RM.
13' x 12'

SLOPE   CEILING
CLO.

PORCH
12' x 6'

HEAT & A/C

W.H.

ATTIC STAIRS

GARAGE
22' x 21'

AREAS

Living	1420 sq. ft.
Porches	189 sq. ft.
Garage & Storage	540 sq. ft.
Total	2149 sq. ft.

Exterior walls are 2x6 construction.
Specify crawlspace or slab foundation.

52'

Blueprint Price Code A

Plan E-1426

TO ORDER THIS BLUEPRINT,
CALL TOLL-FREE 1-800-547-5570
(prices and details on pp. 12-15.)

The Solid Look of Permanence

- Exterior design lends an air of quality and elegance which is carried on throughout the home.
- Large, centered living room decor includes 10' ceilings, detailed fireplace, and ceiling fans.
- Side porch can be entered through living/dining area.
- Minimum halls generate maximum living space.
- Secluded master suite has romantic sitting area and designer bath.

Plan E-1435

Bedrooms: 3	Baths: 2

Space:	
Total living area:	1,442 sq. ft.
Garage and storage:	516 sq. ft.
Porches:	128 sq. ft.

Exterior Wall Framing:	2x4

Foundation options:
Crawlspace.
Slab.
(Foundation & framing conversion diagram available — see order form.)

Blueprint Price Code:	A

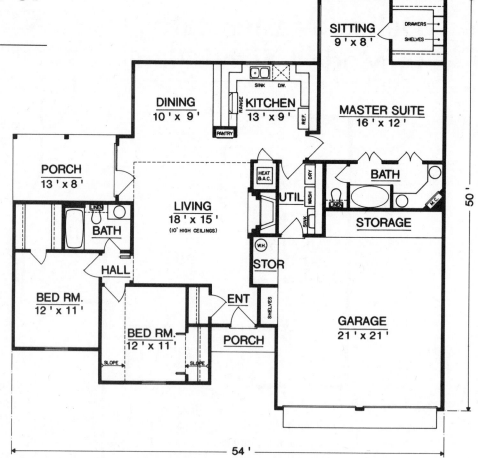

Plan E-1435

Cozy, Compact One-Story Home

- Central living room and attached dining room feature 11' ceilings.
- Cleverly positioned between the main living areas is a unique fireplace, wet bar, and book shelves combination.
- Isolated master suite boasts private bath and large walk-in closet.
- Secondary bedrooms have king-sized closets, and share a full bath.

Plan E-1427

Bedrooms: 3	Baths: 2

Space:

Total living area:	1,444 sq. ft.
Garage and storage:	540 sq. ft.
Porches:	160 sq. ft.

Exterior Wall Framing:	2x4

Foundation options:
Crawlspace.
Slab.
(Foundation & framing conversion diagram available — see order form.)

Blueprint Price Code:	A

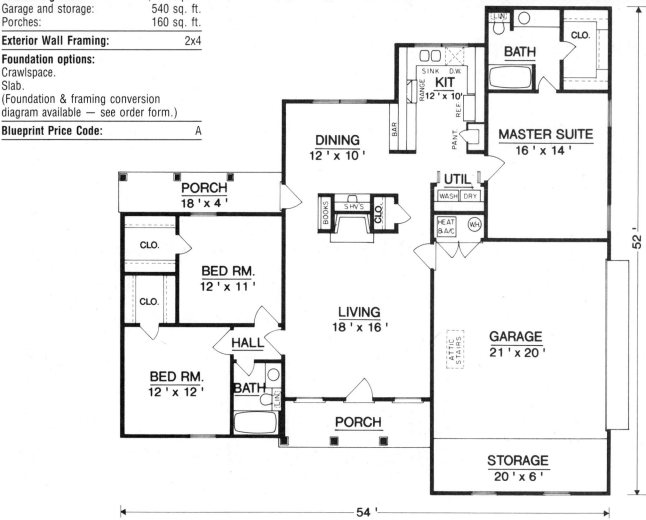

Plan E-1427

Kitchen Faces Wrap-Around Porch

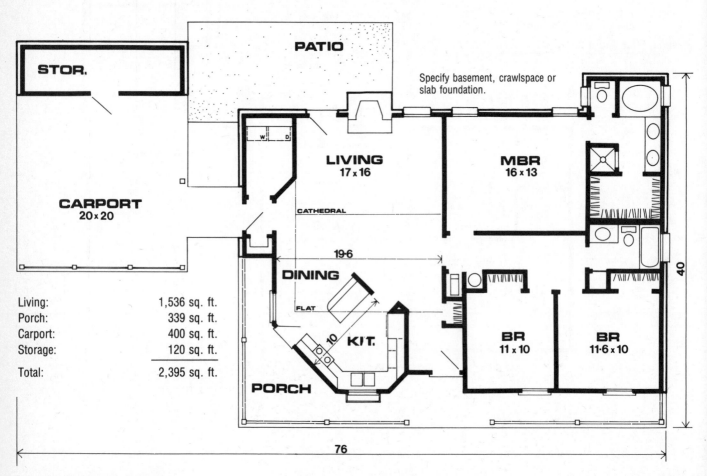

PATIO

STOR.

Specify basement, crawlspace or slab foundation.

CARPORT
20 x 20

LIVING
17 x 16

MBR
16 x 13

CATHEDRAL

19-6

DINING

FLAT

Living:	1,536 sq. ft.
Porch:	339 sq. ft.
Carport:	400 sq. ft.
Storage:	120 sq. ft.
Total:	2,395 sq. ft.

10

KIT.

BR
11 x 10

BR
11·6 x 10

PORCH

40

76

Blueprint Price Code B
Plan J-86142

Rustic Comfort

- While rustic in exterior appearance, this home is completely modern inside and loaded with the amenities preferred by today's builders.
- A large living room is made to seem immense by use of 16' ceilings, and an impressive fireplace and hearth dominate one end of the room.
- A formal dining room adds to the spaciousness, since it is separated from the living room only by a divider and a 6" step.
- The large U-shaped kitchen is adjoined by a convenient sewing and utility area, which in turn leads to the garage. A storage area is included in the garage, along with a built-in workbench.

- The sumptuous master suite features a sitting area, enormous walk-in closet and deluxe private bath.
- The two secondary bedrooms share another full bath and are zoned for privacy.

Plan E-1607	
Bedrooms: 3	**Baths: 2**

Space:	
Total living area:	1,600 sq. ft.
Basement:	approx. 1,600 sq. ft.
Garage:	484 sq. ft.
Storage:	132 sq. ft.
Porch:	295 sq. ft.

Exterior Wall Framing:	2x6

Foundation options:
Standard basement.
Crawlspace.
Slab.
(Foundation & framing conversion diagram available — see order form)

Blueprint Price Code:	B

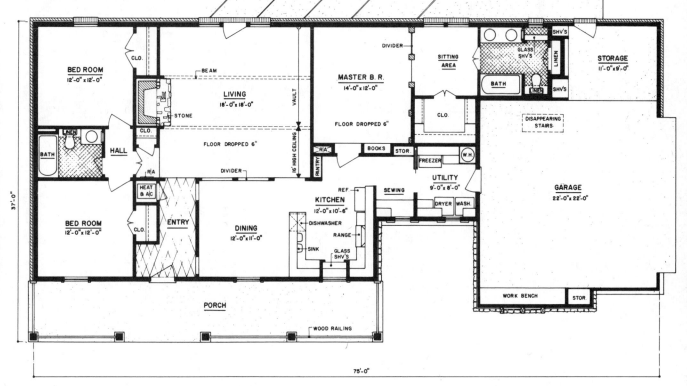

Plan E-1607

Photo by: Karl Bischoff

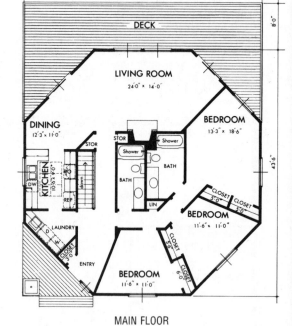

DEN
8'-6" x 13'-3"

up

GARAGE
18'-9" x 21'-0"

BEDROOM
10'-0" x 18'-3"

STOR

BATH

Shr

CLOSET
5'-0"

CLOSET
5'-0"

GENERAL USE
41'-6" x 14'-0"

BASEMENT

DECK

43'-6"

8'-0"

LIVING ROOM
24'-0" x 14'-0"

DINING
12'-3" x 11'-0"

STOR

Shower

BEDROOM
13'-3" x 18'-6"

Shower

KITCHEN
10'-6" x 9'-0"

DW

REF

down

BATH

BATH

LIN

CLOSET
5'-0"

CLOSET
5'-0"

43'-6"

LAUNDRY

D W

CLOSET
3'-0"

ENTRY

BEDROOM
11'-6" x 11'-0"

BEDROOM
11'-6" x 11'-0"

CLOSET
5'-0"

CLOSET
6'-0"

MAIN FLOOR

Unique Octagon Design

- Irregularly shaped rooms are oriented around an entrance hall paralleling the octagonal exterior.
- Short directional hallways eliminate cross-room traffic and provide independent room access to the front door.
- Spacious living and dining rooms form a continuous area more than 38' wide.
- Oversized bathroom serves a large master suite which features a deck view and dual closets.
- This plan is also available with a stucco exterior (Plans H-942-2, with daylight basement, and H-942-2A, without basement).

1/16" = 1'

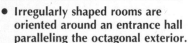

Plans H-942-1 & -1A (Wood)
Plans H-942-2 & -2A (Stucco)

Bedrooms: 3-4	Baths: 2-3
Space:	
Main floor:	1,564 sq. ft.
Basement:	approx. 1,170 sq. ft.
Total with basement:	2,734 sq. ft.
Garage:	394 sq. ft.
Exterior Wall Framing:	2x6

Foundation options:
Daylight basement (Plans H-942-1 & -2).
Crawlspace (Plans H-942-1A & -2A).
(Foundation & framing conversion diagram available — see order form.)

Blueprint Price Code:

Without basement:	B
With basement:	D

Plans H-942-1/1A & -2/2A

Great Room Features Cathedral Ceiling

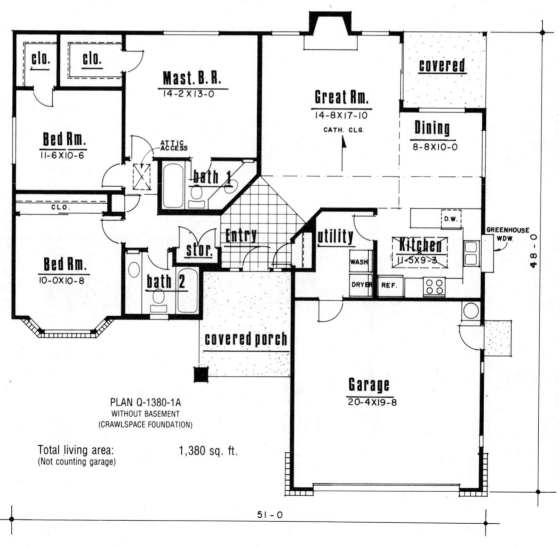

clo. clo.

Mast. B.R.
14-2X13-0

Bed Rm.
11-6X10-6

ATTIC ACCESS

CLO.

Bed Rm.
10-0X10-8

bath 1

bath 2

stor.

Entry

Great Rm.
14-8X17-10
CATH. CLG.

covered

Dining
8-8X10-0

utility

WASH

DRYER   REF.

D.W.

Kitchen
11-5X9-3

GREENHOUSE WDW.

covered porch

Garage
20-4X19-8

48 - 0

51 - 0

PLAN Q-1380-1A
WITHOUT BASEMENT
(CRAWLSPACE FOUNDATION)

Total living area: 1,380 sq. ft.
(Not counting garage)

Deluxe Private Master Bedroom Suite

Living area: 1,380 sq. ft.
Utility & storage: 84 sq. ft.
Garage: 440 sq. ft.
Porch: 80 sq. ft.
_____
1,984 sq. ft.

PLAN E-1311
WITHOUT BASEMENT
(BOTH CRAWLSPACE AND
SLAB FOUNDATION AVAILABLE)

Exterior walls are 2x6 construction.

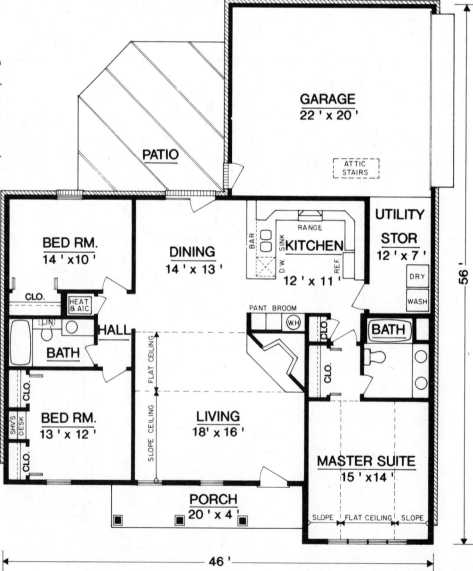

**TO ORDER THIS BLUEPRINT,
CALL TOLL-FREE 1-800-547-5570**
(prices and details on pp. 12-15.)

Blueprint Price Code A
Plan E-1311

Three-Tiered Ranch

- A three-tiered roof externally defines the various internal areas of this traditional-styled ranch.
- An arched front portico and colonial details preview the inviting features you'll find inside, such as the large, dramatic living room; a cathedral ceiling, built-in bookshelves and a stunning two-way brick fireplace are highlights here.
- Opposite, the rear family room reveals a corner wet bar, sliders that access a backyard patio and the other side of the fireplace.
- A wraparound bay window creates an "alfresco" dining experience; across the snack bar is a U-shaped kitchen with pantry and view to the adjoining family room.
- The sleeping tier offers three bedrooms, the master with a walk-in closet and convenient half bath, and two additional bedrooms which share a full bath.

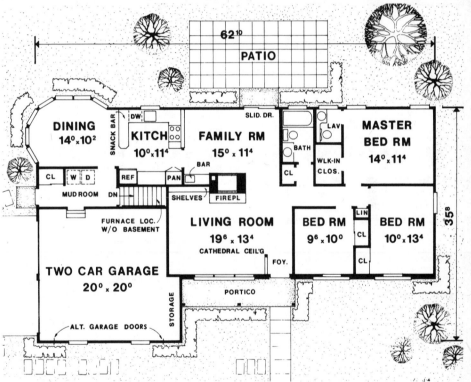

Plan AX-97624-A

Bedrooms: 3	Baths: 1½

Space:

Total living area:	1,396 sq. ft.
Partial basement:	900 sq. ft.
Full basement:	1,396 sq. ft.
Garage:	400 sq. ft.

Exterior Wall Framing:	2x4

Foundation options:
Partial basement.
Standard basement.
Slab.
(Foundation & framing conversion diagram available — see order form.)

Blueprint Price Code: A

Plan AX-97624-A

Open Plan in Traditional Design

- This modest-sized design is popular for its simple yet stylish exterior, making it suitable for either country or urban settings.
- A covered front porch and gabled roof extension accent the facade while providing sheltered space for outdoor relaxing.
- Inside, the living room with a cathedral ceiling and fireplace is combined with an open dining area and kitchen with island to create one large gathering spot for family and guests.

- The master bedroom features a private bath, large closet and ample sleeping area.
- Two other bedrooms share a second full bath.
- A convenient utility area and walk-in pantry are found in the passageway to the carport; also note the large outdoor storage closet.

Plan J-86155

Bedrooms: 3	Baths: 2
Total living area:	1,385 sq. ft.
Basement:	1,385 sq. ft.
Carport:	380 sq. ft.
Exterior Wall Framing:	2x4

Foundation options:
Standard basement.
Crawlspace.
Slab.
(Foundation & framing conversion diagram available — see order form.)

Blueprint Price Code:	A

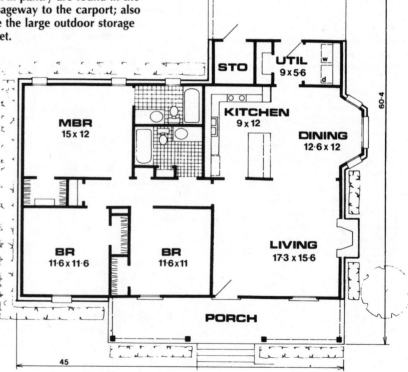

Plan J-86155

Oriented for Scenic Rear View

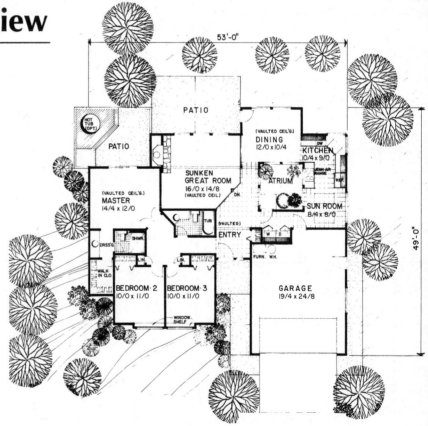

PLAN P-6533-2D
WITH DAYLIGHT BASEMENT

Main floor: 1,484 sq. ft.
(Not counting garage)
Basement level: 1,484 sq. ft.

PLAN P-6533-2A
WITHOUT BASEMENT
(CRAWLSPACE FOUNDATION)

Total living area: 1,399 sq. ft.
(Not counting garage)

Blueprint Price Code A

Plans P-6533-2A & -2D

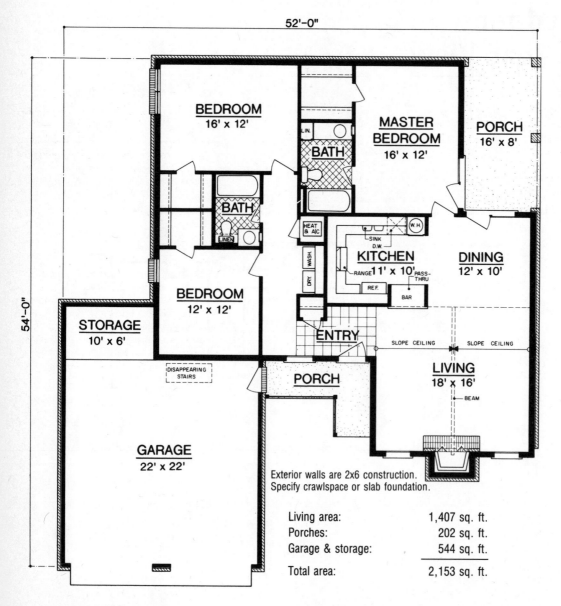

Compact One-Story Home

PLAN E-1425
WITHOUT BASEMENT

52'-0"

54'-0"

BEDROOM
16' x 12'

LIN.

BATH

MASTER
BEDROOM
16' x 12'

PORCH
16' x 8'

BATH

LINEN

HEAT & A/C

W.H.

SINK
D.W.

KITCHEN
11' x 10'

PASS-THRU

DINING
12' x 10'

DRY WASH

RANGE

REF.

BAR

BEDROOM
12' x 12'

STORAGE
10' x 6'

ENTRY

SLOPE CEILING   SLOPE CEILING

DISAPPEARING STAIRS

PORCH

LIVING
18' x 16'

BEAM

GARAGE
22' x 22'

Exterior walls are 2x6 construction.
Specify crawlspace or slab foundation.

Living area:	1,407 sq. ft.
Porches:	202 sq. ft.
Garage & storage:	544 sq. ft.
Total area:	2,153 sq. ft.

**TO ORDER THIS BLUEPRINT,
CALL TOLL-FREE 1-800-547-5570**
(prices and details on pp. 12-15.)

Blueprint Price Code A

Plan E-1425

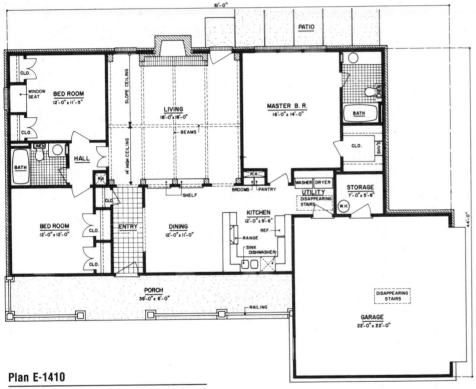

Vaulted Ceiling in Living Room

- This home packs a lot of grace and space into 1,418 square feet.
- Note the large living room with its beamed, vaulted ceiling and massive fireplace.
- The formal dining room lies off the foyer, and adjoins the efficient kitchen, which also includes a pantry and utility area.
- The master suite features a large walk-in closet and roomy master bath.
- At the other end of the home, two secondary bedrooms with abundant closet space share another full bath.
- The house-spanning porch invites guests to come in for a relaxing visit.

Plan E-1410

Bedrooms: 3	Baths: 2

Space:

Total living area:	1,418 sq. ft.
Garage:	484 sq. ft.
Storage:	38 sq. ft.
Porch:	238 sq. ft.

Exterior Wall Framing:	2x4

Foundation options:
Crawlspace.
Slab.
(Foundation & framing conversion diagram available — see order form.)

Blueprint Price Code:	A

Plan E-1410

Appealing Contemporary Styling

- Contemporary wood exterior allows for economical construction.
- Spacious, open floor plan permits easy traffic flow, minimal wasted hall space.
- U-shaped kitchen includes pantry and eating bar.
- Isolated master suite features generous walk-in closet with built-in drawers and shelves and a private bath with separate sinks and large whirlpool.

Plan E-1430

Bedrooms: 3	Baths: 2

Space:

Total living area:	1,430 sq. ft.
Garage and storage:	465 sq. ft.
Porches:	128 sq. ft.

Exterior Wall Framing: 2x4

Foundation options:
Crawlspace.
Slab.
(Foundation & framing conversion diagram available — see order form.)

Blueprint Price Code: A

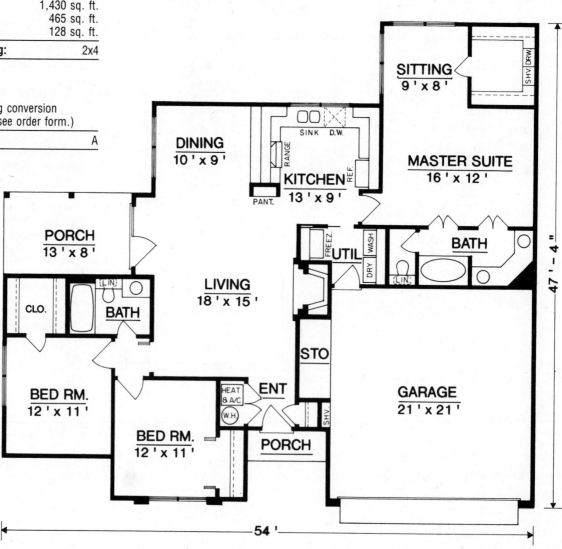

SITTING 9' x 8'

DINING 10' x 9'

SINK   D.W.

RANGE

KITCHEN 13' x 9'

PANT.

MASTER SUITE 16' x 12'

PORCH 13' x 8'

CLO.

LIN.

BATH

FREEZ.

UTIL

WASH   DRY

LIN.

BATH

LIVING 18' x 15'

BED RM. 12' x 11'

STO

ENT

BED RM. 12' x 11'

HEAT & A/C   W.H.

SHV.

PORCH

GARAGE 21' x 21'

47' - 4"

54'

Plan E-1430

Angles Add Interior Excitement

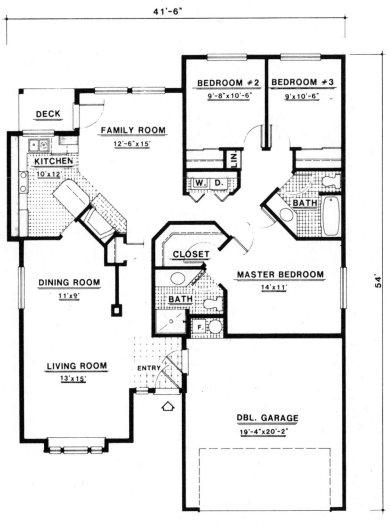

41'-6"

DECK

FAMILY ROOM
12'-6"x15'

KITCHEN
10'x12'

BEDROOM #2
9'-8"x10'-6"

BEDROOM #3
9'x10'-6"

LIN.

W. D.

BATH

DINING ROOM
11'x9'

CLOSET

MASTER BEDROOM
14'x11'

BATH

F.

LIVING ROOM
13'x15'

ENTRY

54'

DBL. GARAGE
19'-4"x20'-2"

- Eye-catching exterior leads into exciting interior.
- You'll find cathedral ceilings throughout the living and dining area.
- Angular kitchen includes eating bar, plenty of cabinet and counter space.
- Master suite includes angled double-door entry, private bath and large walk-in closet.
- Family room and kitchen join together to make large casual family area.
- Main bathroom continues the angled motif, and the washer and dryer are conveniently located in the bedroom hallway.

Plan NW-864

Bedrooms: 3	Baths: 2
Total living area:	1,449 sq. ft.
Garage:	390 sq. ft.
Exterior Wall Framing:	2x6

Foundation options:
Crawlspace only.
(Foundation & framing conversion diagram available — see order form.)

Blueprint Price Code:	A

Plan NW-864

Distinctive Exterior, Economical Construction

- A modest-sized and fairly simple one-story design, this home will fit the budget of many young families.
- To make optimum use of a limited space, the living and dining rooms are combined to make more space for entertaining large groups.
- The open kitchen faces a sunny nook, with bay windows to brighten the entire area.
- An adjoining family room includes a corner wood stove for heat and a cozy atmosphere on chilly days.
- A pleasant master suite includes a double-door entry, skylighted bath and large closet.
- Bedrooms 2 and 3 share another full bath, and the utility area is convenient to all three bedrooms.

Plan R-1063

Bedrooms: 3	Baths: 2

Space:

Total living area:	1,585 sq. ft.
Garage:	408 sq. ft.

Exterior Wall Framing:	2x4

Foundation options:
Crawlspace only.
(Foundation & framing conversion diagram available — see order form.)

Blueprint Price Code:	B

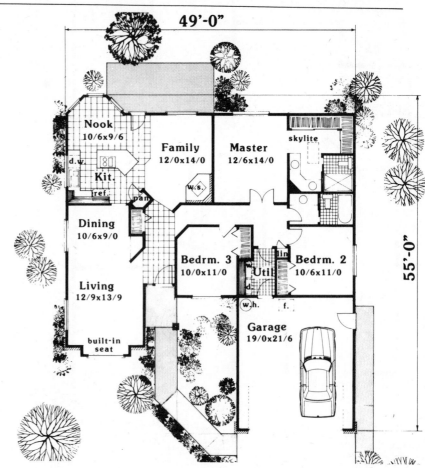

Plan R-1063

Open Plan Includes Circular Dining Room

- Innovative architectural features and a functional, light-filled floor plan are the hallmarks of this attractive design.
- The facade is graced by a stone chimney and a circular glass bay which houses the spectacular dining room with its domed ceiling.
- A bright, sunny kitchen is set up for efficient operation and adjoins a dinette area which echoes the circular shape of the formal dining room.
- The living room features a stone fireplace, and opens to the dining room to make a great space for entertaining.
- The bedrooms are zoned to the left, with the master suite including a private bath, large walk-in closet and access to an outdoor terrace.

Plan K-663-N

Bedrooms: 3	Baths: 2

Space:	
Total living area:	**1,560 sq. ft.**
Basement:	1,645 sq. ft.
Garage:	453 sq. ft.
Mudroom & stairs:	122 sq. ft.

Exterior Wall Framing:	2x4/2x6

Foundation options:
Standard basement.
Slab.
(Foundation & framing conversion diagram available — see order form.)

Blueprint Price Code:	B

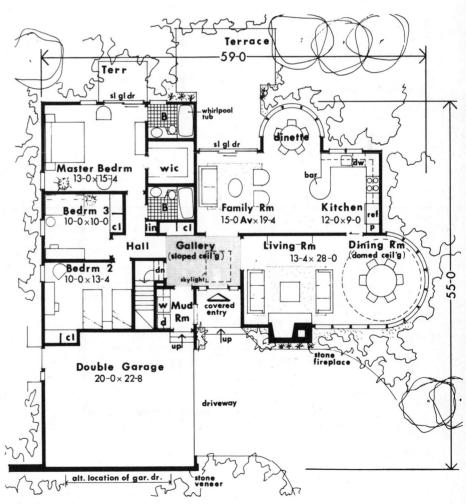

Plan K-663-N

TO ORDER THIS BLUEPRINT, CALL TOLL-FREE 1-800-547-5570
(prices and details on pp. 12-15.)

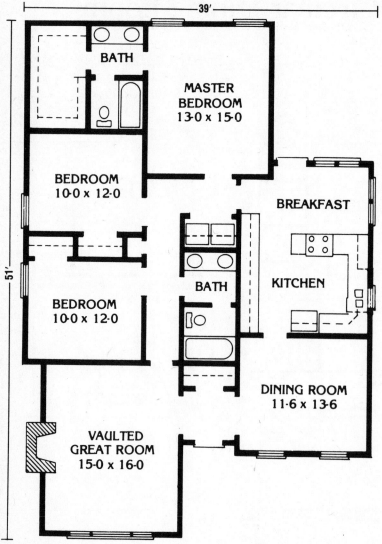

BATH

MASTER
BEDROOM
13-0 x 15-0

BEDROOM
10-0 x 12-0

BREAKFAST

BATH

KITCHEN

BEDROOM
10-0 x 12-0

DINING ROOM
11-6 x 13-6

VAULTED
GREAT ROOM
15-0 x 16-0

39'

51'

Appealing French Details

Authentic French details adorn the facade of this appealing one-story design. The slightly recessed doorway, arched windows, and curved shutters all add interest to this beautifully proportioned residence.

The vaulted ceiling of the Great Room makes this room appear much larger than its dimensions state. An oversized Palladian window creates a dramatic focal point and floods the room with natural light. The kitchen contains an unusual amount of cabinets and counter space.

Abundant closet space is provided for the inhabitants of the master bedroom. Also, note the convenient location of the laundry center, handy to both kitchen and bedroom areas.

PLAN V-1586
WITHOUT BASEMENT
(CRAWLSPACE FOUNDATION)

Total living area: 1,586 sq. ft.

9'-0" CEILINGS THROUGHOUT

Blueprint Price Code B
Plan V-1586

Choice of Exterior Designs for Practical Plan

PLAN N-117-HB-1 (with basement)
PLAN N-117-HB-2 (with crawlspace or slab)

PLAN N-117-HA-1 (with basement)
PLAN N-117-HA-2 (with crawlspace or slab)

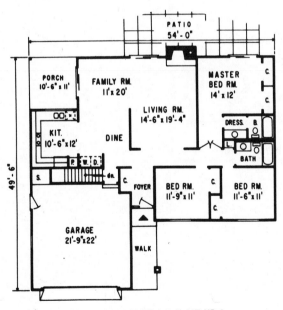

PLANS N-117-HA-1 & N-117-HB-1
WITH BASEMENT

Total living area: 1,555 sq. ft.
(Not counting basement or garage)

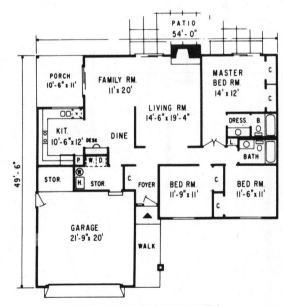

PLANS N-117-HA-2 & N-117-HB-2
WITHOUT BASEMENT

Specify crawlspace or slab foundation.

Total living area: 1,565 sq. ft.
(Not counting garage)

Blueprint Price Code B

Plans N-117-HA-1 & -2, N-117-HB-1 & -2

TO ORDER THIS BLUEPRINT,
CALL TOLL-FREE 1-800-547-5570
(prices and details on pp. 12-15.)

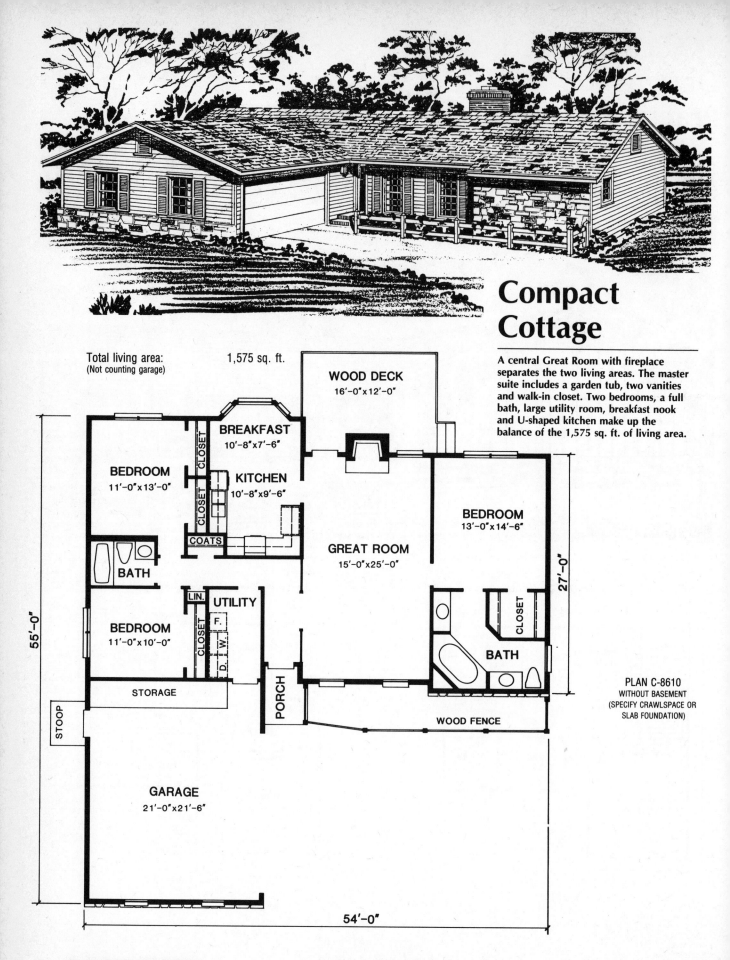

Compact Cottage

Total living area: 1,575 sq. ft.
(Not counting garage)

A central Great Room with fireplace separates the two living areas. The master suite includes a garden tub, two vanities and walk-in closet. Two bedrooms, a full bath, large utility room, breakfast nook and U-shaped kitchen make up the balance of the 1,575 sq. ft. of living area.

WOOD DECK
16'-0" x 12'-0"

BREAKFAST
10'-8" x 7'-6"

CLOSET

CLOSET

BEDROOM
11'-0" x 13'-0"

KITCHEN
10'-8" x 9'-6"

COATS

BATH

GREAT ROOM
15'-0" x 25'-0"

BEDROOM
13'-0" x 14'-6"

LIN.

UTILITY

F.

CLOSET

D. W.

BEDROOM
11'-0" x 10'-0"

CLOSET

BATH

27'-0"

55'-0"

STORAGE

PLAN C-8610
WITHOUT BASEMENT
(SPECIFY CRAWLSPACE OR
SLAB FOUNDATION)

STOOP

PORCH

WOOD FENCE

GARAGE
21'-0" x 21'-6"

54'-0"

Blueprint Price Code B
Plan C-8610

PLAN H-1381-1
WITH BASEMENT

Total living area: 1,596 sq. ft.
(Not counting basement or garage)

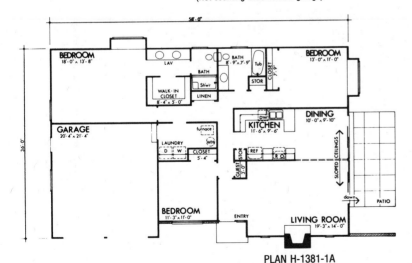

PLAN H-1381-1A
WITHOUT BASEMENT
(CRAWLSPACE FOUNDATION)

Total living area: 1,587 sq. ft.
(Not counting garage)

Popular Contemporary

This low-slung contemporary design contains a lot more space than is apparent from the outside. Oriented towards the outdoor sideyard, it features a pair of sliding glass doors offering outside access from both the living and dining room.

Effective zoning is the rule here: Bedrooms are secluded on one side to the rear; living areas and active kitchen space are grouped on the opposite side of the home.

All of these rooms are easily reached from a central hallway that provides excellent traffic flow, precluding unnecessary cross-room traffic.

Note the convenient location of the laundry room and staircase to the basement. Access to the garage is also available from the interior of the home. A generous assortment of plumbing facilities is grouped at the rear of the home. One bath serves the master bedroom privately. Another complete unit serves the balance of the house.

The attractive low silhouette is embellished with architectural touches such as the interesting window seats, the extension of the masonry wall that shields the side patio, and the low pitched roof.

Overall width of the home is 58' and greatest depth measures 36'. Exterior walls are 2x6 construction.

Blueprint Price Code B

Plans H-1381-1 & -1A

Updated Traditional

- "Updated traditional," is how you might describe this 1,571 sq. ft. home. The exterior combines traditional materials, such as lap siding, divided light windows and an inviting entry with flanking side lights.
- Inside, the home has the design features the move-up or empty nesters markets desire. From the vaulted entry, there is a long view over the open railed stairs to the Great Room with fireplace and sliders to a deck.
- The island kitchen overlooks a breakfast eating area and has a pass-through to the Great Room eating area.
- The master bedroom has a vaulted ceiling, walk-in closet, and private bath with additional vanity in the dressing area.
- The third bedroom can be used as a den or study.

Plan B-88039

Bedrooms: 2-3	Baths: 2
Space:	
Total living area:	1,571 sq. ft.
Basement:	1,571 sq. ft.
Garage:	440 sq. ft.
Exterior Wall Framing:	2x4

Foundation options:
Standard basement.
(Foundation & framing conversion diagram available — see order form.)

Blueprint Price Code:	B

***TO ORDER THIS BLUEPRINT,
CALL TOLL-FREE 1-800-547-5570***
(prices and details on pp. 12-15.)

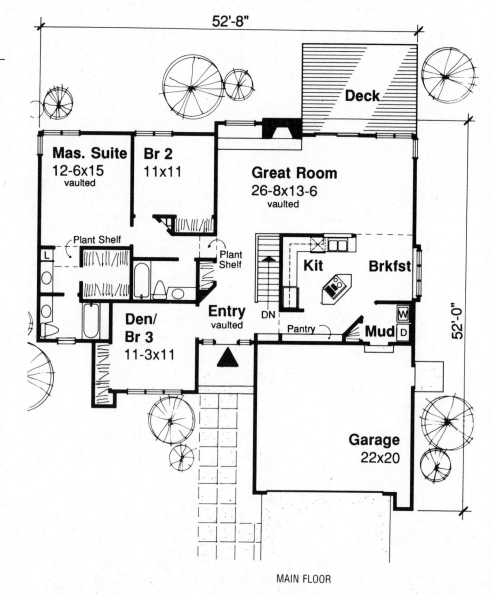

52'-8"

Deck

Mas. Suite 12-6x15 vaulted

Br 2 11x11

Great Room 26-8x13-6 vaulted

Plant Shelf

Plant Shelf

L

Den/ Br 3 11-3x11

Entry vaulted

Kit

Brkfst

DN

Pantry

Mud

W

D

52'-0"

Garage 22x20

MAIN FLOOR

Plan B-88039

Vaulted Living Room Featured

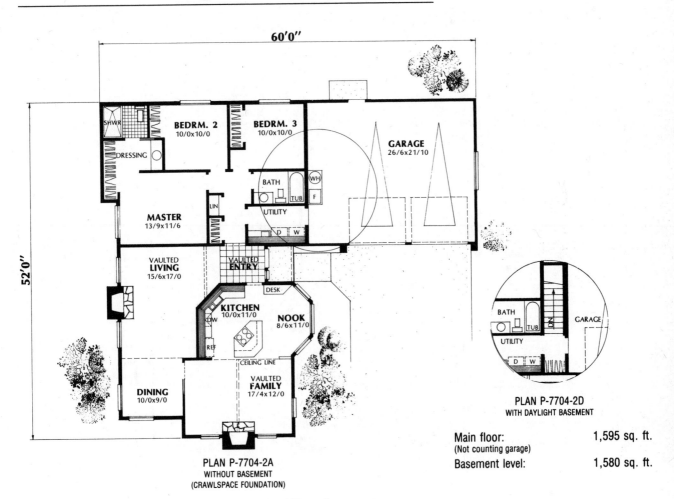

PLAN P-7704-2A
WITHOUT BASEMENT
(CRAWLSPACE FOUNDATION)

Total living area: 1,535 sq. ft.
(Not counting garage)

PLAN P-7704-2D
WITH DAYLIGHT BASEMENT

Main floor: 1,595 sq. ft.
(Not counting garage)
Basement level: 1,580 sq. ft.

Blueprint Price Code B

Plans P-7704-2A & -2D

TO ORDER THIS BLUEPRINT,
CALL TOLL-FREE 1-800-547-5570
(prices and details on pp. 12-15.)

Angular Interior Adds Spark

- Mediterranean-style exterior encloses a creatively modern interior.
- Living and dining rooms form a "V", with the kitchen at the center.
- Master suite includes a triangular bath with separate tub and shower, which is in a five-sided enclosure.
- The study is also angled, and would make a great home office if needed for that purpose.
- A sunny breakfast nook adjoins the kitchen which is also angled for visual interest and efficiency.
- Laundry area is found in the garage entryway, next to the second bath.

Plan Q-1449-1A

Bedrooms: 2	Baths: 2
Total living area:	1,449 sq. ft.
Garage:	387 sq. ft.
Exterior Wall Framing:	2x4

Foundation options:
  Slab only.
(Foundation & framing conversion diagram available — see order form.)

Blueprint Price Code:	A

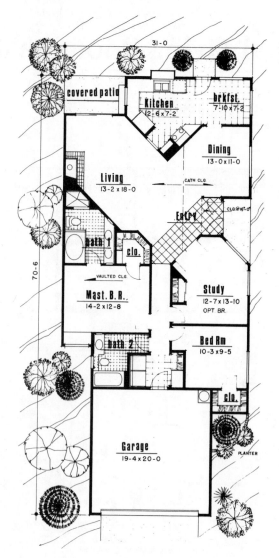

Plan Q-1449-1A

Economical Design

FRONT VIEW

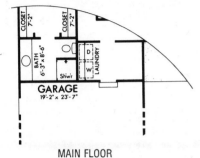

MAIN FLOOR
PLAN H-868-1A
WITHOUT BASEMENT

REAR VIEW

- Uninterrupted glass and a full, rear deck afford a sweeping view of the outdoors.
- Rear orientation provides a seclusion from street and neighbors.
- Open, flexible family living areas allow for efficient traffic flow.
- Optional daylight basement plan offers recreation room, additional bedroom and third bath.

Plans H-868-1 & -1A	
Bedrooms: 3-4	**Baths: 2-3**
Space: Main floor:	1,525 sq. ft.
Total living area:	1,525 sq. ft.
Basement:	1,420 sq. ft.
Garage:	426 sq. ft.
Exterior Wall Framing:	2x4

Foundation options:
Daylight basement (Plan H-868-1).
Crawlspace (Plan H-868-1A).
(Foundation & framing conversion diagram available — see order form.)

Blueprint Price Code:
Without basement   B
With basement   D

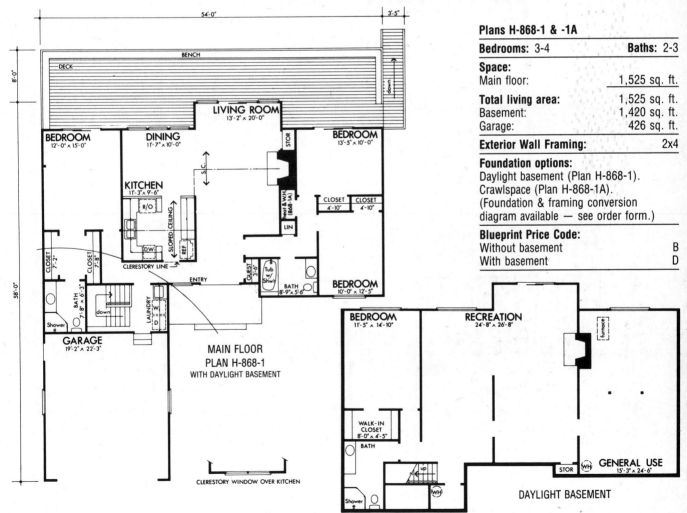

MAIN FLOOR
PLAN H-868-1
WITH DAYLIGHT BASEMENT

CLERESTORY WINDOW OVER KITCHEN

DAYLIGHT BASEMENT

Plans H-868-1 & -1A

Compact Contemporary With Clerestory

This 1,457 square foot contemporary design features a large family room with a stone fireplace, double doors to the rear patio, dining area, open stairwell to the full basement and a vaulted ceiling with exposed wood beams and triple clerestory windows. The master suite includes two walk-in closets and a private bath. Both front bedrooms have a walk-in closet and share a second full bath. The eat-in kitchen includes access from the dining area as well as the front opening garage. Additional features include a coat closet off the foyer, vertical wood siding with stone, and a recessed entry with a front porch.

Total living area: 1,457 sq. ft.
(Not counting basement or garage)

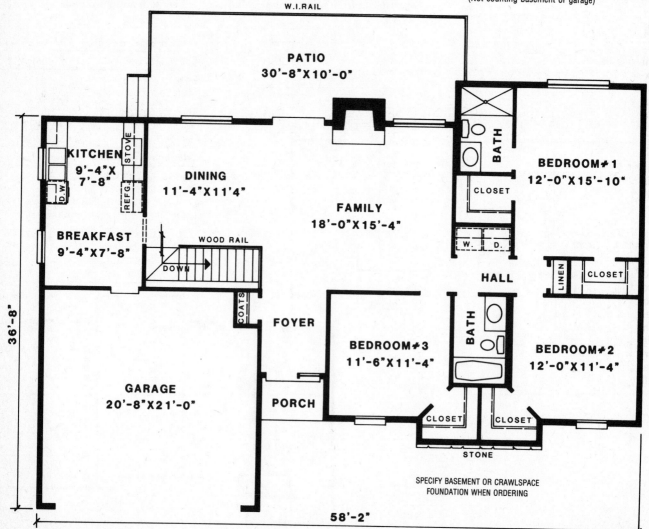

Blueprint Price Code A
Plan C-8356

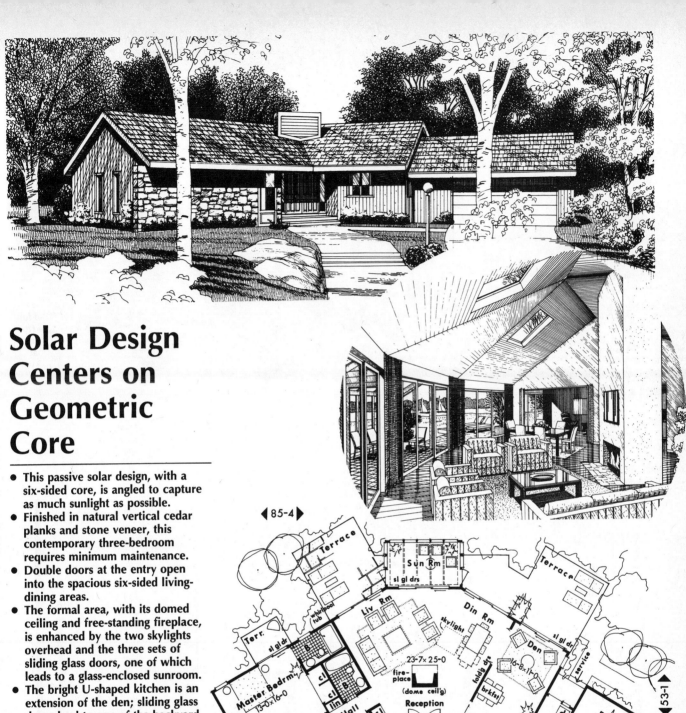

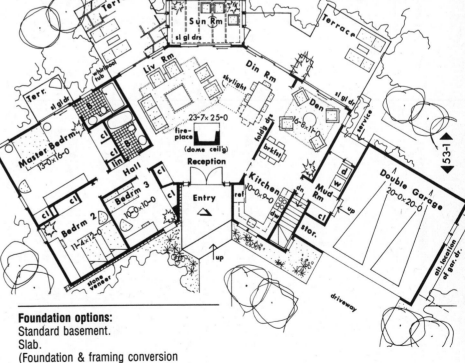

Solar Design Centers on Geometric Core

- This passive solar design, with a six-sided core, is angled to capture as much sunlight as possible.
- Finished in natural vertical cedar planks and stone veneer, this contemporary three-bedroom requires minimum maintenance.
- Double doors at the entry open into the spacious six-sided living-dining areas.
- The formal area, with its domed ceiling and free-standing fireplace, is enhanced by the two skylights overhead and the three sets of sliding glass doors, one of which leads to a glass-enclosed sunroom.
- The bright U-shaped kitchen is an extension of the den; sliding glass doors lead to one of the backyard terraces.
- The master bedoom, in a quiet sleeping wing, boasts ample closets, private terrace and a luxurious bath, complete with a whirlpool tub.

Plan K-534-L

Bedrooms: 3	Baths: 2

Space:	
Total living area:	**1,495 sq. ft.**
Basement:	1,505 sq. ft.
Garage:	400 sq. ft.
Mud room, etc.:	152 sq. ft.
Exterior Wall Framing:	2x4 or 2x6

Foundation options:
Standard basement.
Slab.
(Foundation & framing conversion diagram available — see order form)

Blueprint Price Code:	A

Plan K-534-L

Cathedral Ceiling Featured

The open floor plan of this modified A-Frame design virtually eliminates wasted hall space. The centrally located Great Room features a 15'4" cathedral ceiling with exposed wood beams and large areas of fixed glass on both front and rear. Living and dining areas are visually separated by a massive stone fireplace.

The isolated master suite features a walk-in closet and sliding glass doors opening onto the front deck.

A walk-thru utility room provides easy access from the carport and outside storage area to the compact kitchen. On the opposite side of the Great Room are two additional bedrooms and a second full

bath. All this takes up only 1,454 square feet of heated living area. A full length deck and vertical wood siding with stone accents on the corners provide a rustic yet contemporary exterior.

Total living area: 1,454 sq. ft.
(Not counting basement or garage)

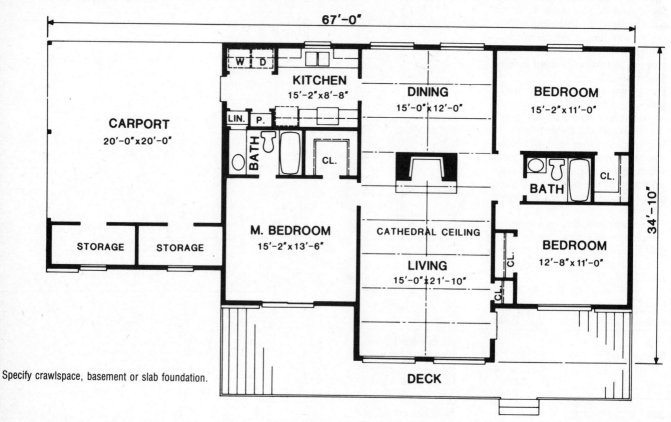

Specify crawlspace, basement or slab foundation.

TO ORDER THIS BLUEPRINT,
CALL TOLL-FREE 1-800-547-5570
(prices and details on pp. 12-15.)

Blueprint Price Code A
Plan C-7360

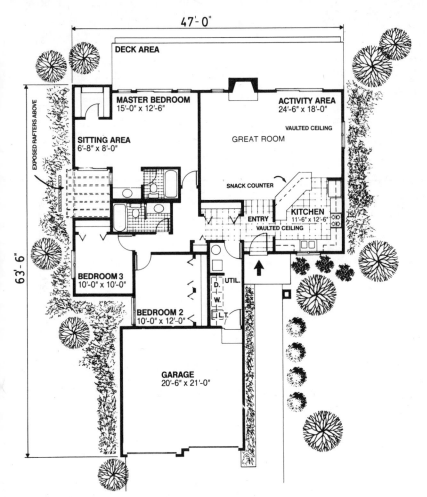

Affordable Three-Bedroom with Open Kitchen and Great Room

Multiple gabled roofs with dramatic overhangs add to the exterior charm of this three-bedroom contemporary home. The interior is cozy, with plenty of features for folks who love outdoor living indoors. There's a garden area located just off the master bedroom's sitting area with privacy fence. Vaulted ceilings add a sense of the great outdoors to the large activity area, corner kitchen, and entry. The activity room also enjoys its own fireplace and snack bar and shares access to a rear wood deck with the master bedroom.

PLAN N-1276-1
WITH BASEMENT

PLAN N-1276-2
WITHOUT BASEMENT
(CRAWLSPACE WITH
OPTIONAL SLAB-ON-GRADE)

Total living area: 1,533 sq.. ft.

Small Home with a Big Look

- Vaulted ceilings and an open floor plan bring a big look to the interior spaces of this modestly sized home.
- Twin gables, a modified hip roof and a mixture of brick and wood siding give added dimension to the exterior.
- The recessed entry opens to the foyer, where the spectacular living and dining rooms come into immediate view. Vaulted ceilings, a fireplace and plenty of windows overlooking the patio lend a bright, airy feel to these two rooms.
- The combination kitchen and breakfast area is also vaulted. The kitchen features a wall cutout to the dining room, while the breakfast area includes a convenient laundry closet.
- The angled wall in the foyer branches to the bedroom hallway. The master bedroom offers a vaulted ceiling, his and hers closets and a private bath with a garden tub. The two smaller bedrooms share a hall bath.

Plan APS-1305

Bedrooms: 3	**Baths:** 2
Space:.	
Main floor	1,302 sq. ft.
Total Living Area	**1,302 sq. ft.**
Garage	380 sq. ft.
Exterior Wall Framing	2x4

Foundation options:

Slab

(Foundation & framing conversion diagram available—see order form.)

Blueprint Price Code	**A**

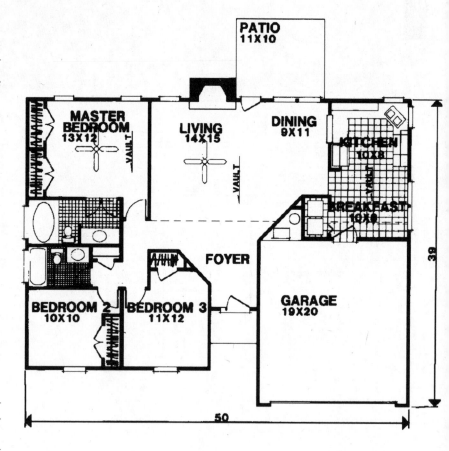

MAIN FLOOR

Plan APS-1305

Simple Plan for Economical Construction

Total living area:	1,522 sq. ft.
Carport:	397 sq. ft.
Storage:	39 sq. ft.
Front porch:	213 sq. ft.
Total area:	2,171 sq. ft.

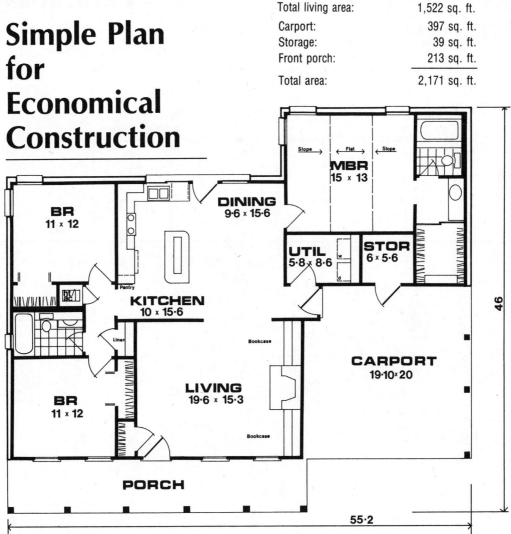

Specify basement, crawlspace or slab foundation.

Blueprint Price Code B

Plan J-8670

TO ORDER THIS BLUEPRINT,
CALL TOLL-FREE 1-800-547-5570
(prices and details on pp. 12-15.)

Solarium Brightens This Economical 3-Bedroom Home

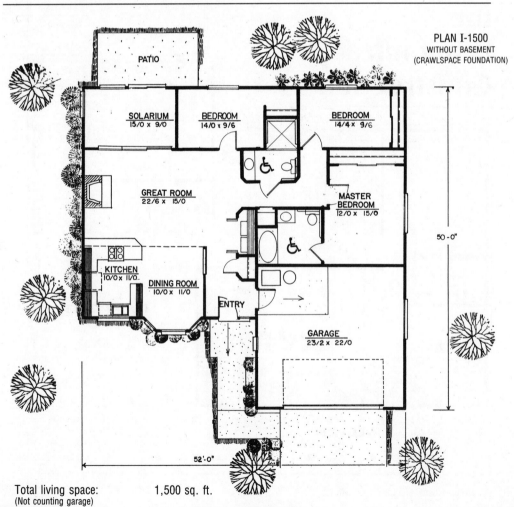

PLAN I-1500
WITHOUT BASEMENT
(CRAWLSPACE FOUNDATION)

PATIO

SOLARIUM
15/0 x 9/0

BEDROOM
14/0 x 9/6

BEDROOM
14/4 x 9/6

GREAT ROOM
22/6 x 15/0

MASTER BEDROOM
12/0 x 15/0

KITCHEN
10/0 x 11/0

DINING ROOM
10/0 x 11/0

ENTRY

GARAGE
23/2 x 22/0

50'-0"

52'-0"

Total living space: 1,500 sq. ft.
(Not counting garage)

**TO ORDER THIS BLUEPRINT,
CALL TOLL-FREE 1-800-547-5570**

(prices and details on pp. 12-15.)

Blueprint Price Code B

Plan I-1500-H

Passive Solar with Many Orientation Options

This angled passive solar design is planned to suit almost any plot and many orientation alternatives. Exterior siding of vertical natural wood and a high front chimney give the house an interesting appearance.

Inside, the central focus is the light-filled south-facing sun garden that greets occupants and visitors as they enter the reception hall. The large combination living room and dining room are highlighted by a dramatic sloped ceiling and a high-efficiency wood-burning fireplace. Glass around and above the fireplace contributes more light and provides a panoramic view of the rear landscaping. Sharing a second fireplace is the informal area that includes the family room and U-shaped kitchen.

Three bedrooms are located in the left wing of the house. The large master suite has a cheerful sitting area which borders on the sun garden. Living area, excluding the sun garden, is 1,574 sq. ft.; optional basement is 1,522 sq. ft.; garage is 400 sq. ft.

Total living area: 1,574 sq. ft.
(Not counting basement or garage)

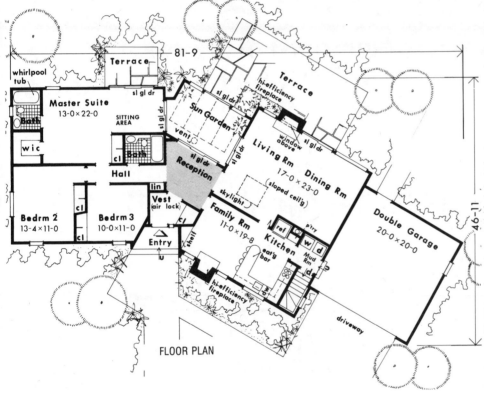

FLOOR PLAN

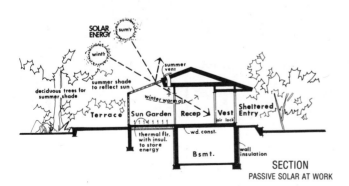

SECTION
PASSIVE SOLAR AT WORK

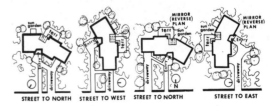

IMAGINE THE ORIENTATION POSSIBILITIES

Blueprint Price Code B

Plan K-526-C

Narrow-Lot Home with Distinctive Appearance

SECOND FLOOR

PLAN Q-1520-1A
WITHOUT BASEMENT
(SLAB FOUNDATION)

First floor: 984 sq. ft.
Second floor: 536 sq. ft.

Total living area: 1,520 sq. ft.
(Not counting garage)

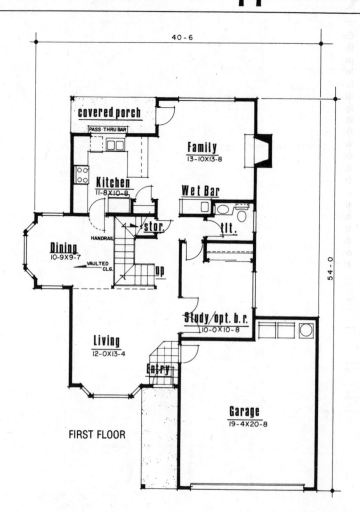

FIRST FLOOR

TO ORDER THIS BLUEPRINT,
CALL TOLL-FREE 1-800-547-5570
(prices and details on pp. 12-15.)

Blueprint Price Code B
Plan Q-1520-1A

Low-Cost Comfort

Conceived to weather energy-tight times, this single-story passive solar home provides year-round comfort at much lower fuel costs. Inside, the open airy plan is a delight. In winter, the sun's warming rays penetrate deeply into the living spaces; warmth settles in the thermal stone wall and floors. After sundown, the floors and walls steadily radiate all the warmth saved during the day. Eave overhangs shade the interior during the summer; operable clerestory windows create a cooling air draft by convection.

The compact plan is suitable for many sites and conditions. With minor modifications, the design is also adaptable to a zero lot line or attached condominium developments. Living area is 1,495 sq. ft.; optional basement is 634 sq. ft.; garage, etc. is 504 sq. ft.

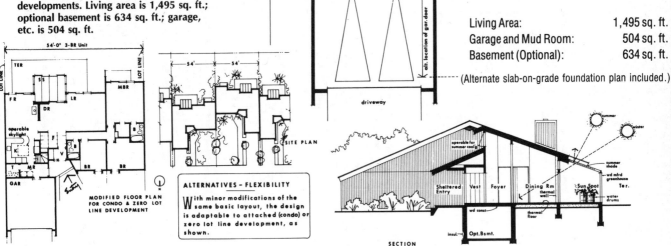

MODIFIED FLOOR PLAN FOR CONDO & ZERO LOT LINE DEVELOPMENT

SITE PLAN

ALTERNATIVES – FLEXIBILITY

With minor modifications of the same basic layout, the design is adaptable to attached (condo) or zero lot line development, as shown.

Living Area:	1,495 sq. ft.
Garage and Mud Room:	504 sq. ft.
Basement (Optional):	634 sq. ft.

(Alternate slab-on-grade foundation plan included.)

SECTION

Compact Plan For Gracious Living

PLAN N-1220-1
WITH BASEMENT

PLAN N-1220-2
CRAWLSPACE WITH OPTIONAL SLAB

Total living area: 1,540 sq. ft.
(Not counting basement or garage)

- Great room, accessible from foyer, offers cathedral ceiling with exposed beams, brick fireplace and access to rear patio.
- Kitchen-breakfast area with center island and cathedral ceiling is accented by the round top window.
- Master bedroom suite includes full bath and walk-in closet.
- Two additional bedrooms and bath help make this an ideal plan for any growing family.

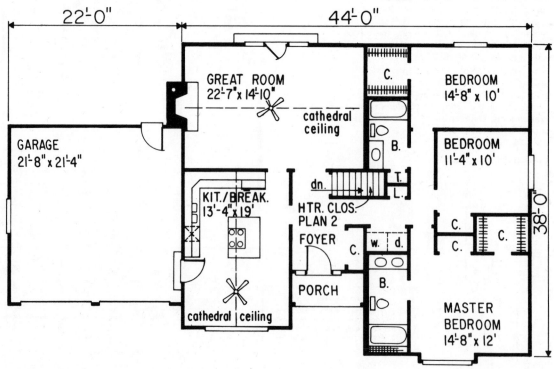

Blueprint Price Code B
Plans N-1220-1 & -2

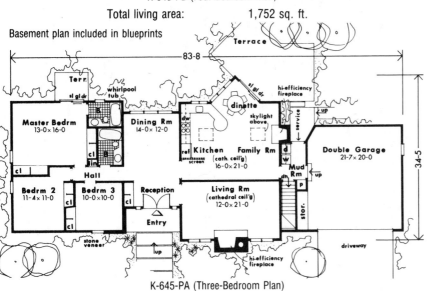

K-645-PB (Four-Bedroom Plan)

Total living area: 1,752 sq. ft.

Basement plan included in blueprints

K-645-PA (Three-Bedroom Plan)

Total living area: 1,548 sq. ft.

Choice of Three- or Four-Bedroom Design

This distinctive contemporary ranch offers a three-bedroom or a four-bedroom version of a nearly identical basic plan. Natural stone and wood finish generates an exterior appeal and requires little maintenance. Double doors at the entry open onto a wide reception hall and a stunning view of the rear garden.

A dramatic cathedral ceiling crowns the living room and the family room/kitchen area. The living room features a woodburning fireplace amid a glass wall. Overlooking the backyard is the informal area; the family room is graced with operable skylights and a second fireplace. An efficient kitchen serves both the cheerful dinette and the formal dining room.

The privately zoned sleeping wing comes with either three bedrooms or four bedrooms. The master bedroom suite boasts a private terrace, ample closet space and a full bath. Living area is 1,548 sq. ft. for the three-bedroom and 1,752 sq. ft. for the four. Garage, mud room, etc., total 563 sq. ft.

Blueprint Price Code B

Plans K-645-PA & K-645-PB

TO ORDER THIS BLUEPRINT,
CALL TOLL-FREE 1-800-547-5570
(prices and details on pp. 12-15.)

One-Level Design Features Vaulted Ceilings

- Compact L-shaped kitchen features corner windows at sink and pass-through to dining room.
- Vaulted master suite features luxurious spa tub, large closets and double vanities.
- Living room focuses on corner fireplace and also opens to outdoor deck.
- Both living and dining rooms boast large window areas.

Plan B-89043

Bedrooms: 2	Baths: 2
Total living area:	1,540 sq. ft.
Basement:	1,540 sq. ft.
Garage:	410 sq. ft.

Exterior Wall Framing:	2x4

Foundation options:
Standard basement.
(Foundation & framing conversion diagram available — see order form.)

Blueprint Price Code:	B

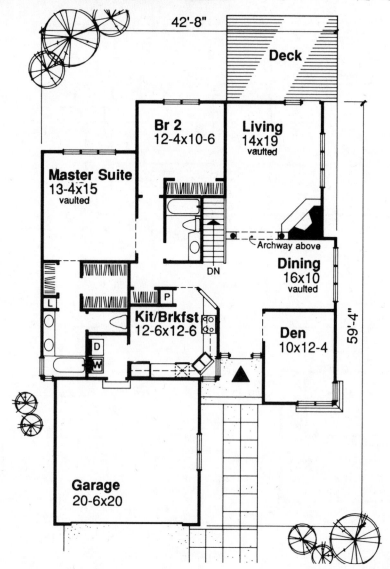

 (prices and details on pp. 12-15.)

Plan B-89043

Flexible Floor Plan Featured

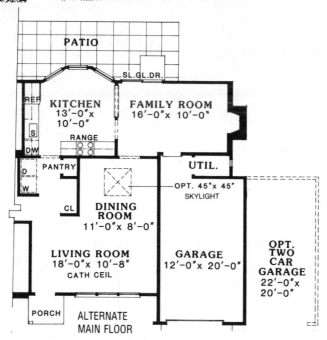

ALTERNATE MAIN FLOOR

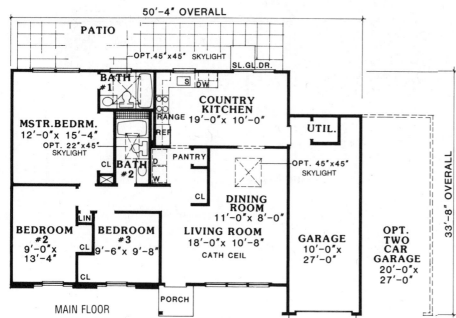

MAIN FLOOR

Plan AX-98818

- This compact cottage-style home has a lot to offer, all within an economical 1,190 sq. ft. What's more, the flexible floor plan gives you several options.
- The low, tiered roofline and covered front entry distinguish the exterior.
- The entry opens to the huge combination living/dining room. Cathedral ceilings, a skylight and the front picture window create an open, airy atmosphere.
- An arched opening connects the dining room to the large country kitchen. An alternate first-floor plan gives the option of a family room and bayed kitchen in place of the country kitchen. In both versions of the plan, sliding glass doors open to a full-width patio.
- The master bedroom also overlooks the rear patio and features a private bath brightened by a skylight.
- Another skylit bath is across from the the two smaller bedrooms.
- Note the central coat closet, laundry area and pantry.
- The plan includes your choice of a one- or two-car garage with a handy utility/storage area, in addition to the two floor plans.

Plan AX-98818

Bedrooms: 3	Baths: 2
Space:	
Main floor	1,190 sq. ft.
Alternate Main floor	1,296 sq. ft.
Total Living Area	**1,190/1,296 sq. ft.**
Basement	1,296 sq. ft.
Garage	270/540 sq. ft.
Exterior Wall Framing	2x4

Foundation options:
Standard Basement
Slab
(Foundation & framing conversion diagram available—see order form.)

Blueprint Price Code	**A**

TO ORDER THIS BLUEPRINT,
CALL TOLL-FREE 1-800-547-5570
(prices and details on pp. 12-15.)

Cottage in the City

- Picturesque rooflines and a stucco and brick exterior resemble turn-of-the-century cottages.
- Inside, this compact, but open ranch offers space for three bedrooms and a roomy kitchen.
- The combination living and dining room features a cathedral ceiling, fireplace, rear view and adjoining deck; the kitchen has an eating bar peninsula open to both.
- Double doors open to a dramatic master suite with cathedral ceiling, Palladian window, walk-in closet and private bath with separate tub and shower, plus dual vanities.

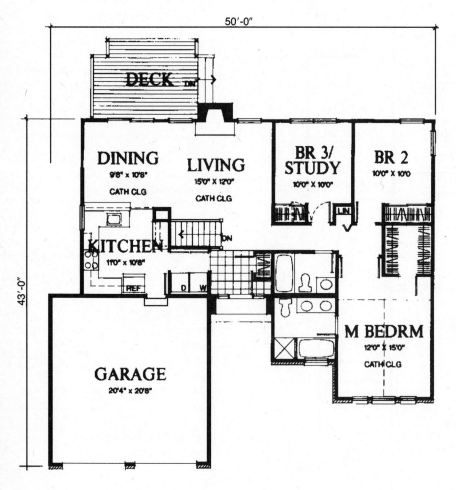

Plan OH-105

Bedrooms: 2-3	Baths: 2
Space:	
Main floor	1,239 sq. ft.
Total Living Area	**1,239 sq. ft.**
Basement	1,239 sq. ft.
Garage	420 sq. ft.
Exterior Wall Framing	2x4
Foundation options:	
Standard Basement	
(Foundation & framing conversion diagram	
available—see order form.)	
Blueprint Price Code	A

Plan OH-105

Small Home
Has Big Impact

- Small in area but big on function, this angled, three-bedroom ranch glows with charm.
- The central foyer neatly channels traffic to the bedroom wing, the formal areas to the rear and the kitchen and family room to the left.
- Highlighted by a sloped ceiling and a stone fireplace, the living and dining rooms combine for a dramatic setting that overlooks a backyard terrace.
- The family room and kitchen also flow together smoothly for a casual family atmosphere.
- Two skylighted bathrooms and three bedrooms are secluded to the right of the home.

Plan K-696-T

Bedrooms: 3	Baths: 2½
Living Area:	
Main floor	1,272 sq. ft.
Total Living Area:	**1,272 sq. ft.**
Standard basement	1,232 sq. ft.
Garage	509 sq. ft.
Exterior Wall Framing:	2x4 or 2x6

Foundation Options:

Standard basement
Slab
(Typical foundation & framing conversion diagram available—see order form.)

BLUEPRINT PRICE CODE: **A**

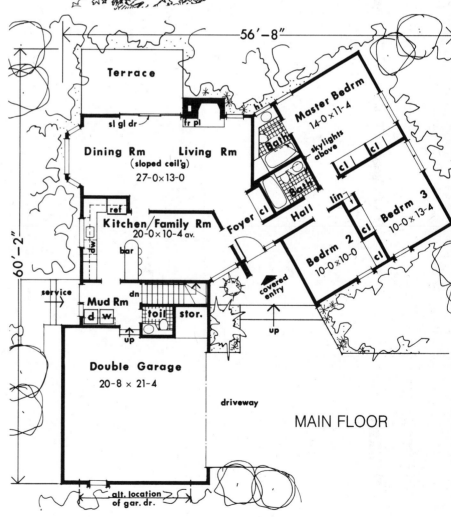

MAIN FLOOR

Plan K-696-T

Economy with Amenities

- The rear-facing living room in this economical three-bedroom ranch merges with the kitchen and breakfast peninsula and the dining area to form an informal family setting.
- The spaciousness is enhanced by an entry that allows a view of the rear yard.
- The generous master suite, also oriented to the rear of the home, offers a private bath with dressing area and walk-in closet.
- Two secondary bedrooms have closet space and a nearby second bath.
- A double-car garage has extra storage space; the handy main-floor laundry room is conveniently located near the garage entrance.

Plan SDG-81115

Bedrooms: 3	**Baths:** 2

Space:

Main floor	1,296 sq. ft.
Total Living Area	**1,296 sq. ft.**
Garage	400 sq. ft.
Exterior Wall Framing	2x4

Foundation options:
Slab
(Foundation & framing conversion diagram available—see order form.)

Blueprint Price Code	**A**

TO ORDER THIS BLUEPRINT,
CALL TOLL-FREE 1-800-547-5570
(prices and details on pp. 12-15.)

Plan SDG-81115

Pretty as a Picture

- A lovely front porch and half-round window combine to give this one-story a picturesque exterior.
- The accommodating foyer reveals a large sunken living room with beamed cathedral ceiling and a massive, corner see-through fireplace open to the dining room and kitchen on the opposite side.
- The dining room shares a counter bar with the adjoining kitchen and offers access to a rear garden court through sliding glass doors.
- Convenient main-floor laundry facilities are located near the kitchen and garage entrance.
- The secluded master bedroom features a generous dressing area with dual closets and a vanity separate from the toilet and shower.

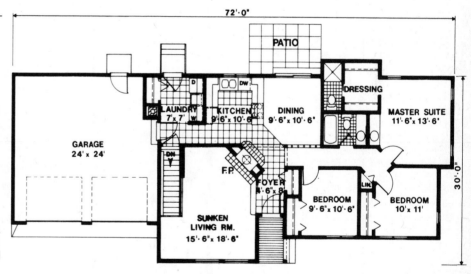

Plan CPS-1105-C

Bedrooms: 3	**Baths:** 2

Space:	
Main floor	1,338 sq. ft.
Total Living Area	**1,338 sq. ft.**
Basement	1,267 sq. ft.
Garage	576 sq. ft.

Exterior Wall Framing	2x6

Foundation options:
Standard Basement
(Foundation & framing conversion diagram available—see order form.)

Blueprint Price Code	**A**

Plan CPS-1105-C

Quaint Cottage-Style Home

- The heartwarming simplicity of this quaint cottage-style home is undeniable, its appeal universal.
- The home's square footage is maximized by a straightforward floor plan and the use of 9-ft. ceilings throughout.
- The Great Room is the hub of the home, featuring a fireplace with built-in cabinetry on both sides.
- The Great Room flows into the large combination dining room/kitchen. Adjoining the U-shaped kitchen is a laundry room with access to the backyard. The dining room has sliding glass doors to the backyard.
- The master bedroom is secluded on one side of the home. It includes a private bath that is compartmentalized.
- The two smaller bedrooms at the other side of the home are separated by another full bath.

Plan V-1365

Bedrooms: 3	Baths: 2
Space:	
Main floor	1,365 sq. ft.
Total Living Area	**1,365 sq. ft.**
Exterior Wall Framing	2x6

Foundation options:

Crawlspace

(Foundation & framing conversion diagram available—see order form.)

Blueprint Price Code	**A**

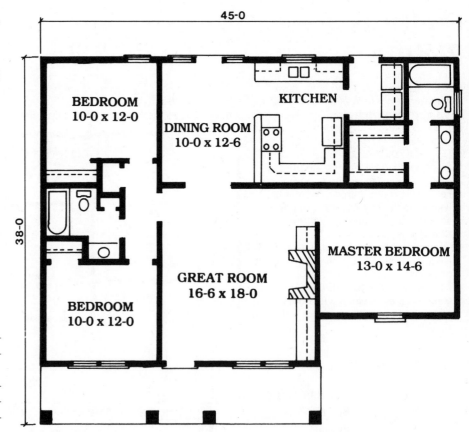

Plan V-1365

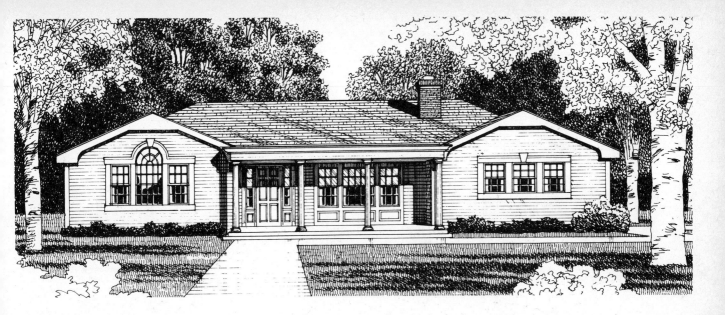

Design Harmony

- This house combines several different architectural styles to achieve a design harmony all its own.
- The columns of the front porch are reminiscent of ancient Greece, while the Palladian window in the master bedroom originates from the Renaissance period. The sleek rectangular shape of the home is in keeping with more contemporary times.
- The columns are repeated inside, where they are used to visually divide the foyer from the living room and to dramatize the cathedral ceiling. Columns also frame the heat-circulating fireplace.
- Note the twin closets in the foyer. Straight ahead is the combination dining room and kitchen, which basks in an abundance of natural light from two skylights, a large bow window, plus a sliding glass door that opens to the terrace.
- Another back entrance separates the kitchen from the large mud room. The mud room has loads of closet space, with two closets and cabinets above the washer and dryer.
- The sleeping wing has three large bedrooms and two full baths. Here, as elsewhere, closet space is well accounted for.

View into living room from entry foyer.

Plan HFL-1200-FH

Bedrooms: 3	Baths: 2
Space:	
Main floor	1,397 sq. ft.
Total Living Area	**1,397 sq. ft.**
Basement	1,434 sq. ft.
Garage and Storage	463 sq. ft.
Exterior Wall Framing	2x6

Foundation options:
Standard Basement
Slab
(Foundation & framing conversion diagram available—see order form.)

Blueprint Price Code	A

(floor plan)

73'-0"

2x6 studs for added insulation

TERRACE

sl. gl. dr.

skylight   skylight

BED RM 13'-4"x11'-6"

BED RM 11'-4"x10'-0"

DINING RM 13'-0" x 11'-0"

KITCHEN 14'-0"x12'-0"

laundry   COVERED PORCH

d. w.

dn

dw

MUD RM

high ceiling

range

cl.   opt.

ref.   s.

cl.   cl.

30'-0"

cl.   cl.   lin.

HALL

cl.

cl.

BATH

cl.

FOYER

cl.

cathedral ceiling

LIVING RM 23'-0" x 13'-4"

TWO CAR GARAGE 20'-0" x 20'-0"

MASTER BED RM 13'-4"x13'-4"

BATH

heat-circul. fireplace

stor.

whirlpool tub

PORTICO

Plan HFL-1200-FH

Economical One-Level Comfort

- This charming one-level home was designed with economy in mind.
- The plan is based on the Great Room concept, which makes the most of available square footage and creates an open feeling throughout the house.
- A dining area is defined by the sunny bay windows in the Great Room near the kitchen.
- The open-plan kitchen is combined with a sunny nook for an open, airy feeling.
- The private area of the home features a master suite which is impressive for a home of this size. It features two walk-in closets as well as a private bath with double-bowl vanity.
- Two secondary bedrooms share another full bath.
- A utility area in the garage entryway includes space for a washer and dryer.

Plan S-52191

Bedrooms: 3	Baths: 2
Space:	
Main floor	1,441 sq. ft.
Total Living Area	**1,441 sq. ft.**
Basement	1,441 sq. ft.
Garage	473 sq. ft.
Exterior Wall Framing	2x6

Foundation options:
Standard Basement
Crawlspace
(Foundation & framing conversion diagram available—see order form.)

Blueprint Price Code	**A**

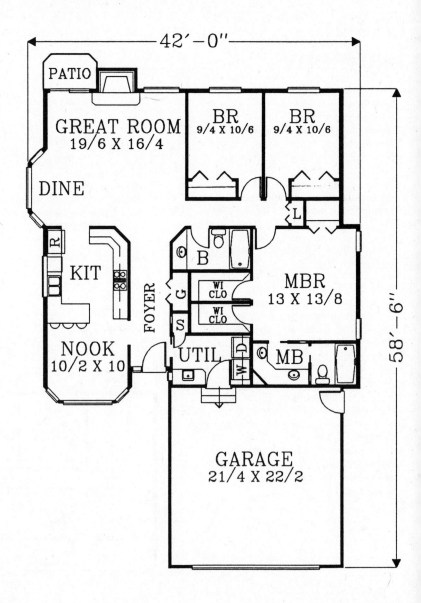

Plan S-52191

One-Story Country-Style

- This country-looking one-story home features a covered front porch with decorative posts and railings.

- The gabled roof, shuttered windows and L-shaped floor plan give the home added definition.
- The Great Room is at the center of the design and is highlighted by a large fireplace.
- The dining room boasts a sunny bay window and a breakfast bar that faces the spacious kitchen.
- A full bath is just off the Great Room, adjacent to the two smaller bedrooms. A compact laundry closet is conveniently located in the bedroom hallway.
- The master bedroom is quietly positioned at the rear of the home, away from the activity areas. The private master bath is compartmentalized for dual use. The vanity area, which adjoins the walk-in closet, also serves as a dressing room.

Plan V-1452

Bedrooms: 3	Baths: 2
Space:	
Main floor	1,452 sq. ft.
Total Living Area	**1,452 sq. ft.**
Garage	528 sq. ft.
Exterior Wall Framing	2x6

Foundation options:

Crawlspace

(Foundation & framing conversion diagram available—see order form.)

Blueprint Price Code	**A**

Floor Plan

62-0

MASTER BEDROOM
12-6 X 16-6

DINING
8-0 X 11-6   KITCHEN

51-0

BEDROOM
9-6 X12-6

GARAGE
22-0 x 24-0

GREAT ROOM
19-6 X 17-0

BEDROOM
13-6 X 13-0

Plan V-1452

High-Style Ranch Home

- A Palladian window, shuttered windows with planter boxes and recessed entry distinguish this unusual ranch home.
- To the right of the central foyer is a large living room with a cathedral ceiling, oversized fireplace and elegant windows.
- The living room flows into the dining room, which has sliding glass doors to a large rear terrace for even more entertainment space.
- The centrally located kitchen adjoins a sunny dinette with window walls overlooking the terrace.
- A service entrance leads from the terrace to the mud room and laundry area.
- The spacious master bedroom features his and her closets and a private bath.
- The second bath includes a double-sink vanity and a whirlpool tub.

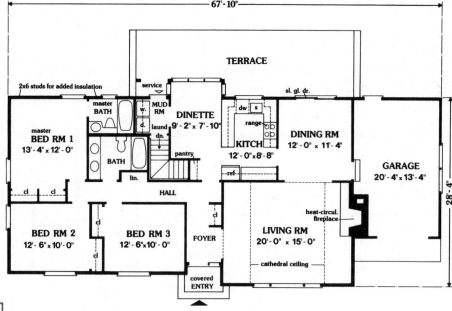

VIEW INTO LIVING ROOM FROM DINING ROOM.

Plan HFL-1420-BL

Bedrooms: 3	**Baths:** 2

Space:

Main floor	1,492 sq. ft.
Total Living Area	**1,492 sq. ft.**
Basement	1,428 sq. ft.
Garage	274 sq. ft.

Exterior Wall Framing	2x6

Foundation options:
Standard Basement
Slab
(Foundation & framing conversion diagram available—see order form.)

Blueprint Price Code	**A**

*TO ORDER THIS BLUEPRINT,
CALL TOLL-FREE 1-800-547-5570*

Plan HFL-1420-BL

Modest Ranch Big on Space

- This contemporary ranch offers three generous-sized bedrooms and abundant living space in just over 1,500 square feet.
- The large living room boasts a massive corner fireplace and shares the front, formal areas of the home with the adjacent dining room.
- Adjoining the kitchen, the family room provides an open atmosphere, a handy snack bar and sliders to the rear.
- Two full baths and convenient main-floor laundry facilities service the bedrooms.

Plan AX-8595-A

Bedrooms: 3	Baths: 2
Space:	
Main floor	1,520 sq. ft.
Total Living Area	**1,520 sq. ft.**
Basement	1,520 sq. ft.
Garage	452 sq. ft.
Exterior Wall Framing	2x4

Foundation options:

Standard Basement

Slab

(Foundation & framing conversion diagram available—see order form.)

Blueprint Price Code	**B**

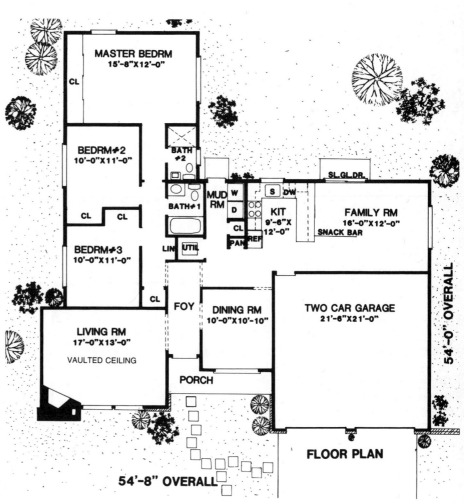

Plan AX-8595-A

Attractive Details

- This appealing ranch offers dramatic 12-foot ceilings in the foyer, living room, dining room and kitchen.
- Half-round windows add excitement to the sunken living room. Half-round windows are also found above the kitchen sink and above the patio doors in the dining room.
- The roomy kitchen is situated between the family room and the dining room for easy food service and efficient traffic flow; it features a pantry, and an eating bar overlooking the family room with fireplace.
- Railings around the living room and plant ledges off the foyer and hallway add decorative touches.
- Secluded to the rear of the home, the master suite has a private dressing area, walk-in closet and compartmentalized toilet and shower.

Plan U-87-101

Bedrooms: 3	Baths: 2

Space:

Main floor without basement	1,546 sq. ft.
Main floor with basement	1,588 sq. ft.
Total Living Area	**1,546/1,588 sq. ft.**
Basement	1,588 sq. ft.
Garage	564 sq. ft.
Exterior Wall Framing	**2x6**

Foundation options:

Standard Basement
Crawlspace
Slab

(Foundation & framing conversion diagram available—see order form.)

Blueprint Price Code	**B**

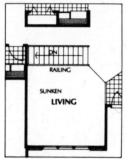

STAIR LOCATION FOR BASEMENT OPTION

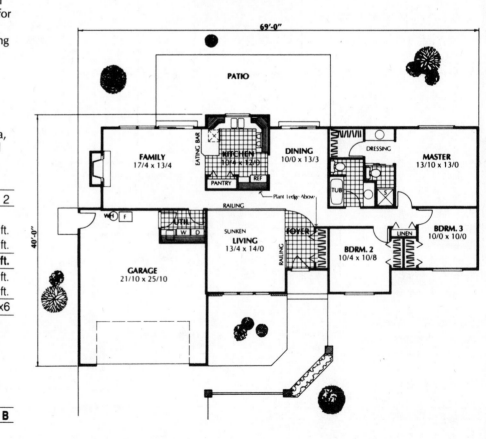

Plan U-87-101

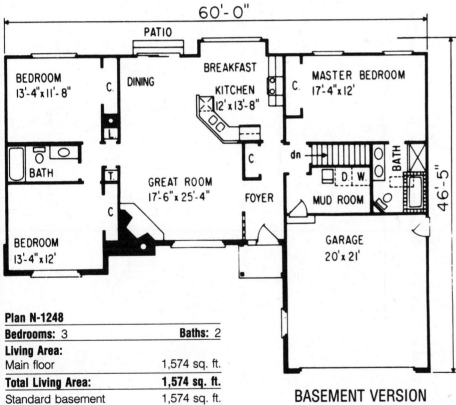

60'-0"

PATIO

BEDROOM
13'-4"x11'-8"

C.

DINING

BREAKFAST

KITCHEN
12'x13'-8"

MASTER BEDROOM
17'-4"x12'

C.

BATH

GREAT ROOM
17'-6"x 25'-4"

C

FOYER

dn

D. W.

BATH

MUD ROOM

46'-5"

BEDROOM
13'-4"x12'

GARAGE
20'x 21'

BASEMENT VERSION

Plan N-1248	
Bedrooms: 3	**Baths:** 2
Living Area:	
Main floor	1,574 sq. ft.
Total Living Area:	**1,574 sq. ft.**
Standard basement	1,574 sq. ft.
Garage	420 sq. ft.
Exterior Wall Framing:	2x4
Foundation Options:	
Standard basement	
Slab	
(Typical foundation & framing conversion diagram available—see order form.)	
BLUEPRINT PRICE CODE:	B

Striking Great Room

- A combination of brick and siding lends a solid look of permanence to this attractive design.
- An enormous Great Room is the focus of this exciting, inviting plan. The large open area includes a dining space, and also leads into a breakfast nook and an efficient kitchen.
- A splendid master bedroom with a private skylighted master bath is isolated to the right, while two secondary bedrooms are placed to the left of the Great Room.
- A mud room is conveniently located in the garage entry area.

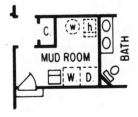

C. w h

MUD ROOM

BATH

W. D.

SLAB VERSION

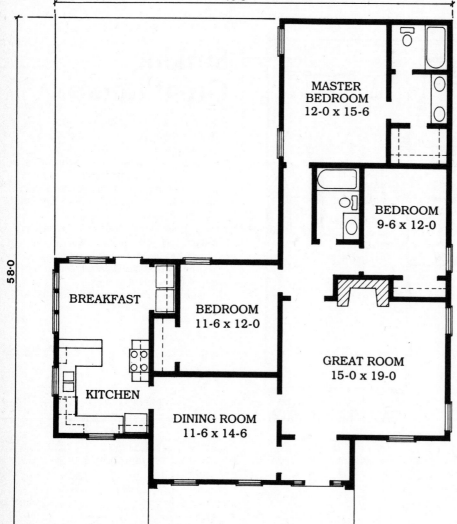

46·0

58·0

MASTER
BEDROOM
12-0 x 15-6

BEDROOM
9-6 x 12-0

BREAKFAST

BEDROOM
11-6 x 12-0

KITCHEN

GREAT ROOM
15-0 x 19-0

DINING ROOM
11-6 x 14-6

Charming and Efficient

- The facade of this charming home is highlighted by a porch and eye-catching entryway.
- Inside, the foyer leads into a spacious dining room and exceptionally grand Great Room warmed by a fireplace.
- A large, sunny kitchen opens to a brightly lit breakfast area that also houses a convenient washer and dryer.
- The three bedrooms are spaced apart from each other to provide privacy and quiet.
- The master suite is located at the rear of the home for additional privacy; it has a personal bath with twin vanities and a walk-in closet.

Plan V-1580

Bedrooms: 3	**Baths:** 2
Space:	
Main floor	1,580 sq. ft.
Total Living Area	**1,580 sq. ft.**
Exterior Wall Framing	2x6

Foundation options:
Crawlspace
(Foundation & framing conversion diagram available—see order form.)

Blueprint Price Code	B

Plan V-1580

Striking One-Story Home

- Eye-catching angles, both inside and out, are the keynotes of this luxurious one-story home.
- The striking double-door entry is illuminated by a skylight. The foyer is just as impressive, with its cathedral ceiling and skylight.
- The sunken living room also features a cathedral ceiling, and a bay-window alcove faces the front.
- A low partition separates the living room from the formal dining room. Here, too, a cathedral ceiling and bay windows add interesting angles and spaciousness to the room.
- The open family room, breakfast room and kitchen offer plenty of space for casual family living. The family room includes a corner fireplace with adjacent built-in shelves. The bayed breakfast area boasts a cathedral ceiling and French doors to the backyard. An angled snack counter faces the U-shaped kitchen.
- The master bedroom also has a bay window facing the backyard, plus a large walk-in closet. Also included is a private bath with a whirlpool tub.
- Two more bedrooms, another full bath and a utility area complete the design.

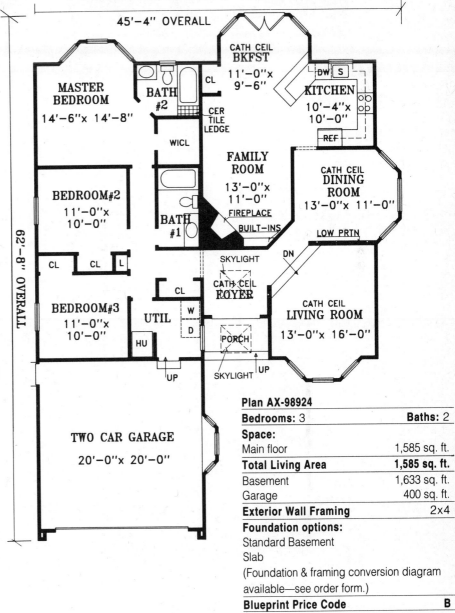

Plan AX-98924

Bedrooms: 3	Baths: 2
Space:	
Main floor	1,585 sq. ft.
Total Living Area	**1,585 sq. ft.**
Basement	1,633 sq. ft.
Garage	400 sq. ft.
Exterior Wall Framing	2x4

Foundation options:
Standard Basement
Slab
(Foundation & framing conversion diagram available—see order form.)

Blueprint Price Code	**B**

Plan AX-98924

(prices and details on pp. 12-15.) **111**

Handsome Ranch Offers Symmetry

- A dramatic facade with stone chimney, vertical siding and stone veneer accents gives this ranch a distinctive custom appearance.
- Double doors at the entry open to a skylit gallery and a well-zoned floor plan.
- The formal living and dining rooms at the front of the home are highlighted by a vaulted ceiling and a stone-finished fireplace.
- The expansive informal areas at the rear are ideal for casual family living and entertaining. A vaulted ceiling hovers above a sunny, angular dinette area, an open island kitchen and a family room with built-in media center.
- Included in the sleeping wing is an isolated master bedroom with a private terrace and a personal bath with whirlpool tub.

VIEW OF DINETTE AND FAMILY ROOM FROM KITCHEN.

Plan K-673-R

Bedrooms: 3	Baths: 2
Space:	
Main floor	1,704 sq. ft.
Total Living Area	**1,704 sq. ft.**
Basement	1,600 sq. ft.
Garage	400 sq. ft.
Exterior Wall Framing	2x4 or 2x6

Foundation options:
Standard Basement
Slab
(Foundation & framing conversion diagram available—see order form.)

Blueprint Price Code	B

TO ORDER THIS BLUEPRINT, CALL TOLL-FREE 1-800-547-5570

Plan K-673-R

Vaulted Ceiling in Spacious Family Room

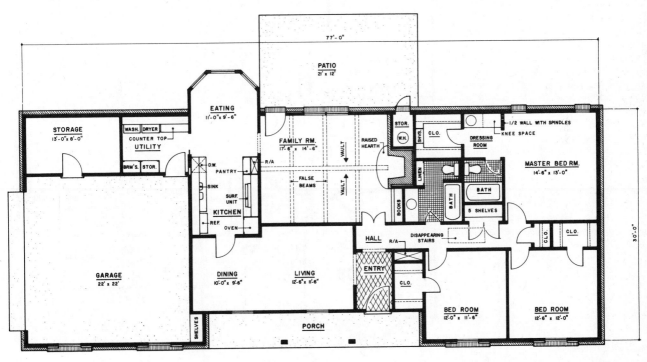

PLAN E-1601
WITHOUT BASEMENT

Specify crawlspace or slab foundation.

AREAS

Living	1630 sq. ft.
Garage & Storage	610 sq. ft.
Porch	116 sq. ft.
Total	2356 sq. ft.

Blueprint Price Code B

Plan E-1601

Large, Dramatic Rooms

- At the center of this stylish brick home is a modern kitchen, Great Room and dining room combination that will please today's close-knit family. A large fireplace, sloped ceiling and a rear window wall with an adjoining patio add to the drama of this intimate setting.
- The opposite end of the kitchen offers a pantry and handy access to the laundry room and garage.
- Separated from the other two bedrooms, the master bedroom is ideally located and spaciously designed. A tray ceiling in the bedroom and a luxurious corner tub in the private bath are a few of its amenities.
- The third bedroom off the foyer could serve as a den or home office; it features lovely double doors and a front bay window.

Plan SDG-91188	
Bedrooms: 2-3	**Baths: 2**
Space:	
Main floor	1,704 sq. ft.
Total Living Area	**1,704 sq. ft.**
Garage	484 sq. ft.
Exterior Wall Framing	2x4
Foundation options:	
Slab	
(Foundation & framing conversion diagram available—see order form.)	
Blueprint Price Code	**B**

TO ORDER THIS BLUEPRINT, CALL TOLL-FREE 1-800-547-5570

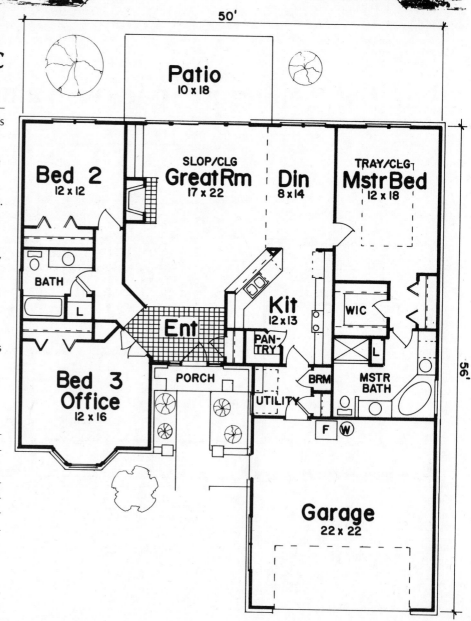

Plan SDG-91188

Dynamic Three-Bedroom Home

- The gabled roof, arched windows and design details such as the window planter make this a hot, new design.
- The covered front entry is highlighted by exposed beams that echo the shape of the arched window above the door.
- The foyer opens to the den on the left, which features an overhead plant shelf, and the vaulted Great Room straight ahead.
- The Great Room offers a corner fireplace and adjoins the rear deck and the vaulted dining room.
- The spacious kitchen has an island cooktop and a tucked-away laundry area. Note the convenient access to both a sheltered deck and patio and the two-car garage.
- The luxurious master suite includes a romantic window seat, vaulted ceilings and a walk-in closet. The private bath includes an elegant spa tub.
- Another full bath is adjacent to the second bedroom.

Plan B-87153

Bedrooms: 2-3	Baths: 2
Space:	
Main floor	1,709 sq. ft.
Total Living Area	**1,709 sq. ft.**
Basement	1,709 sq. ft.
Garage	462 sq. ft.
Exterior Wall Framing	2x4

Foundation options:

Standard Basement

(Foundation & framing conversion diagram available—see order form.)

Blueprint Price Code	**B**

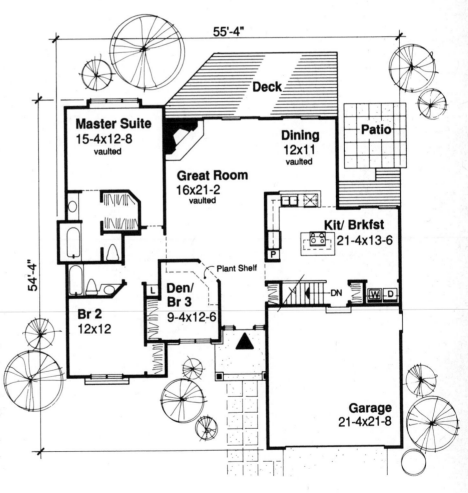

Plan B-87153

Panoramic Rear View

- This rustic but elegant country home offers an open, airy interior.
- At the center of the floor plan is a spacious living room with a sloped ceiling, fireplace and an all-glass circular wall giving a panoramic view of the backyard.
- The adjoining dining room shares the sloped ceiling and offers sliders to the rear terrace.
- The bright kitchen has a large window, an optional skylight and a counter bar that separates it from the bayed dinette.
- The bedroom wing includes two secondary bedrooms and a large, bayed master bedroom with dual walk-in closets and a private bath with a sloped ceiling and a garden whirlpool tub.

VIEW OF LIVING AND DINING ROOMS.

Plan K-685-DA	
Bedrooms: 3	**Baths:** 2 ½
Space:	
Main floor	1,760 sq. ft.
Total Living Area	**1,760 sq. ft.**
Basement	1,700 sq. ft.
Garage	482 sq. ft.
Exterior Wall Framing	2x4 or 2x6
Foundation options:	
Standard Basement	
Slab	
(Foundation & framing conversion diagram available—see order form.)	
Blueprint Price Code	**B**

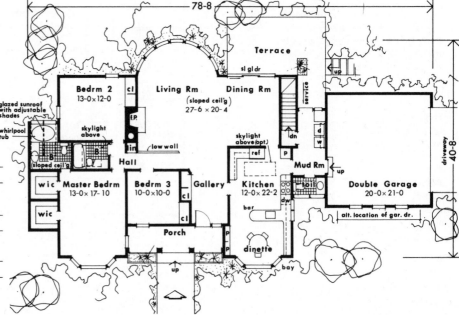

Plan K-685-DA

Impressive Great Room

- Symmetrical lines add height and drama to this great one-story home. The hipped rooflines are perfectly balanced to highlight the elegant front entry.
- The vaulted foyer provides an immediate view of the impressive Great Room, which features a tray ceiling, angled glass walls at the rear and a focal-point fireplace.
- The island kitchen is bordered by a formal dining room and a casual, bay-windowed dinette.
- A half-bath and a large laundry room are close to the home's activity areas, with a mud room leading to the garage entrance.
- The sleeping wing includes a large master suite with a charming window alcove, large walk-in closet and private bath with a whirlpool tub.
- The two smaller bedrooms share a second full bath and have windows facing the backyard. Privacy to all bedrooms is enhanced by eliminating sideyard windows.

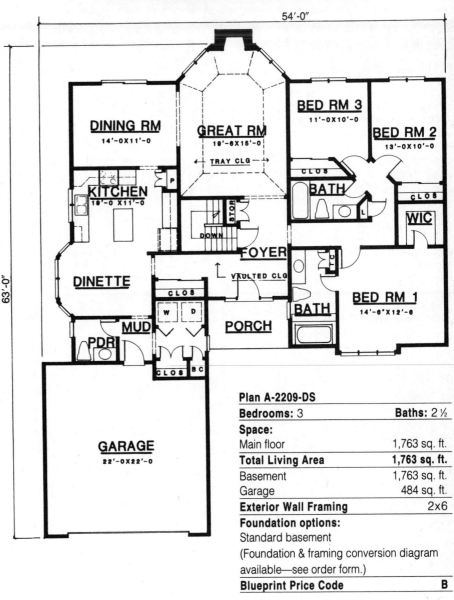

Plan A-2209-DS

Bedrooms: 3		Baths: 2 ½
Space:		
Main floor		1,763 sq. ft.
Total Living Area		**1,763 sq. ft.**
Basement		1,763 sq. ft.
Garage		484 sq. ft.
Exterior Wall Framing		2x6
Foundation options:		
Standard basement		
(Foundation & framing conversion diagram available—see order form.)		
Blueprint Price Code		B

Plan A-2209-DS

Luxury-Filled One-Story

- Interesting roof angles and refined window treatments make this handsome one-story home stand out in any neighborhood.
- Luxurious features abound within, starting with the raised-ceiling reception hall. The adjacent living room is open to the formal dining room and boasts cathedral ceilings, a central fireplace and lots of glass.
- The combination kitchen, dinette and family room is flooded with light to create a warm, bright atmosphere. The bay-windowed dinette overlooks the rear terrace, with access through patio doors in the family room. A built-in entertainment center adds more versatility to the family room area.
- The master bedroom suite is magnificent, featuring a double-door entry, sliders to a private terrace, a large walk-in closet and a great master bath.
- Another full bath, brightened by a skylight, is convenient to both of the secondary bedrooms as well as to the mud room. The efficient air-locked mud room provides access to the garage and the optional basement.

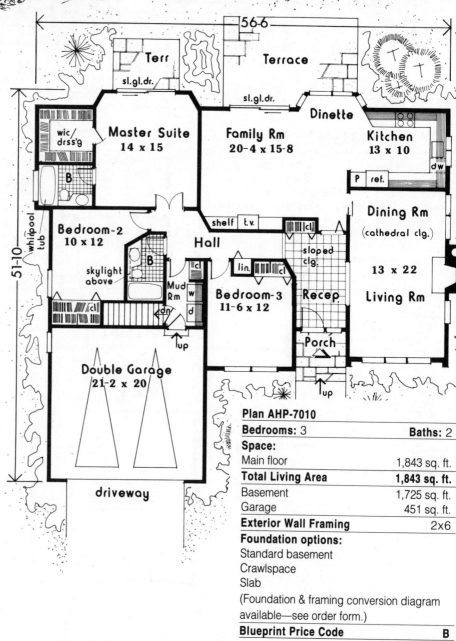

Plan AHP-7010

Bedrooms: 3	Baths: 2
Space:	
Main floor	1,843 sq. ft.
Total Living Area	**1,843 sq. ft.**
Basement	1,725 sq. ft.
Garage	451 sq. ft.
Exterior Wall Framing	2x6

Foundation options:
Standard basement
Crawlspace
Slab
(Foundation & framing conversion diagram available—see order form.)

Blueprint Price Code	B

Plan AHP-7010

Two-Way Fireplace

- Here's a design that offers an abundance of popular features.
- A clean-lined graceful exterior includes an inviting entry in the front, and plenty of access to natural light and outdoor living in the rear. (The deck shown is not included in the working drawings.)
- The living room and the activity area share a vaulted ceiling and an interesting two-way fireplace.
- The kitchen/nook combination is large, airy and convenient to the activity area.
- The master bedroom includes a large walk-in closet and also boasts a bath that's lit by two large skylights.
- The second bedroom also includes a large closet, and an optional third bedroom will serve equally well as a den or home office.

Plan N-1255

Bedrooms: 2-3	Baths: 2
Living Area:	
Main floor	1,850 sq. ft.
Total Living Area:	**1,850 sq. ft.**
Partial basement	1,008 sq. ft.
Garage	462 sq. ft.
Exterior Wall Framing:	2x4

Foundation Options:
Partial basement
Slab
(Typical foundation & framing conversion diagram available—see order form.)

BLUEPRINT PRICE CODE:	**B**

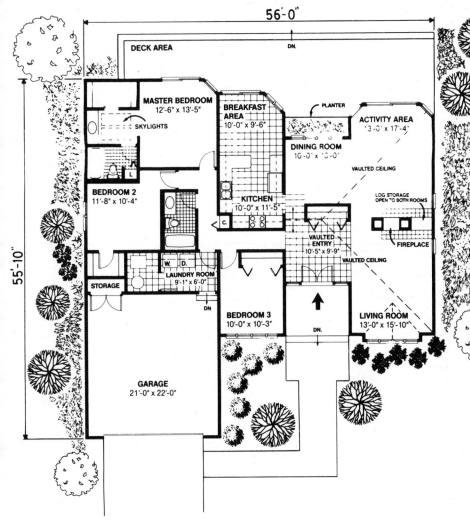

56'-0"

55'-10"

DECK AREA DN.

MASTER BEDROOM
12'-6" x 13'-5"

SKYLIGHTS

BREAKFAST AREA
10'-0" x 9'-6"

PLANTER

ACTIVITY AREA
13'-0" x 17'-4"

DINING ROOM
10'-0" x 10'-0"

VAULTED CEILING

BEDROOM 2
11'-8" x 10'-4"

KITCHEN
10'-0" x 11'-5"

LOG STORAGE
OPEN TO BOTH ROOMS

C.

VAULTED ENTRY
10'-5" x 9'-9"

FIREPLACE

W. D.

LAUNDRY ROOM
9'-1" x 6'-0"

STORAGE

DN.

VAULTED CEILING

BEDROOM 3
10'-0" x 10'-3"

DN.

LIVING ROOM
13'-0" x 15'-10"

GARAGE
21'-0" x 22'-0"

Plan N-1255

A Real Original

- This home is a real head-turner. The round window, elegant entry and transom windows to the right of the fireplace create an original look.
- Inside, high ceilings let the eyes wander. The cozy den, to the right of the foyer, even has its own fireplace.
- Straight ahead is the living room, which features high ceilings and a second fireplace. Tall windows frame the fireplace, offering a view to the expansive deck and patio with spa. The adjoining dining room has vaulted ceilings and also overlooks the deck.
- The spacious kitchen/breakfast area has access to a large screened porch. The laundry room is close by, just off the garage entrance. Note the handy storage area at the rear of the garage.
- The deluxe master suite views out to the patio and has a private entrance to the deck. The dynamite bath features a corner spa tub, separate shower and large walk-in closet.
- A second bedroom and bath complete the main floor, which has 1,889 sq. ft. of living area (excluding the screened porch).

Plan B-90065

Bedrooms: 2-3	Baths: 2
Space:	
Main floor	1,889 sq. ft.
Total Living Area	**1,889 sq. ft.**
Basement	1,889 sq. ft.
Garage	406 sq. ft.
Exterior Wall Framing	2x6

Foundation options:
Standard Basement
(Foundation & framing conversion diagram available—see order form.)

Blueprint Price Code	B

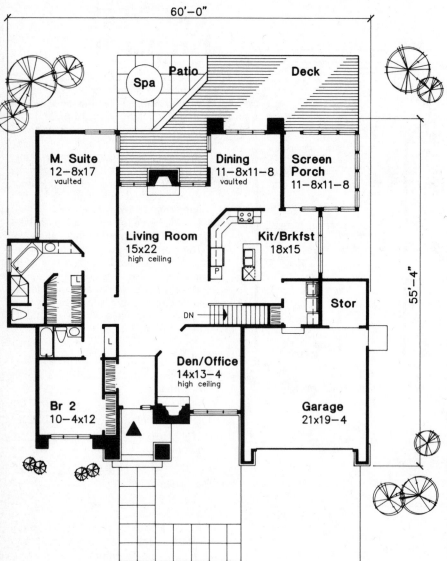

TO ORDER THIS BLUEPRINT,
CALL TOLL-FREE 1-800-547-5570
120 (prices and details on pp. 12-15.)

Plan B-90065

Distinctive One-Story Design

- Angles and curves define the exterior of this distinctive home. A hipped roof with deep overhangs caps the main part of the house. A gabled roof provides contrast and emphasizes the picture window with charming planter box.
- A trellised walkway leads to the double-door entry. The foyer is brightened by a half-round roof window that accentuates the semi-circular ceiling.
- The living room, straight ahead, is highlighted by a cathedral ceiling and a fireplace framed by angled glass walls. A French door opens to a large backyard terrace.
- The dining room is open to the living room, but a lower ceiling in the dining room helps visually separate the two rooms.
- A large combination family room, dinette and kitchen is adjacent to the formal living areas. The family room has sliding glass doors to the terrace, the dinette is distinguished by a bayed eating alcove, and the kitchen has a snack bar.
- Convenient to the family living areas are a spacious laundry room, a mud room and a utility area with a pantry closet plus two additional closets.
- The sleeping wing is well isolated from the activity areas. The spacious master bedroom includes twin closets plus a large walk-in closet. The private bath features an oversized whirlpool tub and double-bowl vanity.

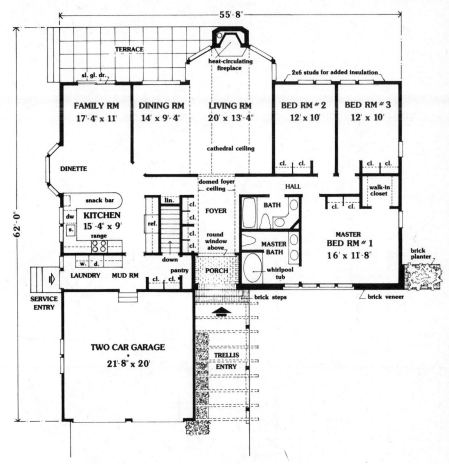

Plan HFL-1320-MG	
Bedrooms: 3	**Baths:** 2
Space:	
Main floor	1,895 sq. ft.
Total Living Area	**1,895 sq. ft.**
Basement	1,760 sq. ft.
Garage	441 sq. ft.
Exterior Wall Framing	2x6
Foundation options:	
Standard Basement	
Slab	
(Foundation & framing conversion diagram available—see order form.)	
Blueprint Price Code	**B**

VIEW OF LIVING AND DINING ROOMS.

Plan HFL-1320-MG

Contemporary Sunbelt Design

- Exposed entry rafters, wide overhanging gable roof lines and vertical windows make this design appealing and stylish.
- Near the entry, a stunning kitchen/breakfast room invites family and visitors alike.
- The activity area beyond leads to an equally dazzling sun room, which in turn offers easy access to a rear deck, patio or terrace.
- A master bedroom fit for royalty includes two large closets, a private bath and easy access to the cozy sun room.
- Two other bedrooms share another full bath. Also note the large laundry room in the bedroom zone.

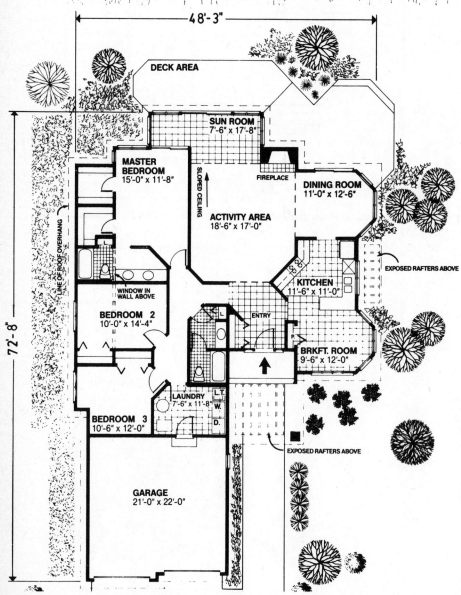

48'-3"

DECK AREA

SUN ROOM
7'-6" x 17'-8"

MASTER BEDROOM
15'-0" x 11'-8"

FIREPLACE

DINING ROOM
11'-0" x 12'-6"

SLOPED CEILING

ACTIVITY AREA
18'-6" x 17'-0"

EXPOSED RAFTERS ABOVE

WINDOW IN WALL ABOVE

KITCHEN
11'-6" x 11'-0"

BEDROOM 2
10'-0" x 14'-4"

ENTRY

72'-8"

LINE OF ROOF OVERHANG

BRKFT. ROOM
9'-6" x 12'-0"

LAUNDRY
7'-6" x 11'-8"

L.T.
W.
D.

BEDROOM 3
10'-6" x 12'-0"

EXPOSED RAFTERS ABOVE

GARAGE
21'-0" x 22'-0"

Plan N-1271	
Bedrooms: 3	**Baths:** 2
Living Area:	
Main floor	1,907 sq. ft.
Total Living Area:	**1,907 sq. ft.**
Partial basement	1,040 sq. ft.
Garage	462 sq. ft.
Exterior Wall Framing:	2x4

Foundation Options:
Partial basement
Slab
(Typical foundation & framing conversion diagram available—see order form.)

BLUEPRINT PRICE CODE:	B

**TO ORDER THIS BLUEPRINT,
CALL TOLL-FREE 1-800-547-5570**

Plan N-1271

Skylights Bring in Outdoors

- Skylights brighten the interior of this three-bedroom ranch.
- Cathedral ceilings hover above the spacious family room, central living room, bayed breakfast room and dining room.
- Only a half-wall separates the breakfast area from the family room, which features a fireplace and sliders to the patio.
- A roomy master bedroom is secluded to the rear; it offers a generous walk-in closet and a private bath with twin vanities and a skylit tub.
- Two additional bedrooms share a second full bath.

Plan AX-91311

Bedrooms: 3	Baths: 2
Space:	
Main floor	1,915 sq. ft.
Total Living Area	**1,915 sq. ft.**
Basement	1,915 sq. ft.
Garage	387 sq. ft.
Exterior Wall Framing	2x4

Foundation options:
Standard Basement
Slab
(Foundation & framing conversion diagram available—see order form.)

Blueprint Price Code	**B**

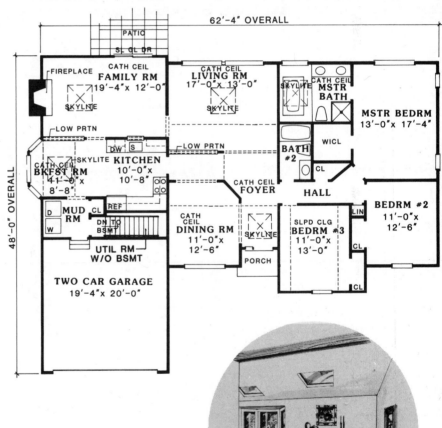

VIEW OF FAMILY ROOM AND BREAKFAST ROOM.

Plan AX-91311

TO ORDER THIS BLUEPRINT, CALL TOLL-FREE 1-800-547-5570 (prices and details on pp. 12-15.)

Designed for Gracious Living

- A hospitable Spanish/Mediterranean facade welcomes family and visitors alike to this thoroughly modern home.
- A large lanai at the rear greatly extends the living room in good weather, and lets in an abundance of natural light under any conditions.
- The Great-Room-concept activity area boasts an impressive fireplace and a vaulted ceiling.
- The majestic master bedroom includes a private bath with both shower and tub and two vanity sinks.
- The second bedroom also features a large closet and provides easy access to a second full bath.
- Note the huge kitchen/nook combination with its abundance of cabinets and counter space. Also check the inviting entry area, which includes a cathedral ceiling.

Plan N-1253

Bedrooms: 2	Baths: 2

Living Area:	
Main floor	1,966 sq. ft.

Total Living Area:	**1,966 sq. ft.**
Standard basement	1,966 sq. ft.

Exterior Wall Framing:	2x4

Foundation Options:
Standard basement
Slab
(Typical foundation & framing conversion diagram available—see order form.)

BLUEPRINT PRICE CODE:	B

**TO ORDER THIS BLUEPRINT,
CALL TOLL-FREE 1-800-547-5570**

124 (prices and details on pp. 12-15.)

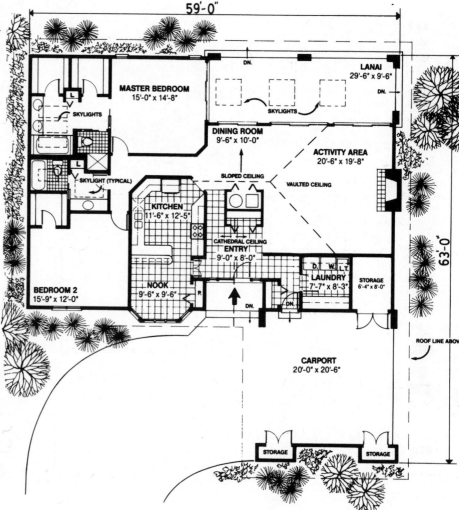

Plan N-1253

Ultra-Modern Mediterranean Home

Plan APS-2010

Bedrooms: 3	Baths: 2

Space:

Main floor	2,020 sq. ft.
Total Living Area	**2,020 sq. ft.**
Garage	448 sq. ft.
Exterior Wall Framing	2x4

Foundation options:

Slab

(Foundation & framing conversion diagram available—see order form.)

Blueprint Price Code	**C**

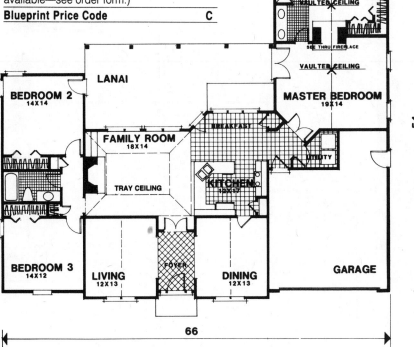

- This attractive Mediterranean ranch design is loaded with ultra-modern, ultra-luxurious features.
- The tiled foyer opens to the formal living and dining rooms, both of which feature vaulted ceilings and tall arched windows.
- Double doors lead to the inviting family room, which has a tray ceiling. A bank of windows lines the rear wall of the family room, offering a sweeping view of the covered porch, or lanai, at the rear of the home.
- The family room's fireplace has an entertainment center built in on one side. On the other side is a short hall to two nice-sized bedrooms and a full bath. The rear-facing bedroom includes a French door to the lanai.
- The kitchen and sunny breakfast area also overlook the lanai. A utility area is tucked into one corner, just off the garage entrance.
- The master bedroom is truly marvelous. Double doors open to the vaulted-ceiling sleeping area with see-through fireplace. Another pair of double doors provides private entrance to the lanai.
- You can really pamper yourself in the master bath. The garden tub is perfectly positioned for enjoying the fireplace, and vaulted ceilings add to the luxurious atmosphere.

Plan APS-2010

TO ORDER THIS BLUEPRINT,
CALL TOLL-FREE 1-800-547-5570
(prices and details on pp. 12-15.) **125**

Comfort and Good Looks

- This three-bedroom design combines comfort and good looks for modern families who want a sense of living outdoors while being indoors.
- An impressive pillared entrance leads into an equally impressive foyer with a large planter.
- The large activity area includes a fireplace, a vaulted ceiling and easy access to the rear.
- A formal dining room receives an abundance of natural light through its bay window.
- A gorgeous kitchen/breakfast area dominates the center of the home.
- The magnificent master bedroom is isolated for privacy, and has its own deluxe bath and huge walk-in closet.
- Two other bedrooms share a second full bath. For more peace and quiet, they are positioned well away from the activity room and the kitchen.

Plan N-1260

Bedrooms: 3		**Baths:** 2	

Living Area:

Main floor	2,190 sq. ft.
Total Living Area:	**2,190 sq. ft.**
Standard basement	2,190 sq. ft.
Garage	473 sq. ft.
Exterior Wall Framing:	2x4

Foundation Options:

Standard basement

Slab

(Typical foundation & framing conversion diagram available—see order form.)

BLUEPRINT PRICE CODE:	**C**

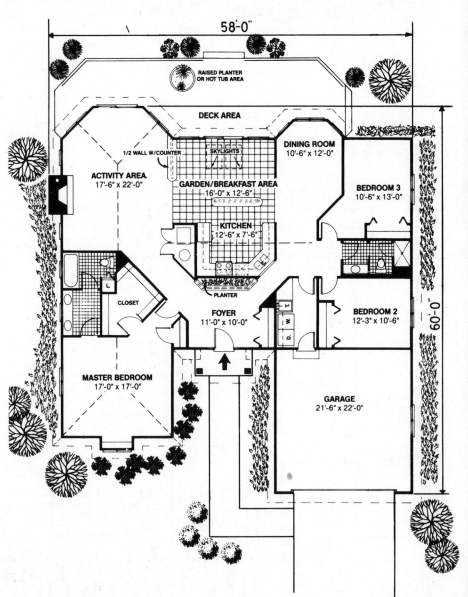

58'-0"

RAISED PLANTER
OR HOT TUB AREA

DECK AREA

1/2 WALL W/COUNTER

SKYLIGHTS

DINING ROOM
10'-6" x 12'-0"

ACTIVITY AREA
17'-6" x 22'-0"

GARDEN/BREAKFAST AREA
16'-0" x 12'-6"

BEDROOM 3
10'-6" x 13'-0"

KITCHEN
12'-6" x 7'-6"

60'-0"

CLOSET

PLANTER

FOYER
11'-0" x 10'-0"

BEDROOM 2
12'-3" x 10'-6"

D W T

MASTER BEDROOM
17'-0" x 17'-0"

GARAGE
21'-6" x 22'-0"

TO ORDER THIS BLUEPRINT,
CALL TOLL-FREE 1-800-547-5570
(prices and details on pp. 12-15.)

Plan N-1260

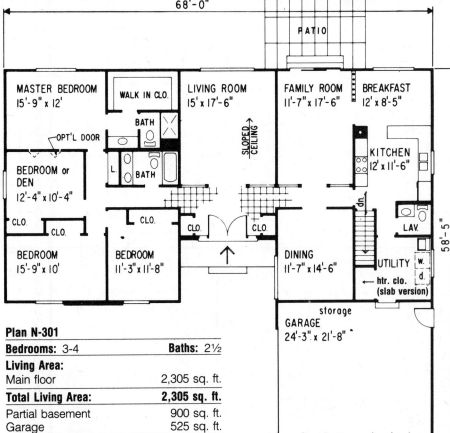

68'-0"

PATIO

MASTER BEDROOM
15'-9" x 12'

WALK IN CLO.

LIVING ROOM
15' x 17'-6"

FAMILY ROOM
11'-7" x 17'-6"

BREAKFAST
12' x 8'-5"

BATH

OPT'L DOOR

L.

BATH

SLOPED CEILING

KITCHEN
12' x 11'-6"

BEDROOM or
DEN
12'-4" x 10'-4"

CLO.

CLO.

CLO.

CLO.

CLO.

LAV.

BEDROOM
15'-9" x 10'

BEDROOM
11'-3" x 11'-8"

DINING
11'-7" x 14'-6"

UTILITY

W.

dn.

d.

← htr. clo.
(slab version)

58'-5"

storage

GARAGE
24'-3" x 21'-8"

alternate garage door location

Plan N-301

Bedrooms: 3-4	**Baths: 2½**

Living Area:

Main floor	2,305 sq. ft.

Total Living Area:	**2,305 sq. ft.**
Partial basement	900 sq. ft.
Garage	525 sq. ft.
Exterior Wall Framing:	2x4

Foundation Options:

Partial basement

Slab

(Typical foundation & framing conversion
diagram available—see order form.)

BLUEPRINT PRICE CODE: **C**

Spacious One-Story

- With 2,305 sq. ft. on one floor, this plan offers plenty of living space for today's busy families.
- A large family room adjoins a roomy breakfast nook and a large kitchen. A half-bath and a utility area are positioned between the kitchen and the garage.
- A formal dining room is conveniently located, with easy access from the foyer and the kitchen.
- The master bedroom includes a large walk-in closet and a private bath.
- The balance of the sleeping zone offers either three bedrooms or two bedrooms and a den. The hall bath includes a built-in vanity with two sinks.
- An attractive central hallway leads into the spacious living room, which offers a great view of the backyard.

Plan N-301

Designed for Easy Living

- Designed for comfort as well as eye appeal, this home will serve a busy family well year after year.
- An impressive entry directs traffic to a sunken living room to the right, or to an open activity/dining room to the left.
- The living and working areas of the home center on a gorgeous kitchen with abundant counter space, an angled breakfast bar and a sloped ceiling extending to the surrounding areas.
- The three bedrooms are well isolated to the right, and noise is buffered by the bathrooms and hallway.
- The master suite boasts a large closet, a deluxe bath and easy access to an outdoor patio or deck with hot tub.
- Two secondary bedrooms share another full bath, and a laundry area is conveniently located in the bedroom zone.

Plan N-1266

Bedrooms: 3	**Baths:** 2

Living Area:

Main floor	2,466 sq. ft.
Total Living Area:	**2,466 sq. ft.**
Standard basement	1,950 sq. ft.
Garage	430 sq. ft.
Exterior Wall Framing:	2x4

Foundation Options:

Standard basement

Slab

(Typical foundation & framing conversion diagram available—see order form.)

BLUEPRINT PRICE CODE:	C

TO ORDER THIS BLUEPRINT, CALL TOLL-FREE 1-800-547-5570

Plan N-1266

Floor plan labels

51'-0"

60'-0"

RAIL

DECK AREA

ROOF OVERHANG

RAIL

OPTIONAL HOT TUB

MASTER BEDROOM 12'-0" x 14'-0"

CLOSET

DECK AREA

ACTIVITY AREA 12'-6" x 14'-6"

NOOK 10'-3" x 9'-6"

SLOPED CEILING

BEDROOM 2 9'-0" x 13'-0"

CATHEDRAL CEILING

KITCHEN 11'-0" x 9'-6"

DINING 14'-0" x 10'-0"

SLOPED CEILING

ENTRY

DN

SLOPED CEILING

LAUNDRY ROOM 8'-0" x 7'-0"

D.

W.

T.

BEDROOM 3 9'-0" x 13'-0"

SUNKEN LIVING ROOM 18'-0" x 14'-0"

GARAGE 21'-6" x 20'-0"

Features to Spare

- Vaulted ceilings, an activity area, a library and a master bedroom with private bath are only a few of the modern features found in this attractive plan.
- A beautiful and well-planned kitchen adjoins the activity area on the one side and the formal dining room on the other.
- A spacious living room includes a fireplace, a cathedral ceiling, and built-in bookshelves.
- An impressive master suite boasts a deluxe private bath and two large walk-in closets. A second bedroom also has a private bath.
- Bedroom #3 is also in the front, and the adjoining library could serve as a fourth bedroom, as well as a home office or studio.

Plan N-1264

Bedrooms: 3-4	Baths: 2½
Living Area:	
Main floor	2,773 sq. ft.
Total Living Area:	**2,773 sq. ft.**
Standard basement	2,203 sq. ft.
Garage	484 sq. ft.
Exterior Wall Framing:	2x4

Foundation Options:
Standard basement
Slab
(Typical foundation & framing conversion diagram available—see order form.)

BLUEPRINT PRICE CODE: D

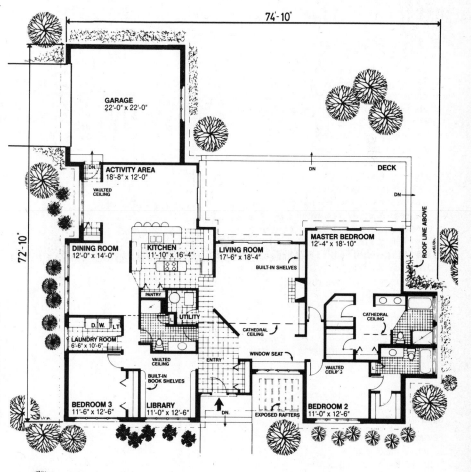

GARAGE
22'-0" x 22'-0"

ACTIVITY AREA
18'-8" x 12'-0"
VAULTED CEILING

DECK

DN

DN

ROOF LINE ABOVE

74'-10"

72'-10"

DINING ROOM
12'-0" x 14'-0"

KITCHEN
11'-10" x 16'-4"

LIVING ROOM
17'-6" x 18'-4"

MASTER BEDROOM
12'-4" x 18'-10"

BUILT-IN SHELVES

CATHEDRAL CEILING

PANTRY

UTILITY

D. W.

LAUNDRY ROOM
6'-6" x 10'-6"

VAULTED CEILING

CATHEDRAL CEILING

WINDOW SEAT

VAULTED CEILING

BUILT-IN BOOK SHELVES

BEDROOM 3
11'-6" x 12'-6"

LIBRARY
11'-0" x 12'-6"

ENTRY

DN.

EXPOSED RAFTERS

BEDROOM 2
11'-6" x 12'-6"

Plan N-1264

Efficiently Elegant

- Brick with corner quoins and entry columns add an elegance to this efficient, narrow, well-planned ranch home.
- The central Great Room, straight ahead of the entry foyer, is graced with a vaulted ceiling, fireplace and bay window.
- The formal dining room, with trayed ceiling and French doors to the rear deck, is separated from the Great Room by handsome columns.
- The island kitchen flows into the breakfast room, with French door to its own deck.
- Both bedrooms have dramatic vaulted ceilings.

Plan B-90004

Bedrooms: 2	Baths: 2
Space:	
Total living area:	1,631 sq. ft.
Basement:	1,631 sq. ft.
Garage:	390 sq. ft.
Exterior Wall Framing:	2x4

Foundation options:
Standard basement.
(Foundation & framing conversion diagram available — see order form.)

Blueprint Price Code:	B

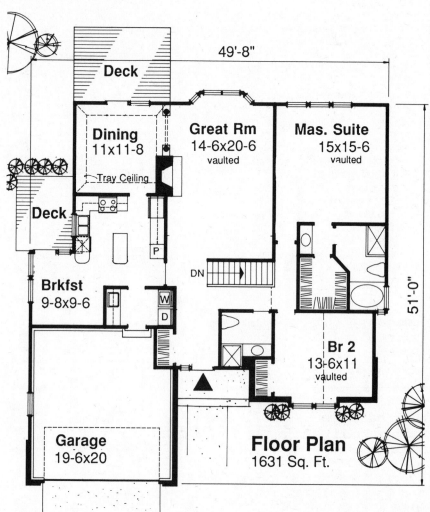

Floor Plan
1631 Sq. Ft.

Deck

Dining 11x11-8
Tray Ceiling

Deck

Great Rm 14-6x20-6 vaulted

Mas. Suite 15x15-6 vaulted

Brkfst 9-8x9-6

DN

Br 2 13-6x11 vaulted

Garage 19-6x20

49'-8"

51'-0"

Plan B-90004

Master Suite Adjoins Spa Solarium

- This elegant mid-sized design includes all the amenities needed for gracious living.
- Especially note the luxurious spa tub located in the solarium conveniently between the master suite and the Great Room.
- The large, vaulted Great Room and dining room combine to create plenty of space for entertaining and family living alike.

Plans P-6562-3A & P-6562-3D

Bedrooms: 3	Baths: 2

Space:

Main floor (non-basement version):	1,639 sq. ft.
Main floor (basement version):	1,699 sq. ft.
(Both figures include 123 sq. ft. solarium.)	
Basement:	1,699 sq. ft.
Garage:	438 sq. ft.

Exterior Wall Framing:	2x4

Foundation options:
Daylight basement (P-6562-3D).
Crawlspace (P-6562-3A).
(Foundation & framing conversion diagram available — see order form.)

Blueprint Price Code:	B

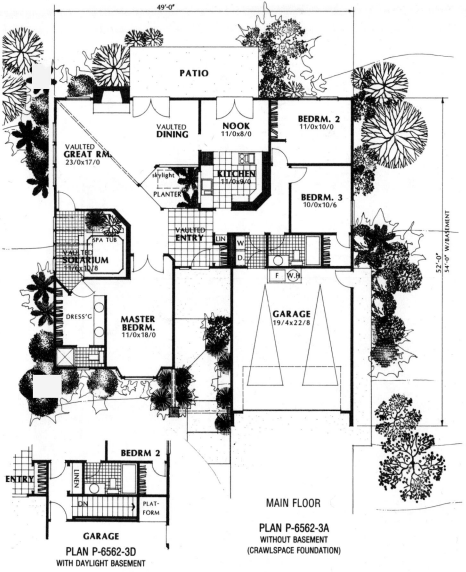

49'-0"

PATIO

VAULTED DINING

NOOK 11/0x8/0

BEDRM. 2 11/0x10/0

VAULTED GREAT RM. 23/0x17/0

skylight
KITCHEN 11/0x9/0
PLANTER

BEDRM. 3 10/0x10/6

VAULTED ENTRY LIN

SPA TUB

VAULTED SOLARIUM

W
D
F W.H.

DRESS'G

MASTER BEDRM. 11/0x18/0

GARAGE 19/4x22/8

52'-0" W/BASEMENT
54'-0" W/BASEMENT

MAIN FLOOR

PLAN P-6562-3A
WITHOUT BASEMENT
(CRAWLSPACE FOUNDATION)

BEDRM 2

ENTRY

LINEN

DN

PLAT-FORM

GARAGE

PLAN P-6562-3D
WITH DAYLIGHT BASEMENT

Plans P-6562-3A & -3D

TO ORDER THIS BLUEPRINT,
CALL TOLL-FREE 1-800-547-5570
(prices and details on pp. 12-15.) **131**

Vaulted Ceilings, Open Planning, Compact Luxury

- A protected entryway opens into a foyer which immediately shows off the impressive fireplace and vaulted ceiling in the living room.
- The dining room, breakfast nook and kitchen flow logically together as an efficient unit, with a pass-through from the kitchen to the breakfast area.
- The master suite is spectacular for a home of this size, with a vaulted ceiling, sunny sitting area, large closet and sumptuous master bath with separate tub and shower.
- The front bedroom, with its beautiful palladian window and vaulted ceiling, would serve equally well as a den or impressive home office.
- Note the convenient placement of the laundry area, garage entrance and basement stairs.

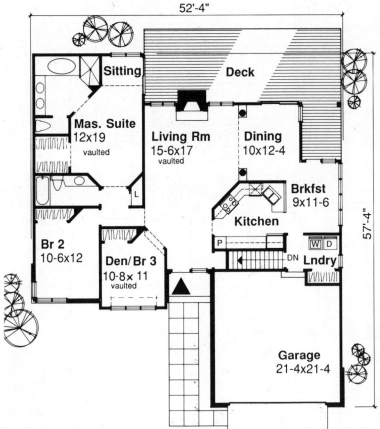

MAIN FLOOR

Plan B-89020

Bedrooms: 2-3	Baths: 2

Space:

Total living area:	1,642 sq. ft.
Basement:	approx. 1,642 sq. ft.
Garage:	455 sq. ft.

Exterior Wall Framing:	2x4

Foundation options:
Standard basement only.
(Foundation & framing conversion diagram available — see order form.)

Blueprint Price Code:	B

TO ORDER THIS BLUEPRINT,
CALL TOLL-FREE 1-800-547-5570

Plan B-89020

Spacious Great Room

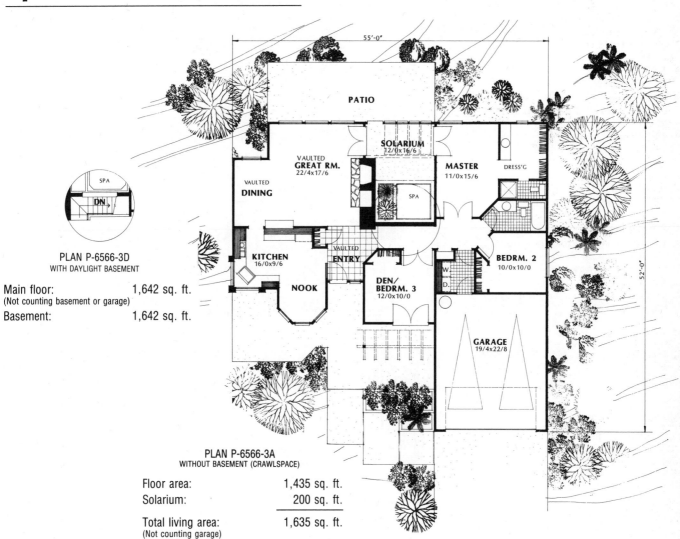

PLAN P-6566-3D
WITH DAYLIGHT BASEMENT

Main floor: 1,642 sq. ft.
(Not counting basement or garage)
Basement: 1,642 sq. ft.

PLAN P-6566-3A
WITHOUT BASEMENT (CRAWLSPACE)

Floor area: 1,435 sq. ft.
Solarium: 200 sq. ft.
Total living area: 1,635 sq. ft.
(Not counting garage)

Blueprint Price Code B

Plans P-6566-3A & -3D

**TO ORDER THIS BLUEPRINT,
CALL TOLL-FREE 1-800-547-5570**
(prices and details on pp. 12-15.) **133**

Elegant Master Suite

- This charming traditional home offers a multitude of fine features inside an attractive and stylish exterior.
- The covered entry and vaulted foyer create an inviting atmosphere.
- The vaulted Great Room features a fireplace, covered patio, bar and lots of windows.
- The splendid gourmet kitchen adjoins a sunny nook on one side and the dining area of the Great Room on the other.
- With a vaulted ceiling, the master suite also includes a reading area, large walk-in closet and superb bath with separate tub and shower.
- Two secondary bedrooms share another full bath and are connected by a skylit hallway.
- A utility area is positioned in the garage entryway, conveniently near the bedrooms.

Plans S-4789-A & -B

Bedrooms: 3	Baths: 2
Total living area:	1,665 sq. ft.
Basement:	approx. 1,665 sq. ft.
Garage:	400 sq. ft.

Exterior Wall Framing:	2x6

Foundation options:
Standard basement (Plan S-4789-B).
Crawlspace (Plan S-4789-A).
(Foundation & framing conversion diagram available — see order form.)

Blueprint Price Code:	B

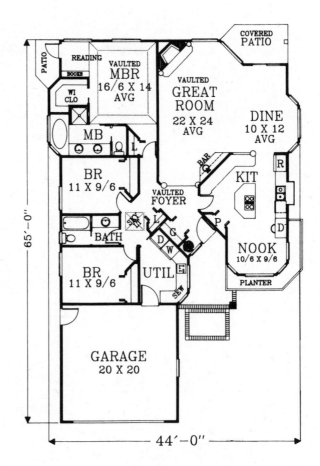

PLAN S-4789-B
WITH BASEMENT

Plans S-4789-A & -B

Ground-Hugging Home Features Atrium

A clean-lined roof with wide, overhanging eaves links this structure to its site. A low-walled entrance court, accentuated by wood trellis and brick facade, adds elegance to the expansive design. The central gallery sets a smooth and logical flow from one area to another. The sleeping wing is separate. Note the master suite with its sky-lighted dressing room, private bath and ample closets. Total living area is 1,768 sq. ft.; optional basement 1,768 sq. ft.; garage, mud room, etc., 684 sq. ft.

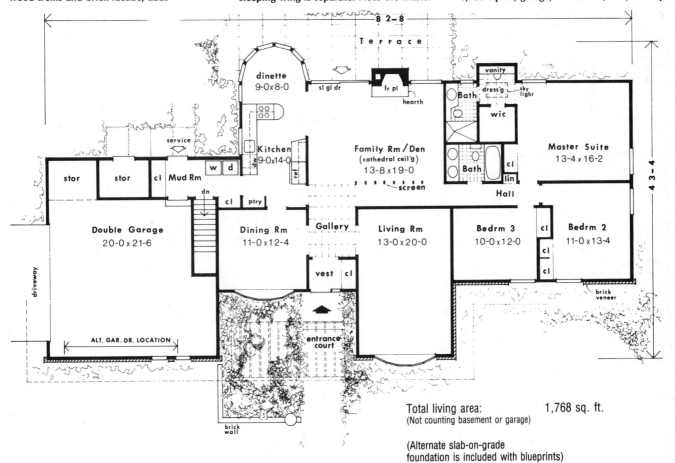

Total living area: 1,768 sq. ft.
(Not counting basement or garage)

(Alternate slab-on-grade foundation is included with blueprints)

Blueprint Price Code B

Plan K-167-R

Grace and Finesse

A graceful brick arch sets off the entry to this beautiful one level home and complements the curve of the heightened windows found in the vaulted living room.

Measuring 1,685 sq. ft., this home has plenty of finesse but still manages to keep the square footage at an affordable level.

A barrel vaulted ceiling highlights the living room for a striking effect, while the adjoining dining room provides an added dimension of spaciousness.

The centrally located kitchen is spectacular. It not only has abundant counter and cabinet space, but is also designed as an integral part of the family room and nook. Note how the angled counter provides the cook a work area that encourages interaction with others in the adjoining living areas. The solarium windows that highlight the nook also provide plenty of natural light to brighten the kitchen as well.

The master bedroom doesn't skimp on any of the extras home buyers have come to expect. It boasts a private bath with dual vanities, illuminating skylight and a fantastic walk-in closet.

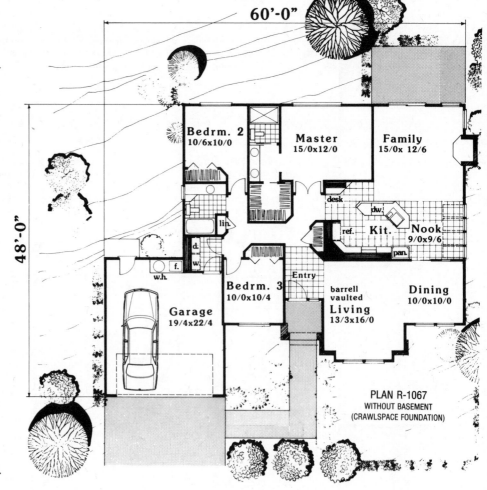

Total living area: 1,685 sq. ft.
(Not counting garage)

Blueprint Price Code B
Plan R-1067

Open Floor Plan

The open floor plan of this modified A-Frame design virtually eliminates wasted hall space. The centrally located great room features a 15'4" cathedral ceiling with exposed wood beams and large areas of fixed glass on both front and rear. Living and dining areas are visually separated by a massive stone fireplace. The isolated master suite features a walk-in closet and sliding glass doors opening onto the front deck.

A walk-thru utility room provides easy access from the carport and outside storage areas to the compact kitchen. On the opposite side of the great room are two additional bedrooms and a second full bath. All this in only 1,669 sq. ft. of heated living area. A full length deck and vertical wood siding with stone accents on the corners provide a rustic yet contemporary exterior.

Total living area: 1,669 sq. ft.
(Not counting basement or carport)

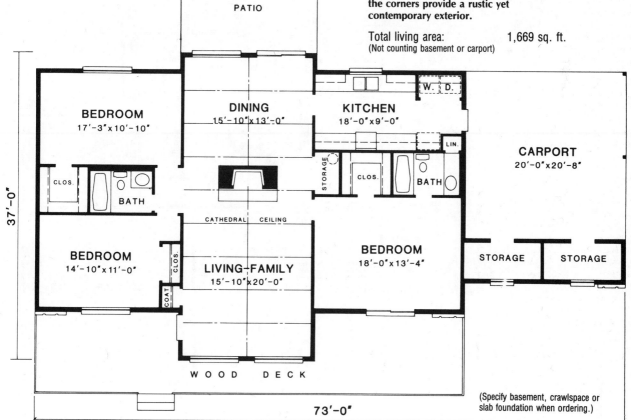

Blueprint Price Code B

Plan C-8160

TO ORDER THIS BLUEPRINT, CALL TOLL-FREE 1-800-547-5570
(prices and details on pp. 12-15.)

Angled, Vaulted Kitchen

- A corner fireplace and angled wall in the vaulted living room and bordering kitchen add interest to the interior of this medium-sized three-bedroom.
- The living room is open to the adjoining vaulted dining room, allowing a clear view of the rear deck and yard.
- Uniquely shaped and also oriented to the rear, the vaulted kitchen with eating bar and pantry joins a sunny breakfast nook with private access to the deck.
- The sleeping wing offers a generous-sized master bedroom with a nice bath for two; a step-up tub, separate shower, large walk-in closet and twin vanities make it ideal for two.
- Two secondary bedrooms share the rest of the plan with a second bath and laundry room.

Plan U-90-102	
Bedrooms: 3	**Baths: 2**
Space:	
Main floor	1,689 sq. ft.
Total Living Area	**1,689 sq. ft.**
Basement	1,689 sq. ft.
Garage	576 sq. ft.
Exterior Wall Framing	2x4

Foundation options:

Daylight Basement

(Foundation & framing conversion diagram available—see order form.)

Blueprint Price Code	**B**

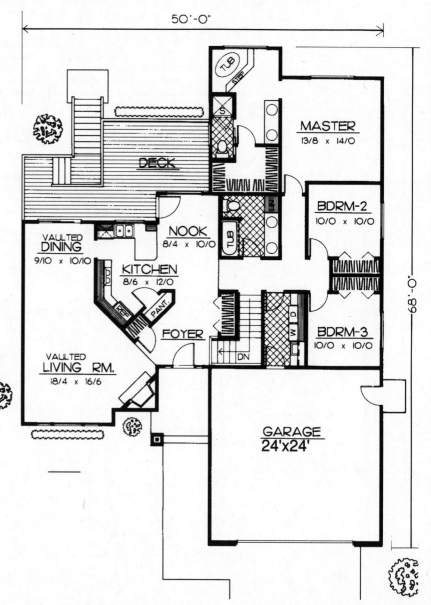

Plan U-90-102

Designed for Livability

- As you enter this excitingly spacious traditional home you see through the extensive windows to the back yard.
- This four-bedroom home was designed for livability of the maturing family with the separation of the master suite.
- The formal dining room expands spatially to the living room while being framed by the column and plant shelves.
- The bay that creates the morning room and sitting area for the master suite also adds excitement to this plan, both inside and out.
- The master bath offers an exciting oval tub under glass and separate shower, as well as a spacious walk-in closet and dressing area.

Plan DD-1696

Bedrooms: 4	Baths: 2
Space:	
Total living area:	1,748 sq. ft.
Garage:	393 sq. ft.

Exterior Wall Framing:	2x4

Foundation options:
Basement.
Crawlspace.
Slab.
(Foundation & framing conversion diagram available — see order form.)

Blueprint Price Code:	B

Floor Plan

54'10"

PATIO

SITTING

MORNING
9⁸ x 9⁴

MASTER BEDROOM
14⁴ x 18⁰

LIVING
15⁰ x 19⁸

BEDROOM 3
12⁴ x 11⁰

KITCHEN
9⁴ x 14⁰

BATH 2

M BATH

UTIL

BEDROOM 4
10⁰ x 10⁴

DINING
11⁴ x 11⁴

50'5"

GARAGE
19⁸ x 20⁰

BEDROOM 2
12⁴ x 10⁴

MAIN FLOOR

Plan DD-1696

Great Room Featured

- In this rustic design, the centrally located Great Room features a cathedral ceiling with exposed wood beams. Living and dining areas are separated by a massive fireplace.
- The isolated master suite features a walk-in closet and compartmentalized bath.
- The gallery type kitchen is between the breakfast room and formal dining area. A large utility room and storage room complete the garage area.
- On the opposite side of the Great Room are two additional bedrooms and a second full bath.

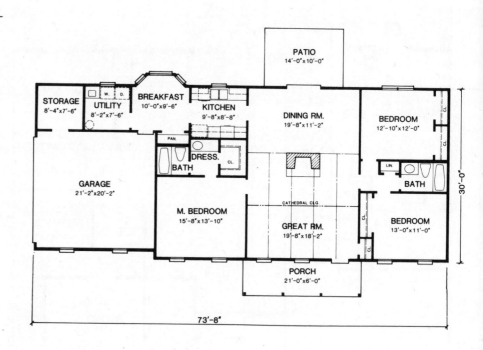

Plan C-8460

Bedrooms: 3	**Baths:** 2

Space:

Total living area:	1,670 sq. ft.
Basement:	approx. 1,600 sq. ft.
Garage:	427 sq. ft.
Storage:	63 sq. ft.

Exterior Wall Framing:	2x4

Foundation options:
Standard basement.
Crawlspace.
Slab.
(Foundation & framing conversion diagram available — see order form)

Blueprint Price Code: B

Plan C-8460

Efficient Dining-Kitchen-Nook Combination

- Here's a four-bedroom design that is beautiful in its simplicity and ease of construction.
- All on one floor, it offers ample space for both family life and entertaining.
- A huge living room soars aloft with vaulted, beamed ceilings and features a massive fireplace to give a Great Room feel to the area.
- The roomy, efficient kitchen is flanked by a sunny informal eating

area protruding into the back yard and a front-facing formal dining room that is right off the elegant foyer.
- A deluxe master suite includes a dressing room, large closet and private bath.
- The three secondary bedrooms are larger than average and also offer ample closet space.
- Convenient storage and utility areas are segmented off the two-car garage.

Plan E-1702	
Bedrooms: 4	**Baths:** 2
Space:	
Total living area:	1,751 sq. ft.
Porch:	64 sq. ft.
Garage:	484 sq. ft.
Storage:	105 sq. ft.
Exterior Wall Framing:	2x4

Foundation options:
Crawlspace.
Slab.
(Foundation & framing conversion diagram available — see order form)

Blueprint Price Code:	B

77'-0"

PATIO
21'-0"x12'-0"

EATING
11'-0"x9'-6"

STORAGE
13'-0"x8'-0"

UTILITY
9'-0"x8'-0"

WASH. DRYER

BRM'S. STOR.

PANTRY
DISHWASHER
KITCHEN
10'-0"x9'-6"

SINK

SURF. UNIT

REF

OVEN

SLOPE

SLOPE

LIVING
19'-0"x16'-0"

BEAMS

BOOKS

SHV'S.

CLO.

LINEN

BOOKS

BATH

BATH

LINEN

POST ON
1/2 WALL

DRESS. ROOM

MASTER B.R.
16'-0"x13'-0"

SHELVES

GARAGE
22'-0"x22'-0"

DINING
11'-0"x10'-0"

ENTRY
10'-0"x5'-0"

DISAPPEARING STAIRS

CLO.

HALL

CLO.

CLO.

PORCH

BED ROOM
12'-0"x10'-6"

CLO.

CLO.

BED ROOM
12'-6"x11'-6"

BED ROOM
12'-6"x12'-6"

32'-0"

Plan E-1702

Design Reflects Finesse

This especially handsome yet simple ranch house attracts admiration with its exterior facade of stone, shingles, and natural tone (unpainted) wood, all used with finesse. The house layout is practical, but with many imaginative touches. There are two entries to the house, one through the mud room, the other a formal, covered front entranceway.

To the left of the welcoming gallery is the dining room-living room area, with elegant cathedral ceiling. The living room has an optional entrance to the family room, covered by folding doors. The dinette, with a curved wall of stock-size windows overlooking the terrace, also has a screen or partition shielding it from the family room. The family room offers a sliding glass exit to the terrace and a built-in fireplace.

To the right of the gallery lie the three bedrooms. The master suite contains a walk-in closet and a surprise: a skylight above the dressing alcove. The master bedroom has its own bath while the other two bedrooms share a bath. There is plenty of closet and storage space throughout. The basic house is 1,672 sq. ft.; optional basement is 1,672 sq. ft.; garage, etc., is 546 sq. ft.

Living area:	1,672 sq. ft.
Basement (opt.):	1,672 sq. ft.
Garage, mud rom, etc.:	546 sq. ft.

(Alternate slab-on-grade foundation plan included.)

TO ORDER THIS BLUEPRINT, CALL TOLL-FREE 1-800-547-5570
142 (prices and details on pp. 12-15.)

Blueprint Price Code B
Plan K-162-J

Rustic Home for Relaxed Living

A screened-in breezeway provides a cool place to dine out on warm summer days and nights, and the rustic front porch is ideal for relaxed rocking or a swing. A Great Room to the left of the entry has a fireplace and connects the dining area to the country kitchen.

The large master suite contains separate shower, garden tub, vanities and walk-in closets.

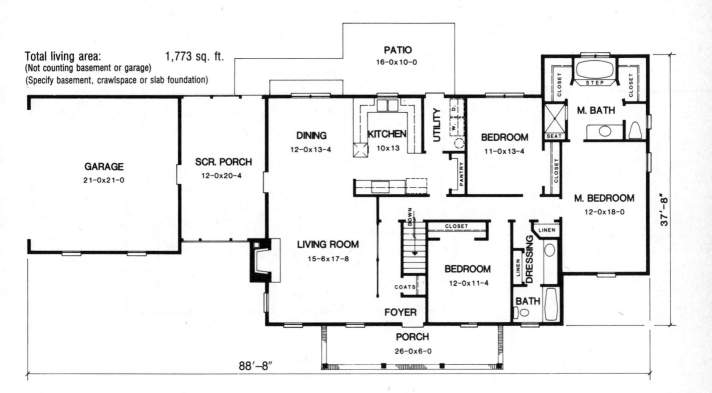

Total living area: 1,773 sq. ft.
(Not counting basement or garage)
(Specify basement, crawlspace or slab foundation)

PATIO
16-0x10-0

GARAGE
21-0x21-0

SCR. PORCH
12-0x20-4

DINING
12-0x13-4

KITCHEN
10x13

UTILITY
W. D.

PANTRY

BEDROOM
11-0x13-4

CLOSET

STEP

CLOSET

M. BATH

SEAT

CLOSET

M. BEDROOM
12-0x18-0

37'-8"

LIVING ROOM
15-6x17-8

DOWN

CLOSET

LINEN

DRESSING

LINEN

COATS

BEDROOM
12-0x11-4

BATH

FOYER

PORCH
26-0x6-0

88'-8"

Rustic Home With Porches Means Relaxation

A spacious screened porch serves as a great place to eat out during warm summer days and nights, while the front porch is ideal for relaxed rocking or a swing. The Great Room to the left of the entry has a fireplace and connects to the dining area and country kitchen. The large master bedroom features a private bath and ample closets.

For entertaining large groups, the combined dining area, living room and screened porch provide lots of space. Also note the large kitchen/utility and pantry area.

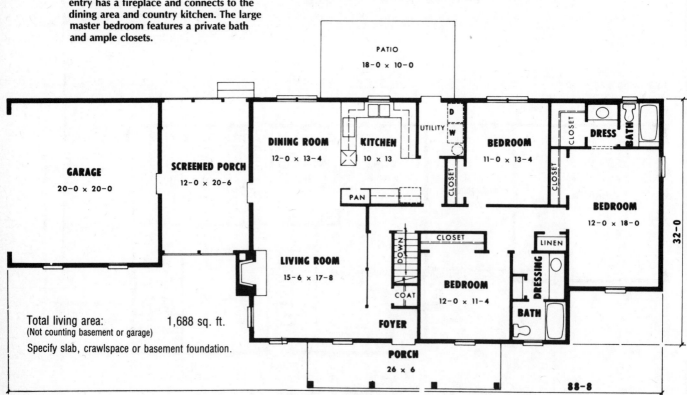

Total living area: 1,688 sq. ft.
(Not counting basement or garage)

Specify slab, crawlspace or basement foundation.

Blueprint Price Code B

Plan C-7557

Traditional Design
For Narrow Lot

Living:	1,626 sq. ft.
Porch:	216 sq. ft.
Storage:	104 sq. ft.
Carport:	410 sq. ft.
Total:	2,356 sq. ft.

Specify basement, crawlspace or slab foundation.

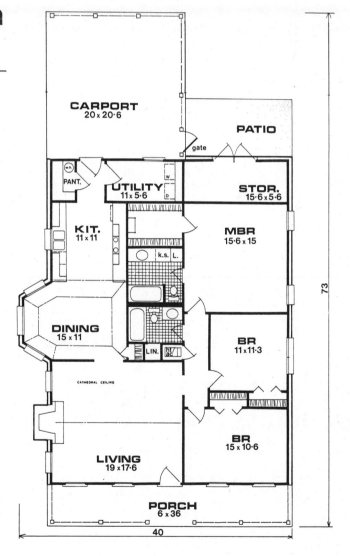

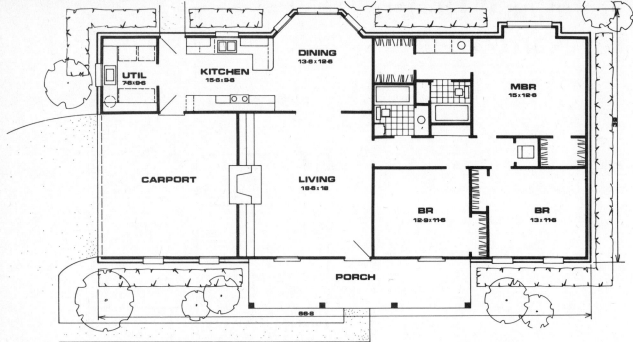

Gracious One-Story with Welcoming Front Porch

- An inviting front porch opens to the large, central living room with fireplace and functional built-ins.
- A view to the backyard is possible through a bayed window in the formal dining room at the rear of the home.
- The walk-through kitchen has lots of counter space and small eating bar adjoining the dining room; convenient laundry facilities are steps away.
- Secluded to the rear corner of the home is a generous-sized master bedroom with lovely boxed window and private bath with second walk-in closet, dressing area and isolated toilet and tub.
- Two additional good-sized bedrooms and a second full bath complete the floor plan.

Plan J-8692	
Bedrooms: 3	Baths: 2
Space:	
Main floor	1,633 sq. ft.
Total Living Area	**1,633 sq. ft.**
Carport	380 sq. ft.
Exterior Wall Framing	2x4
Foundation options:	
Basement	
Crawlspace	
Slab	
(Foundation & framing conversion diagram available—see order form.)	
Blueprint Price Code	B

Plan J-8692

Southwestern Standout

- Contemporary styling with a traditional touch makes this house a standout in any neighborhood.
- The generously sized kitchen contains abundant counter space, a handy pantry and corner windows overlooking an enticing backyard patio. The kitchen is open to the family room and nook for informal living.
- The family room and kitchen can be totally closed off to provide extra privacy for the formal dining and living rooms. Both the family room and the living room feature fireplaces.
- The master bedroom has a private bath and is highlighted by a sunny alcove with a French door that opens to the patio.
- The laundry room is handy to the garage and to the bedrooms.

Plan R-1039

Bedrooms: 3	Baths: 2
Space:	
Main floor	1,642 sq. ft.
Total Living Area	**1,642 sq. ft.**
Garage	517 sq. ft.
Exterior Wall Framing	2x4

Foundation options:

Slab

Crawlspace

(Foundation & framing conversion diagram available—see order form.)

Blueprint Price Code	B

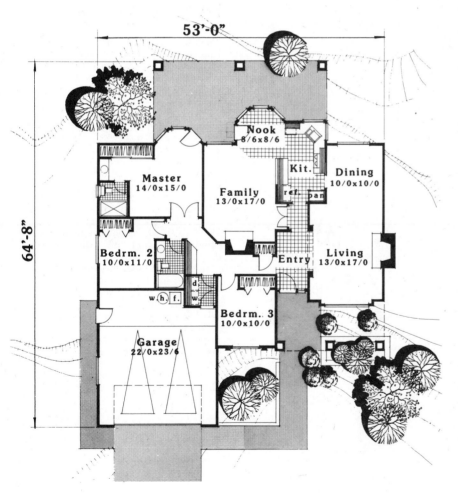

Plan R-1039

A Home for Sun Lovers

This open plan home, brightened by a landscaped atrium, also has a vaulted, glass-ceiling solarium with an optional spa, offering a sunny garden room for sitting or soaking — a bonus in a three-bedroom home of only 1,621 sq. ft.

Intersecting hip roofs with corner notches, a clerestory dormer, vertical board siding and a covered front walkway add design interest and set the house apart from its neighbors. Inside the vaulted, skylighted entry, the hallway angles left past the atrium into the vaulted great room, which has a fireplace and a door leading out to a wood deck or patio.

The spacious L-shaped kitchen also overlooks the atrium and has an adjacent vaulted nook with solarium window and a door to the garage.

To the right of the entry hall is the bedroom wing. Double doors open into the master bedroom, with a private bath and walk-in closet. Doors lead to the solarium and the front courtyard. A second bathroom serves the other two bedrooms, one of which can double as a den and has doors opening into the great room.

In the daylight basement version of the plan, a stairway replaces the atrium.

Main floor:	1,497 sq. ft.
Solarium:	124 sq. ft.
Total living area: (Not counting basement or garage)	1,621 sq. ft.
Basement:	1,514 sq. ft.

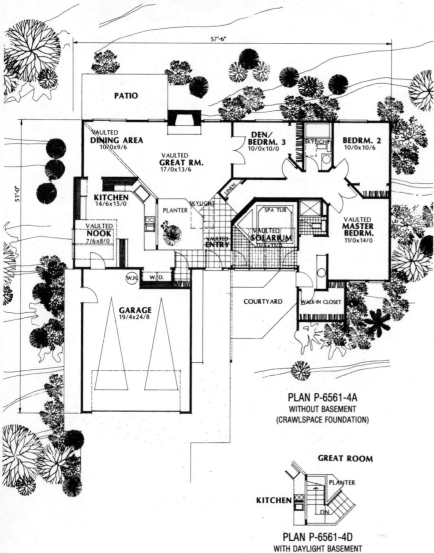

PLAN P-6561-4A
WITHOUT BASEMENT
(CRAWLSPACE FOUNDATION)

PLAN P-6561-4D
WITH DAYLIGHT BASEMENT

Blueprint Price Code B

Plans P-6561-4A & -4D

Photo by Mark Englund/HomeStyles

Exciting Interior Angles

- A relatively modest-looking exterior encloses an exciting interior design that's loaded with surprises.
- The Y-shaped entry directs traffic to the more formal living/dining area or to the family room or bedroom wing.
- Family room features unusual shape, a vaulted ceiling and a fireplace.
- Living room is brightened by a bay window, and also includes a fireplace.
- The dining area, sun room, family room and outdoor patios are grouped around the large kitchen.
- Roomy master suite includes deluxe bath and large closet.
- Daylight basement version adds 1,275 square feet more space.

MAIN FLOOR
PLAN P-7661-3A
WITHOUT BASEMENT

(Floor plan labels:)
55'-0"
54'-0"
PATIO
WALK IN WARDROBE
MASTER 13/0x15/6
VAULTED FAMILY RM. 17/0x13/6
KITCHEN 11/0x10/0
LINEN
WOODSTOVE
EXP. RM.
VAULTED SUN RM.
PATIO
PANTRY
ENTRY
DINING AREA
BEDRM. 2 10/0x10/0
DEN/ BEDRM. 3 10/0x11/6
LIVING RM. 18/4x18/4
GARAGE 21/4x21/8

PLAN P-7661-3D
WITH DAYLIGHT BASEMENT

BAR
MASTER
DN

NOTE:
The above photographed home may have been modified by the homeowner. Please refer to floor plan and/or drawn elevation shown for actual blueprint details.

Plans P-7661-3A & -3D

Bedrooms: 2-3	**Baths:** 2

Space:

Main floor:	1,693 sq. ft.
Basement:	1,275 sq. ft.
Garage:	462 sq. ft.

Exterior Wall Framing:	2x4

Foundation options:
Daylight basement (Plan P-7661-3D).
Crawlspace (Plan P-7661-3A).
(Foundation & framing conversion diagram available — see order form.)

Blueprint Price Code:	B

Plans P-7661-3A & -3D

TO ORDER THIS BLUEPRINT,
CALL TOLL-FREE 1-800-547-5570
(prices and details on pp. 12-15.)

Imposing Form... Outstanding Floor Plan

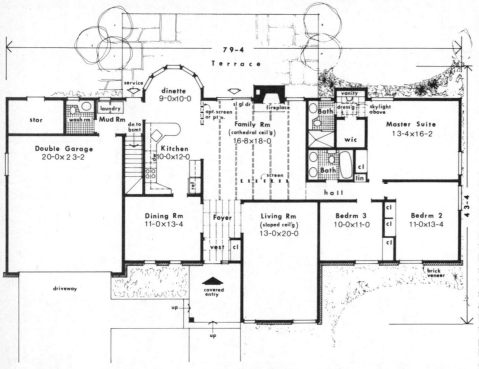

Total living area: 1,725 sq. ft.
Basement (opt.) 1,778 sq. ft.
Gar. & Mud Room, etc. 664 sq. ft.

(Alternate slab-on-grade foundation plan included.)

Stately and imposing, this one-story design has wood-and-brick exterior finish. The focal point of the plan is a grand, spacious family room that has beamed cathedral ceiling, slate-hearth fireplace, and sliding glass doors leading to a rear terrace. Living room with sloped ceiling and high glass panels is located to the front, away from family noise and traffic. Well-organized kitchen and circular dinette, ideally situated between the dining room and family room, are accessible from the service entrance, garage and mud room, and a wash room is conveniently near by. Plan also features a luxurious master suite that includes a sky-lighted dressing room, private bath and ample closet space. Total living area is 1,725 square feet. Basement (which is optional) is 1,778 square feet; garage, mud room, etc., total 664 square feet; energy-saving details are incorporated into the construction plans.

Blueprint Price Code B

Plan K-278-M

Plantation Home Ideal for Several Markets

- An efficient square footage appeals to many different buyers, from first-time, to second-home, to retirement.
- Compact building envelope of 65 x 55 is ideal for a smaller lot.
- A walk-up front porch, lap siding, and Palladian windows convey traditional charm.
- The Grand room features an ale bar, fireplace, and French doors to the rear deck.
- The gourmet kitchen features an island, greenhouse window, and sunny good morning room, and serves the private, formal dining room.
- The master suite features a luxury bath with separate his and her closets.

Plan EOF-25

Bedrooms: 2-3	Baths: 2½
Space:	
Total living area:	1,758 sq. ft.
Garage:	400 sq. ft.
Ceiling Heights:	
Main floor:	9'
Exterior Wall Framing:	2x6

Foundation options:
Slab.
(Foundation & framing conversion diagram available — see order form.)

Blueprint Price Code:	B

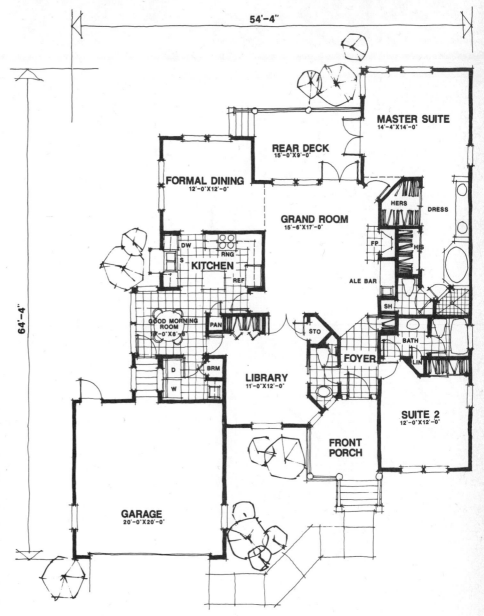

Plan EOF-25

Versatile Octagon

- Popular octagonal design features a secondary raised roof to allow light into the 500 sq. ft. living room.
- Unique framing design allows you to divide the living space any way you choose: left open, with 3 or more bedrooms, a den, library or other options.
- Large, winding deck can accommodate outdoor parties and guests.
- Optional basement expands recreational opportunities.

Plans H-821-1 & -1A

Bedrooms: 3	Baths: 2½
Space:	
Main floor:	1,699 sq. ft.
Total living area:	1,699 sq. ft.
Basement:	approx. 1,699 sq. ft.
Exterior Wall Framing:	2x4

Foundation options:
Daylight basement (Plan H-821-1).
Crawlspace (Plan H-821-1A).
(Foundation & framing conversion diagram available — see order form.)

Blueprint Price Code:	
Without basement	B
With basement	E

MAIN FLOOR

PLAN H-821-1A
WITHOUT BASEMENT

SCALE

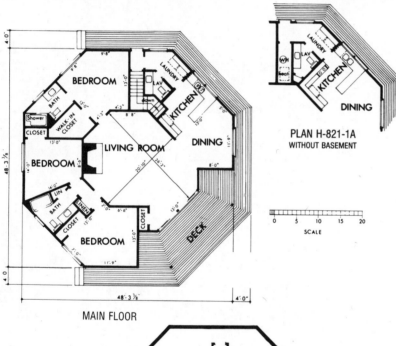

BASEMENT

Plans H-821-1 & -1A

Raised Cottage Design Offers Large Covered Porches

- Twin dormers and covered porch add drama to this raised one-story.
- Large centered living room features 12' ceilings and built-in skylights.
- Kitchen has unusual but functional angular design, sloped ceilings, bar, and eating area that overlooks the adjoining deck.
- Elegant master suite is conveniently located near kitchen.

Plan E-1826

Bedrooms: 3	Baths: 2

Space:	
Total living area:	1,800 sq. ft.
Garage:	550 sq. ft.
Storage:	84 sq. ft.
Porches:	466 sq. ft.

Exterior Wall Framing:	2x6

Foundation options:
Crawlspace.
Slab.
(Foundation & framing conversion diagram available — see order form.)

Blueprint Price Code:	B

Plan E-1826

Fresh New Interior with an Old Favorite Exterior

This Louisiana-style raised cottage features a separate master suite with a connecting showplace bathroom fit for the most demanding taste.

Pairs of French doors in each of the front rooms invite family members and visitors to enjoy the cool and relaxing front porch. The tin roof adds to the comfort and nostalgic appeal of this Creole classic. An unusual, angled eating bar overlooks the cozy covered terrance via a bay window morning room.

The secondary bedroom wing has two full-size bedrooms, maximum closets, and a full-size bath.

This full-feature energy-efficient design is drawn on a raised crawlspace foundation. An alternate concrete slab foundation is available.

PLAN E-1823
WITHOUT BASEMENT

Areas:

Heated:	1,800 sq. ft.
Unheated:	1,100 sq. ft.
Total area:	2,900 sq. ft.

Floor plan labels:

- SHVS
- LIN.
- CLO.
- BATH
- MASTER SUITE 15' x 14'
- CLO.
- SHW'R
- STORAGE 10' x 6'
- FREEZ BRM
- UTILITY 9' x 6'
- DRY WASH
- PANT.
- HALL
- PORCH 15' x 12'
- BED RM. 12' x 11'
- CLO.
- STOR 6' x 4'
- W.H.
- GARAGE 25' x 22'
- ATTIC STAIRS
- DESK
- REF SLOPE CEILING
- EATING 10' x 8'
- COOK TOP
- KIT 13' x 11'
- COMP OVENS
- BAR
- SINK DW
- PANT
- SKYLIGHT
- SLOPE CEILING
- HALL
- LIN
- BATH
- HEAT & A/C
- LIN
- DINING 13' x 12'
- LIVING 22' x 16'
- CLO.
- CLO.
- BED RM. 14' x 11'
- PORCH 44' x 6'
- 60'
- 66'

Exterior walls are 2x6 construction.
Specify crawlspace or slab foundation.

An Energy Efficient Home

Blueprint Price Code B

Plan E-1823

Great Bedroom/Bath Combination

- Dining room has view of entry and living room through surrounding arched openings.
- Living room features 12′ ceilings, fireplace, and a view to the outdoor patio.
- Kitchen has attached eating area with sloped ceilings.
- Tray ceiling adorns the master suite; attached bath has skylight and marble enclosed tub.

Plan E-1830

Bedrooms: 3	Baths: 2

Space:	
Total living area:	1,868 sq. ft.
Garage and storage:	616 sq. ft.
Porch:	68 sq. ft.

Exterior Wall Framing:	2x6

Foundation options:
Crawlspace.
Slab.
(Foundation & framing conversion diagram available — see order form.)

Blueprint Price Code:	B

Plan E-1830

Impressive Master Bedroom Suite

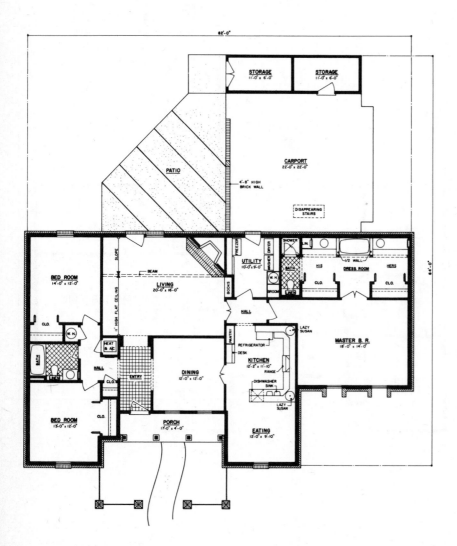

- This updated ranch features an impressive master bedroom with separate dressing areas and closets.
- A lovely front porch opens into a formal dining room and rear-oriented living room with fireplace and attached patio.
- A roomy kitchen and eating area provide plenty of space for work and casual living.

Plan E-1818

Bedrooms: 3	Baths: 2

Space:

Main floor:	1,868 sq. ft.
Total living area:	1,868 sq. ft.
Carport:	484 sq. ft.

Exterior Wall Framing:	2x6

Foundation options:
Crawlspace.
Slab.
(Foundation & framing conversion diagram available — see order form.)

Blueprint Price Code:	B

TO ORDER THIS BLUEPRINT,
CALL TOLL-FREE 1-800-547-5570

Plan E-1818

Master Bedroom Suite Features "His 'n Her" Baths

- A spacious and secluded master bedroom boasts a bath with separate his 'n her dressing areas and closets.
- This traditional ranch also offers a huge central living room with fireplace and adjoining patio.
- A formal dining room is entered through double doors from the roomy kitchen and bayed eating room.

Plan E-1812

Bedrooms: 3	Baths: 2

Space:	
Main floor:	1,860 sq. ft.
Total living area:	1,860 sq. ft.
Carport:	484 sq. ft.

Exterior Wall Framing:	2x6

Foundation options:
Crawlspace.
Slab.
(Foundation & framing conversion diagram available — see order form.)

Blueprint Price Code:	B

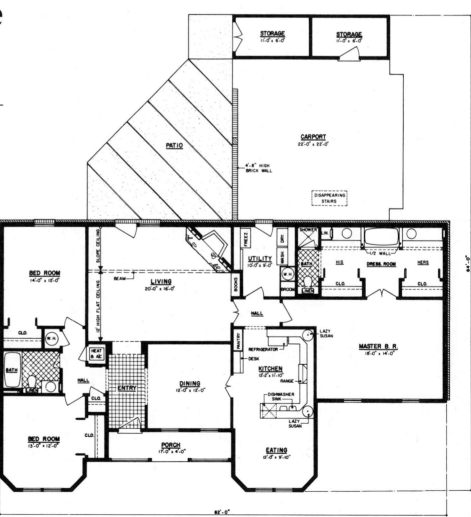

Plan E-1812

Country-Style Home with Welcoming Appeal

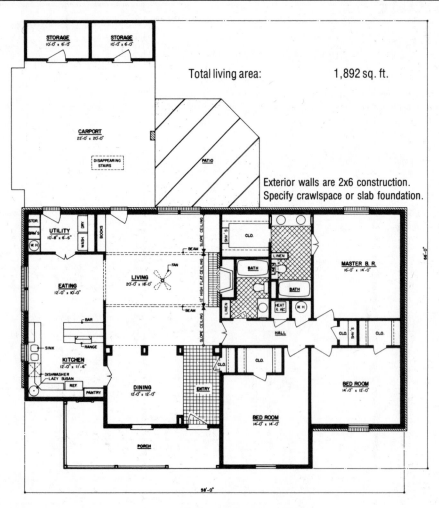

Total living area: 1,892 sq. ft.

Exterior walls are 2x6 construction.
Specify crawlspace or slab foundation.

An Energy Efficient Home
Blueprint Price Code B
Plan E-1813

Elegance and Convenience

- Exterior design presents a dignified, distinctive and solid look.
- Energy-efficient, 2 x 6 exterior walls are used.
- 15' ceilings and a beautifully detailed fireplace are part of the living room decor.
- Octagonal dining room has window walls on three sides to view adjacent porches.
- Master suite features access to a private porch and an attached bath with corner marbled tub and separate shower.

Plan E-1628

Bedrooms: 3	Baths: 2

Space:

Total living area:	1,655 sq. ft.
Garage and storage:	549 sq. ft.
Porches:	322 sq. ft.

Exterior Wall Framing:	2x6

Foundation options:

Crawlspace.
Slab.
(Foundation & framing conversion diagram available — see order form.)

Blueprint Price Code:	B

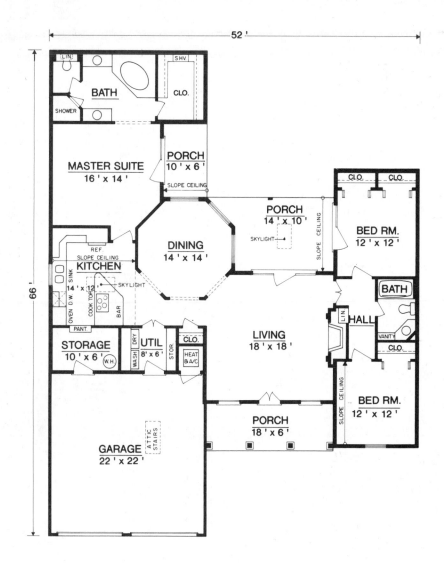

Plan E-1628

Surrounded by Decks

- Wrap-around deck offers a panoramic view of the surroundings as well as space for outdoor living and relaxation.
- Angular arrangement of garage, breezeway, and home provides front-yard privacy and a visual barrier to front bedrooms from street traffic.
- Exciting L-shaped dining room, attached sunken living room, and deck create a perfect atmosphere for entertaining.
- Basement is available with either a concrete floor (Plan H-2083), a framed floor for steep sloping sites (Plan H-2083-B), or on a crawlspace (Plan H-2083-A).

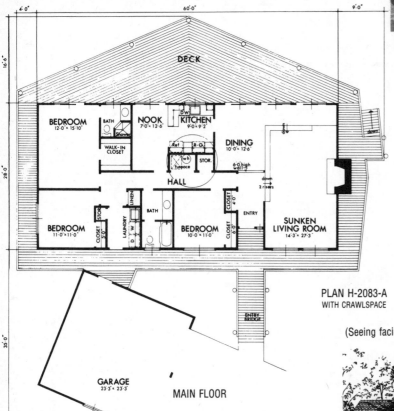

PLAN H-2083-A
WITH CRAWLSPACE

MAIN FLOOR

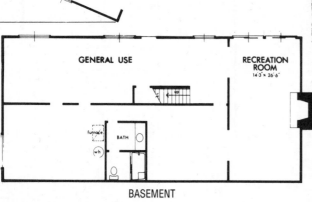

BASEMENT

Plans H-2083, -A & -B

Bedrooms: 3	Baths: 2-3

Space:

Main floor:	1,660 sq. ft.
Basement:	1,660 sq. ft.

Total living area with basement:	3,320 sq. ft.
Garage:	541 sq. ft.

Exterior Wall Framing:	2x4

Foundation options:
Daylight basement (Plans H-2083 & H-2083-B).
Crawlspace (Plan H-2083-A).
(Foundation & framing conversion diagram available — see order form.)

Blueprint Price Code:

Without basement:	B
With basement:	E

(Seeing facing page for alternate floor plan).

PLAN H-2083-B
WITH BASEMENT
WOOD-FRAMED
LOWER LEVEL

PLAN H-2083
WITH CONCRETE BASEMENT

Plans H-2083, -A & -B

FRONT VIEW

Gracious Indoor/ Outdoor Living

- A clean design makes this plan adaptable to almost any climate or setting.
- Perfect for a scenic, hillside lot, the structure and wrap-around deck offers a spanning view.
- Kitchen is flanked by family and dining rooms, allowing easy entrance from both.
- Foundation options include a daylight basement on concrete slab (H-2083-1), a wood-framed lower level (H-2083-1B), and a crawlspace (H-2083-1A).

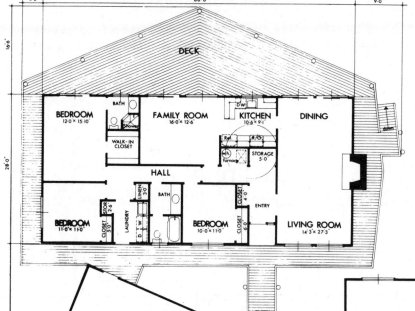

MAIN FLOOR

BASEMENT

PLAN H-2083-1
WITH DAYLIGHT BASEMENT
(ON CONCRETE SLAB)

PLAN H-2083-1B
(WITH WOOD-FRAMED LOWER LEVEL)

(See facing page for both rear view and alternate floor plan.)

Plans H-2083-1, -1A & -1B

Bedrooms: 3	Baths: 2-3

Space:

Main floor:	1,660 sq. ft.
Basement:	1,660 sq. ft.

Total living area: with basement:	3,320 sq. ft.
Garage:	541 sq. ft.

Exterior Wall Framing: 2x4

Foundation options:
Daylight basement (Plan H-2083-1 or -1B).
Crawlspace (Plan H-2083-1A).
(Foundation & framing conversion diagram available — see order form.)

Blueprint Price Code:

Without basement:	B
With basement:	E

Plans H-2083-1, -1A & -1B

Versatile U-Shaped Ranch

- A modern rendition of the popular U-shaped home, this ranch offers a ground-hugging silhouette, a recessed front porch and a large front-facing bay window.
- The lovely sunken living room off the foyer has a corner entrance and adjoining formal dining room; only an open railing separates the two rooms, which creates an elegant and spacious formal entertaining area.
- The dramatic family room includes a sloping cathedral ceiling, a brick-faced, heat-circulating fireplace, sliding doors to the rear patio and a snack bar connecting it to the kitchen.
- The perfect kitchen features a spacious work area with cabinets on four walls.
- The private master suite features an elegant double door entry, a generous walk-in closet and bath.
- Room for one or two additional bedrooms and a utility area are also included.

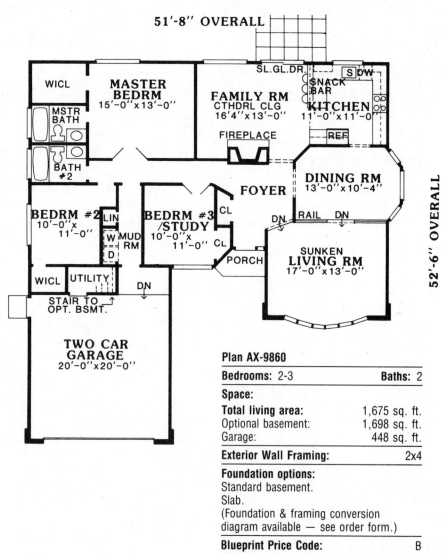

Plan AX-9860

Bedrooms: 2-3	Baths: 2
Space:	
Total living area:	1,675 sq. ft.
Optional basement:	1,698 sq. ft.
Garage:	448 sq. ft.
Exterior Wall Framing:	2x4

Foundation options:
Standard basement.
Slab.
(Foundation & framing conversion diagram available — see order form.)

Blueprint Price Code:	B

Plan AX-9860

Low-profile Country Classic

Total living area:	1,790 sq. ft.
Porches:	352 sq. ft.
Carport:	474 sq. ft.
Storage:	146 sq. ft.
Total:	2,762 sq. ft.

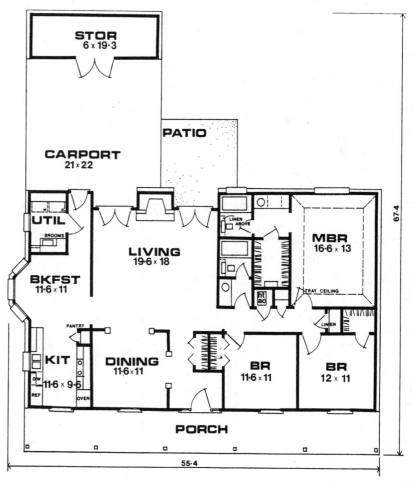

Specify basement, crawlspace or slab foundation.

Blueprint Price Code B

Plan J-8606

Classic Country-Style

- At the center of this rustic country home is an enormous living room with vaulted ceilings, a massive stone fireplace and entrance to a rear porch.
- The adjoining eating area and kitchen provide plenty of room for dining and meal preparation. A sloped ceiling with false beams, porch overlook, pantry, spice cabinet and counter bar are some

attractions found here.
- Formal dining and entertaining can take place in the dining room off the entry.
- For privacy, you'll find the secluded master suite rewarding; it offers a private bath with dressing area, walk-in closet and isolated toilet and tub.
- The two additional bedrooms also have abundant walk-in closet space.

Plan E-1808

Bedrooms: 3	Baths: 2
Space:	
Main floor	1,800 sq. ft.
Total Living Area	**1,800 sq. ft.**
Garage and storage	605 sq. ft.
Porches	354 sq. ft.
Exterior Wall Framing	2x4

Foundation options:
Crawlspace
Slab
(Foundation & framing conversion diagram available—see order form.)

Blueprint Price Code	B

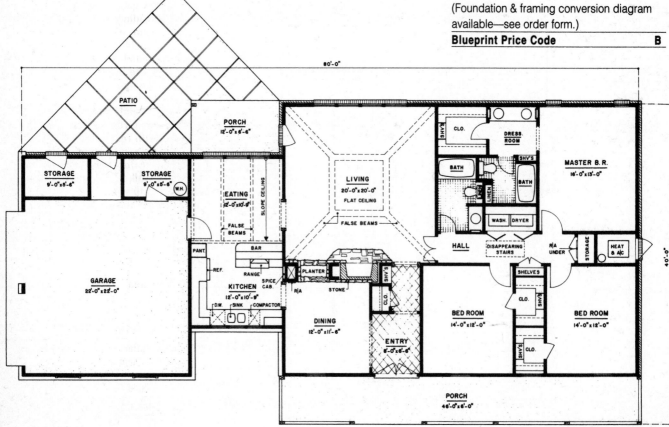

Plan E-1808

New England Farmhouse Charm

- Saltbox design motifs, divided windows, heavy trim and entry columns and shake siding give this one-story a New England farmhouse charm.
- The entry gallery has a vaulted ceiling leading the eye into the living room, with plant shelf and column highlights.
- A three-sided fireplace and wet bar separate the living room from the formal dining room.
- The open kitchen flows into an informal family gathering area. A sun porch further expands the space, with rear patio access.
- The master suite offers such exciting features as a vaulted ceiling, walk-in closet and splendid master bath with separate shower and corner tub under glass.

Plan B-89503

Bedrooms: 2-3	Baths: 2

Space:

Total living area:	1,797 sq. ft.
Basement:	1,797 sq. ft.
Garage:	758 sq. ft.

Exterior Wall Framing:	2x6

Foundation options:
Standard basement.
(Foundation & framing conversion diagram available — see order form.)

Blueprint Price Code:	B

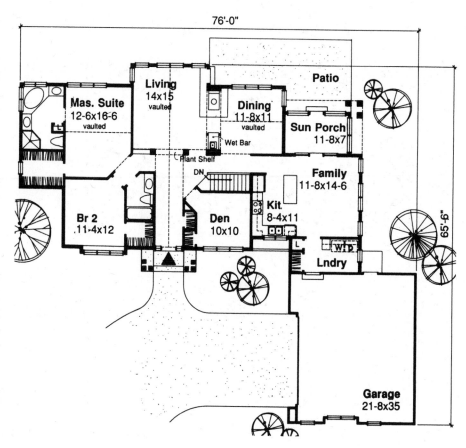

Plan B-89503

A Big First Impression

- A brick covered exterior with dramatic pillared arched entry creates a big first impression.
- Open, flowing spaces create a big first impression inside the front door as well.
- Nine-foot ceilings, with a raised ceiling at the entry, add to the open feeling.
- The living room features a built-in TV center next to the handsome fireplace.
- The formal dining room and a den/fourth bedroom flank the entry.
- The island kitchen incorporates a breakfast eating area, which opens to the covered rear patio.
- The vaulted master suite offers dual walk-in closets and a splashing master bath.

Plan B-90039

Bedrooms: 3-4	Baths: 2
Space:	
Total living area:	1,806 sq. ft.
Garage:	427 sq. ft.
Exterior Wall Framing:	2x6
Ceiling Height:	9'

Foundation options:
Crawlspace.
(Foundation & framing conversion diagram available — see order form.)

Blueprint Price Code:	B

55'-8"

Covered Patio

Brkfst
10x8

niche

Living
13x18-3

M Suite
13-4x16
vaulted

Br 3
12-8x10

raised ceiling

tv

Dining
14x12-8

Den/Br 4
10-6x10-6

Br 3
10x10-4

F
WH

Garage
21-4x20

55'-0"

Plan B-90039

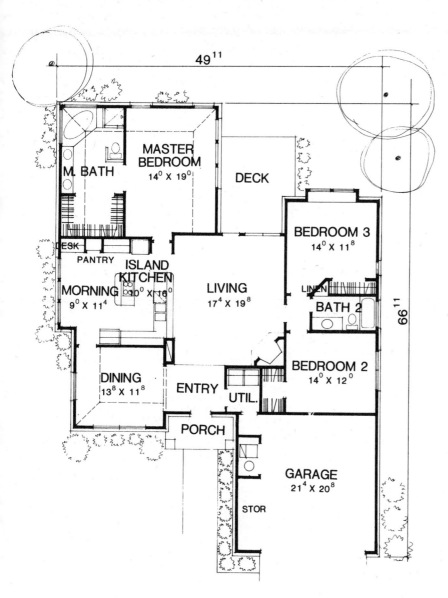

49^{11}

66^{11}

M. BATH

MASTER BEDROOM
14^0 X 19^0

DECK

DESK

PANTRY

ISLAND KITCHEN
10^0 X 16^0

MORNING
9^0 X 11^4

LIVING
17^4 X 19^8

BEDROOM 3
14^0 X 11^8

LINEN

BATH 2

DINING
13^8 X 11^8

ENTRY

UTIL.

BEDROOM 2
14^0 X 12^0

PORCH

GARAGE
21^4 X 20^8

STOR

Single-Level Elegance

- A large living room with corner fireplace lies at the center of this updated ranch. The living room accesses the rear deck and yard.
- The island kitchen incorporates a morning room, built-in desk and handy pantry, and also overlooks the living room for uninterrupted conversation.
- The formal dining room features a trayed ceiling and has a view of the front yard.
- The master suite offers multiple windows overlooking the deck and rear yard. The private bath focuses on a corner luxury tub with separate shower.
- Two extra bedrooms share a second bath, and are well separated from the master suite for privacy.

Plan DD-1836-B

Bedrooms: 3	Baths: 2
Space:	
Main floor	1,836 sq. ft.
Total Living Area	**1,836 sq. ft.**
Basement	1,836 sq. ft.
Garage	441 sq. ft.
Exterior Wall Framing	2x4
Foundation options:	
Standard Basement	
Crawlspace	
Slab	
(Foundation & framing conversion diagram available—see order form.)	
Blueprint Price Code	B

Plan DD-1836-B

Spacious Octagon

- Highly functional main floor plan makes traffic easy and minimizes wasted hall space.
- Double-sized entry opens to spacious octagonal living room with central fireplace and access to all rooms.
- U-shaped kitchen and attached dining area allow for both informal and formal occasions.
- Contiguous bedrooms each have independent deck entrances.
- Exciting deck borders entire home.

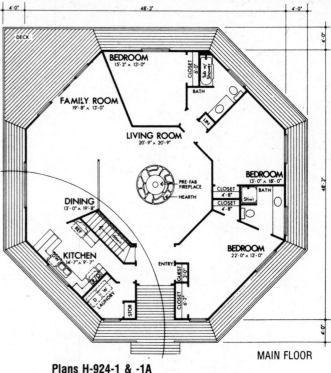

PLAN H-924-1A
WITHOUT BASEMENT

KITCHEN
14'-7" x 13'-0"

MAIN FLOOR

BEDROOM
15'-3" x 13'-0"

FAMILY ROOM
19'-8" x 13'-0"

LIVING ROOM
20'-9" x 20'-9"

PRE-FAB FIREPLACE
HEARTH

BEDROOM
13'-0" x 18'-0"

DINING
13'-0" x 19'-8"

KITCHEN
14'-7" x 9'-7"

BEDROOM
22'-0" x 13'-0"

ENTRY

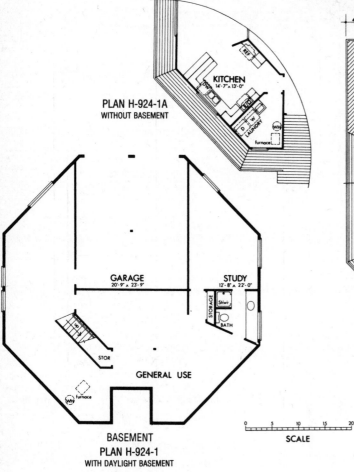

GARAGE
20'-9" x 23'-9"

STUDY
12'-8" x 22'-0"

GENERAL USE

BASEMENT
PLAN H-924-1
WITH DAYLIGHT BASEMENT

SCALE

0 5 10 15 20

Plans H-924-1 & -1A	
Bedrooms: 3-4	**Baths:** 2-3
Space: Main floor:	1,888 sq. ft.
Total without basement:	1,888 sq. ft.
Basement:	1,395 sq. ft.
Total with basement:	3,283 sq. ft.
Garage:	493 sq. ft.
Exterior Wall Framing:	2x4

Foundation options:
Daylight basement (Plan H-924-1).
Crawlspace (Plan H-924-1A).
(Foundation & framing conversion diagram available — see order form.)

Blueprint Price Code:
Without basement: B
With basement: E

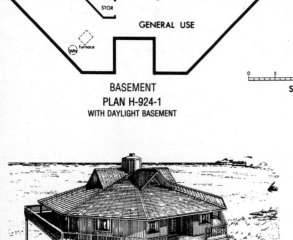

Plans H-924-1 & -1A

Charming Traditional With Great Room, Country Kitchen

- Huge family room features exposed beams in its high cathedral ceilings and a fireplace flanked by French doors and windows.
- A formal living room is partially divided by the dining area with a half-wall.
- Kitchen offers an abundance of work space, further expanded by an eating nook.
- Three large bedrooms complete the plan.

Plan E-1815

Bedrooms: 3	Baths: 2
Space:	
Total living area:	1,898 sq. ft.
Garage and porch:	608 sq. ft.
Exterior Wall Framing:	2x4

Foundation options:
Crawlspace.
Slab.
(Foundation & framing conversion diagram available — see order form.)

Blueprint Price Code:	B

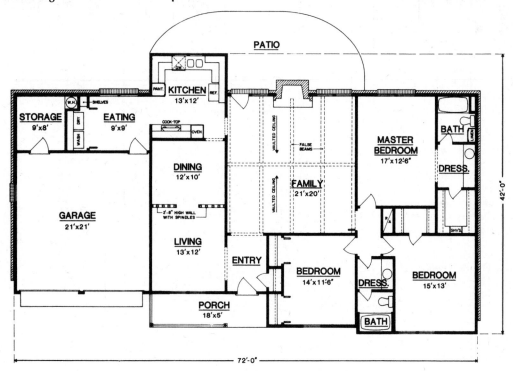

Plan E-1815

A Garden Home with a View

- This clever design proves that privacy doesn't have to be compromised even in high-density urban neighborhoods. From within, all views are oriented to the sideyard and to a lush entry courtyard.
- The exterior view is sheltered, but still offers a warm, welcoming look.
- The innovate interior design centers on a unique kitchen, which directs traffic away from the working areas while still serving the entire home.
- The large sunken family room features a vaulted ceiling and large fireplace.
- The master suite is highlighted by a sumptuous master bath, with separate shower and whirlpool tub, plus a large walk-in closet.
- The formal living room is designed and placed in such a way that it can become a third bedroom, den, office or study room, depending on family needs and lifestyles.

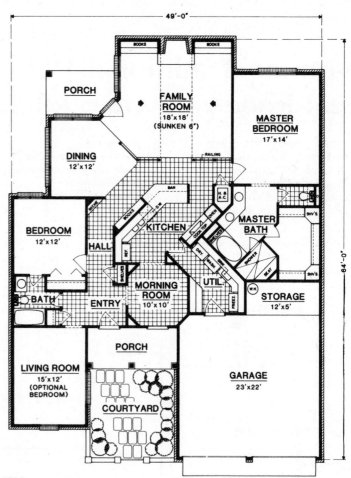

Plan E-1824

Bedrooms: 2-3	Baths: 2
Space:	
Total living area:	1,891 sq. ft.
Garage:	506 sq. ft.
Storage:	60 sq. ft.
Porches:	184 sq. ft.
Exterior Wall Framing:	2x4

Ceiling Heights:	9'
Foundation options:	
Crawlspace.	
Slab.	
(Foundation & framing conversion diagram available — see order form.)	
Blueprint Price Code:	B

TO ORDER THIS BLUEPRINT, CALL TOLL-FREE 1-800-547-5570

Plan E-1824

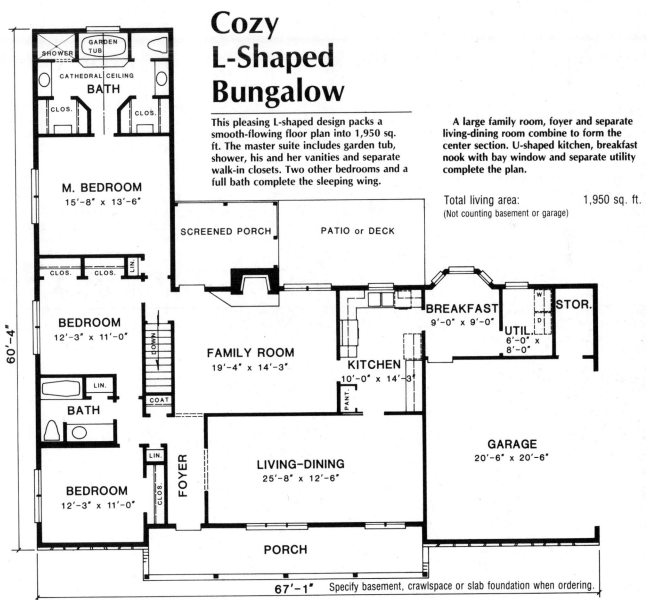

Cozy L-Shaped Bungalow

This pleasing L-shaped design packs a smooth-flowing floor plan into 1,950 sq. ft. The master suite includes garden tub, shower, his and her vanities and separate walk-in closets. Two other bedrooms and a full bath complete the sleeping wing.

A large family room, foyer and separate living-dining room combine to form the center section. U-shaped kitchen, breakfast nook with bay window and separate utility complete the plan.

Total living area: 1,950 sq. ft.
(Not counting basement or garage)

Floor plan labels:

- SHOWER
- GARDEN TUB
- CATHEDRAL CEILING BATH
- CLOS.
- M. BEDROOM 15'-8" x 13'-6"
- CLOS. / CLOS. / LIN.
- BEDROOM 12'-3" x 11'-0"
- LIN.
- BATH
- DOWN
- COAT
- FAMILY ROOM 19'-4" x 14'-3"
- LIN. / CLOS.
- FOYER
- BEDROOM 12'-3" x 11'-0"
- SCREENED PORCH
- PATIO or DECK
- KITCHEN 10'-0" x 14'-3"
- PANT.
- LIVING-DINING 25'-8" x 12'-6"
- BREAKFAST 9'-0" x 9'-0"
- W / D
- STOR.
- UTIL. 6'-0" x 8'-0"
- GARAGE 20'-6" x 20'-6"
- PORCH
- 60'-4"
- 67'-1"

Specify basement, crawlspace or slab foundation when ordering.

Blueprint Price Code B

Plan C-8620

TO ORDER THIS BLUEPRINT,
CALL TOLL-FREE 1-800-547-5570
(prices and details on pp. 12-15.)

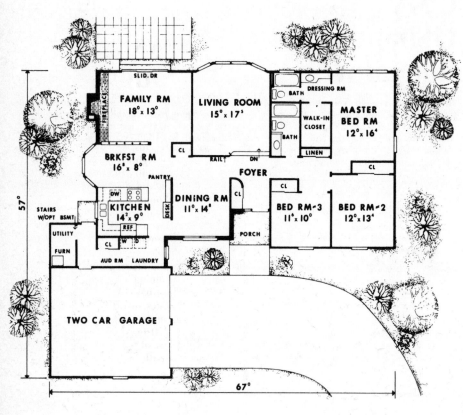

Country Classic

- A variety of siding materials blend together for a classic country exterior look.
- A dramatic sunken living room with bay window-wall is the view that greets arriving guests.
- A front-facing dining room completes the formal living area.
- The family room with fireplace is open to the kitchen and breakfast bay for informal family shared time.
- Three bedrooms and two full baths make up the sleeping wing of the home.

Plan AX-9762

Bedrooms: 3		Baths: 2

Space:	
Total living area:	2,003 sq. ft.
Basement:	2,003 sq. ft.
Garage:	485 sq. ft.
Exterior Wall Framing:	2x4

Foundation options:
Standard basement.
Slab.
(Foundation & framing conversion diagram available — see order form.)

Blueprint Price Code: C

Plan AX-9762

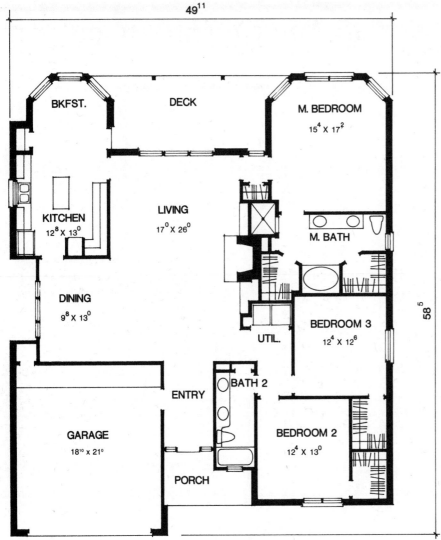

49^{11}

58^5

BKFST.

DECK

M. BEDROOM
15^4 X 17^2

KITCHEN
12^8 X 13^0

LIVING
17^0 X 26^0

M. BATH

DINING
9^8 X 13^0

BEDROOM 3
12^4 X 12^6

UTIL.

ENTRY

BATH 2

GARAGE
18^{10} X 21^0

BEDROOM 2
12^4 X 13^0

PORCH

MAIN FLOOR

Views Through And Out

- This spacious, open feeling plan gains a heightened sense of space from the entry with a long view of the deck and rear yard through the Great Room.
- The formal living area of the Great Room has a showpiece interior fireplace with built-in bookcases on either side.
- The island kitchen serves both the formal dining area and the sunny breakfast bay.
- The master suite is separate from the secondary bedrooms for privacy. It features dual walk-in closets, a sitting bay and a spacious master bath.

Plan DD-1895

Bedrooms: 3	Baths: 2
Space:	
Total living area:	1,964 sq. ft.
Garage:	395 sq. ft.
Exterior Wall Framing:	2x4
Ceiling Heights:	9'
Foundation options: Slab. (Foundation & framing conversion diagram available — see order form.)	
Blueprint Price Code:	B

Plan DD-1895

A Welcome Addition to Any Neighborhood

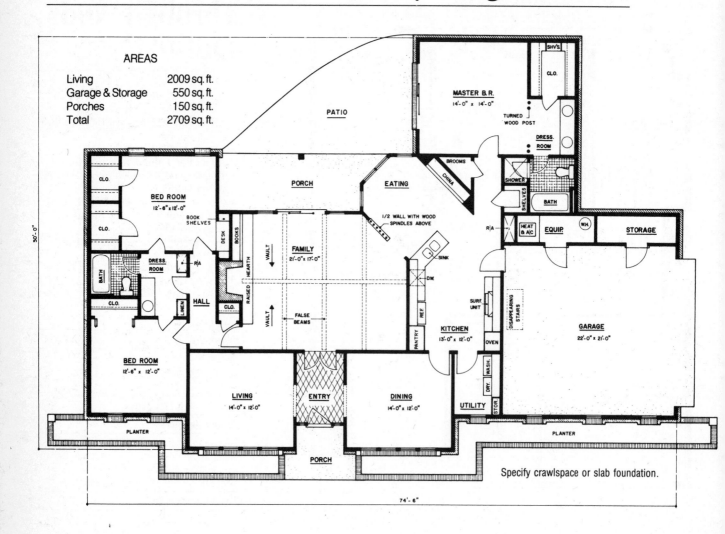

AREAS

Living	2009 sq. ft.
Garage & Storage	550 sq. ft.
Porches	150 sq. ft.
Total	2709 sq. ft.

PATIO

SHV'S

CLO.

MASTER B.R.
14'-0" x 14'-0"

TURNED
WOOD POST

DRESS.
ROOM

BROOMS

PORCH

EATING

CHINA

SHOWER

SHELVES

BATH

BED ROOM
12'-6" x 12'-0"

BOOK
SHELVES

1/2 WALL WITH WOOD
SPINDLES ABOVE

R/A

HEAT
& A/C

EQUIP

W.H.

STORAGE

DESK

BOOKS

VAULT

FAMILY
21'-0" x 17'-0"

SINK

D.W.

BATH

DRESS.
ROOM

R/A

RAISED HEARTH

SURF
UNIT

DISAPPEARING
STAIRS

GARAGE
22'-0" x 21'-0"

CLO.

LINEN

HALL

CLO.

VAULT

FALSE
BEAMS

PANTRY

REF

KITCHEN
13'-0" x 12'-0"

OVEN

BED ROOM
12'-6" x 12'-0"

LIVING
14'-0" x 12'-0"

ENTRY

DINING
14'-0" x 12'-0"

WASH.

DRY

STOR.

UTILITY

PLANTER

PORCH

PLANTER

Specify crawlspace or slab foundation.

50'-0"

74'-6"

Blueprint Price Code C

Plan E-2000

Interior Angles Add Excitement

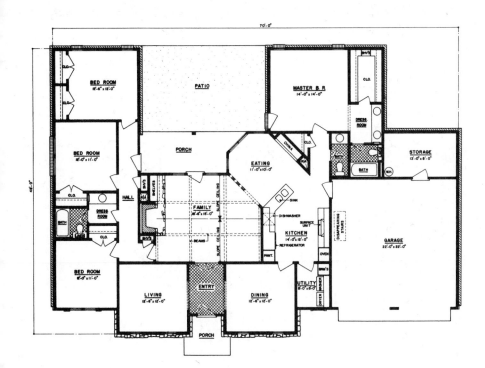

- Interior angles add a touch of excitement to this one-story home.
- A pleasantly charming exterior combines wood and stone to give the plan a solid, comfortable look for any neighborhood.
- Formal living and dining rooms flank the entry, which leads into a large family room complete with fireplace, vaulted and beamed ceiling and built-in bookshelves.
- The adjoining family-eating area with a built-in china cabinet angles off the spacious kitchen.
- Note the pantry and convenient utility area.
- The master bedroom suite is both large and private, and includes a dressing room, large walk-in closet and deluxe bath.
- The three secondary bedrooms are zoned for privacy, also, and share a second full bath.

Plan E-1904

Bedrooms: 4	Baths: 2

Space:

Total living area:	1,997 sq. ft.
Garage:	484 sq. ft.
Storage:	104 sq. ft.
Porches:	157 sq. ft.

Exterior Wall Framing:	2x4

Foundation options:
Crawlspace.
Slab.
(Foundation & framing conversion diagram available — see order form)

Blueprint Price Code:	B

Plan E-1904

Streetscape Interest

- Impressive rooflines with front gables, entry emphasis, and brick highlights give an interesting view of this one-story home from the street.
- The interior features two main, very open feeling living spaces.
- The formal space opens from the entry and reaches from the front to the rear of the house, opening to the lanai with sliders and windows.
- The informal living space includes an island kitchen overlooking the family room with fireplace and sunny breakfast eating area.
- The master suite is well separated from the secondary bedrooms. It has a dressing area, walk-in closet and exciting master bath with spa tub and glass shower.

Plan DD-2025

Bedrooms: 3	Baths: 2

Space:

Total living area:	2,025 sq. ft.
Garage:	494 sq. ft.

Exterior Wall Framing:	2x4

Foundation options:
Slab.
(Foundation & framing conversion diagram available — see order form.)

Blueprint Price Code:	C

***TO ORDER THIS BLUEPRINT,
CALL TOLL-FREE 1-800-547-5570***
176 (prices and details on pp. 12-15.)

MAIN FLOOR

Plan DD-2025

Captivating Great Room

- This charming front has many attractive characteristics from a dramatic bay off the dining room to the ½ round transoms above.
- The tile foyer opens up to an arch which leads you to the overwhelming Great Room. The vaulted ceilings give you a feeling of openness, while a centered fireplace and media center captivates the room.
- Planting shelves and soffits are abundant in every room, adding further charm.
- A separate breakfast nook with bay juts out on to the covered porch for elegant dining.
- The master bedroom overlooks the rear patio through double French doors. It also offers a large walk-in closet and private bath with separate walk-in shower and an elegant step-up spa tub with a decorative glass block window viewing a private solarium.

Plan HDS-90-807

Bedrooms: 4	Baths: 3

Space:	
Total living area:	2,171 sq. ft.
Garage:	405 sq. ft.

Exterior Wall Framing:	2x4 & concrete

Foundation options:
Slab.
(Foundation & framing conversion diagram available — see order form.)

Blueprint Price Code:	C

Floor Plan

- bedrm 2 — 12⁰ · 10⁸
- covered patio
- master bedrm — 18⁸ · 13⁰
- brkfst
- lin
- w.i.c.
- bedrm 3 — 10⁸ · 10⁶
- fireplace
- sink
- rng
- w
- dress
- tub
- family room — 17⁰ · 20⁰
- dw — kit — ref — d
- wh
- bedrm 4 — 10⁴ · 10⁸
- foyer
- dining — 11⁶ · 14⁰
- 19⁰ · 21⁴
- double garage
- living — 10¹⁰ · 14⁸
- ac
- 51'4"
- 60'-0"

Plan HDS-90-807

Charming Exterior, Exciting Interior

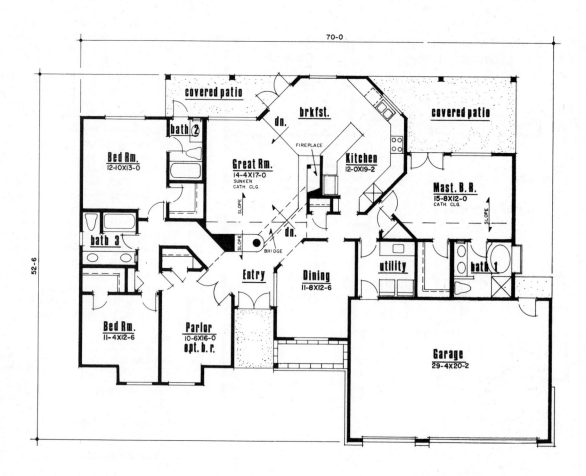

70-0

covered patio

bath 2

Bed Rm.
12-10X13-0

Great Rm.
14-4X17-0
SUNKEN
CATH. CLG.

brkfst.

dn.

FIREPLACE

Kitchen
12-0X19-2

covered patio

Mast. B.R.
15-8X12-0
CATH. CLG.

52-6

bath 3

SLOPE

SLOPE

dn.

BRIDGE

Entry

Dining
11-8X12-6

utility

bath 1

SLOPE

Bed Rm.
11-4X12-6

Parlor
10-6X16-0
opt. b. r.

Garage
29-4X20-2

Total living area:
(Not counting garage)

2,033 sq. ft.

Plan Q-2033-1A
WITHOUT BASEMENT
(SLAB-ON-GRADE FOUNDATION)

Blueprint Price Code C
Plan Q-2033-1A

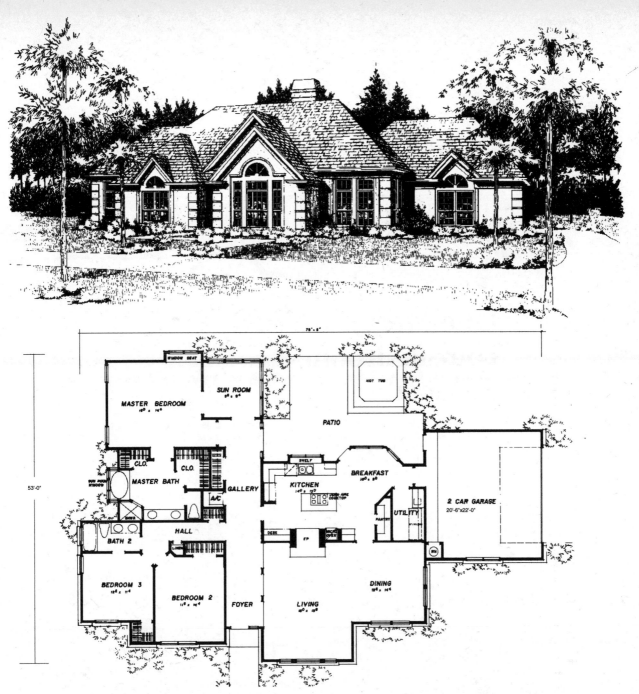

French Flair

- Quoins and semi-circular transoms give this French country home elegance and charm.
- The formal living areas at the front of the home combine for a huge entertainment center; a see-thru fireplace opens to the large island kitchen and bayed breakfast room, opposite.
- A rear patio offers a perfect spot for a hot tub.
- The foyer isolates the bedrooms; a gallery and luxury bath with garden tub and separate shower buffer the master suite and private sun room.

Plan DW-2198

Bedrooms: 3	Baths: 2
Space:	
Main floor	2,198 sq. ft.
Total Living Area	**2,198 sq. ft.**
Basement	2,198 sq. ft.
Garage	451 sq. ft.
Exterior Wall Framing	2x4

Foundation options:
Standard Basement
Crawlspace
Slab
(Foundation & framing conversion diagram available—see order form.)

Blueprint Price Code	C

Plan DW-2198

TO ORDER THIS BLUEPRINT,
CALL TOLL-FREE 1-800-547-5570
(prices and details on pp. 12-15.) **179**

One-Story, Four-Bedroom Colonial

Here's gracious living at its best — North or South. Four bedrooms, two baths, a powder room, separate living and dining rooms, a galley kitchen, bay window breakfast area and large utility room make up the 2,053 sq. ft. of living area in this compact colonial.

Total living area: 2,053 sq. ft.
(Not counting basement or garage)

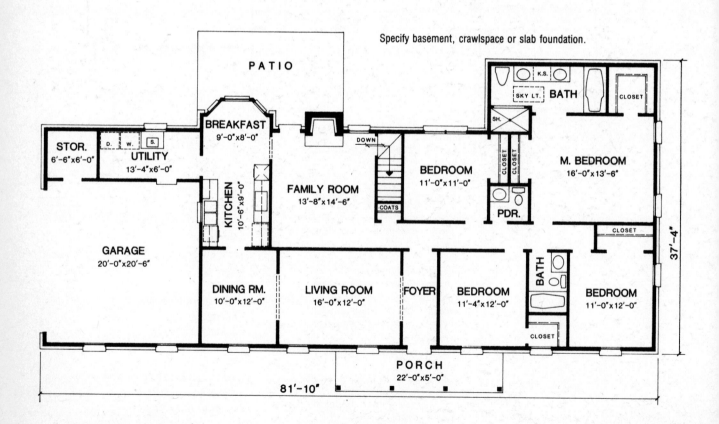

Specify basement, crawlspace or slab foundation.

TO ORDER THIS BLUEPRINT,
CALL TOLL-FREE 1-800-547-5570
180 (prices and details on pp. 12-15.)

Blueprint Price Code C
Plan C-8635

Handsome Hip-Roof Design

- A sleek, contemporary exterior is created with multiple-hip rooflines, quarter-round transom windows and horizontal lap siding with banding accent.
- A dramatic, sunken living room unfolds inside the front door, defined by 3-foot partial walls.
- A formal dining room completes the central entertaining area of the plan.
- The informal family living area is comprised of an island kitchen with walk-in pantry, breakfast nook with French doors to the rear deck and a spacious family room with vaulted ceiling and fireplace.
- The sleeping quarters, to the right of the plan, are highlighted by the vaulted master bedroom with walk-in closet and private bath with garden tub.

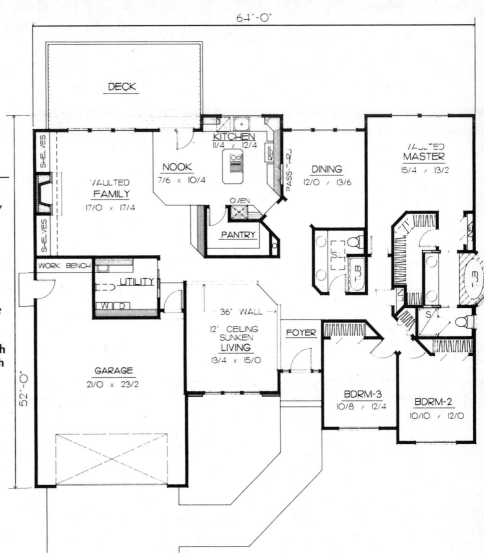

Plan U-89-101

Bedrooms: 3	Baths: 2

Space:

Total living area:	2,255 sq. ft.
Garage:	487 sq. ft.
Storage area:	approx. 75 sq. ft.

Exterior Wall Framing:	2x4

Foundation options:
Crawlspace.
Slab.
(Foundation & framing conversion diagram available — see order form.)

Blueprint Price Code: C

Plan U-89-101

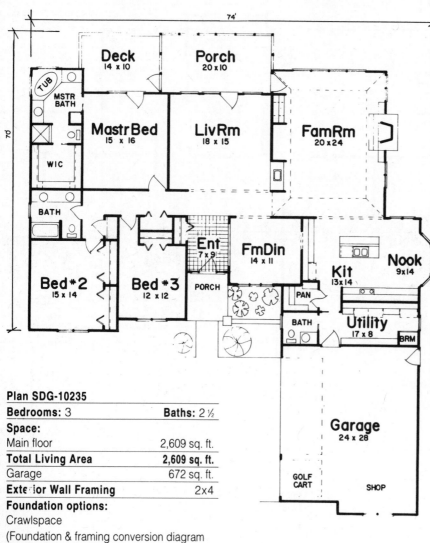

A Classic Brick Beauty

- A brick exterior accented with brick quoins gives a classic look to this luxurious home.
- The generous foyer offers entrance to the formal dining room on the right and the central living room at the rear.
- Both the living room and the adjacent family room with fireplace and rear window wall offer access to a large, screened-in porch.
- An island work area serves the spacious kitchen and nook combination with bay window, pantry and convenient laundry and powder room near the garage entrance.
- Isolated to the rear, the master bedroom has private deck access and a big bath with corner garden tub, separate vanities and large walk-in closet.

Plan SDG-10235	
Bedrooms: 3	Baths: 2 ½
Space:	
Main floor	2,609 sq. ft.
Total Living Area	**2,609 sq. ft.**
Garage	672 sq. ft.
Exterior Wall Framing	2x4
Foundation options:	
Crawlspace	
(Foundation & framing conversion diagram available—see order form.)	
Blueprint Price Code	**D**

Plan SDG-10235

Elegant L-Shaped Ranch

This especially handsome ranch home attracts admiration with its exterior facade of brick and horizontal siding. The house layout is practical and straightforward. From the elegant central foyer, to the left is the sleeping area which is neatly separated from the living and eating quarters. The three bedrooms form a private wing with two full baths and lots of closet space. A central fireplace flanked with bookshelves enhances the beamed-ceiling family room which opens to the rear patio via glass sliding doors. The kitchen/breakfast area is well designed and is adjacent to the lavatory and utility room which opens to the two-car garage.

Total living area: 2,324 sq. ft.
(Not counting basement or garage)

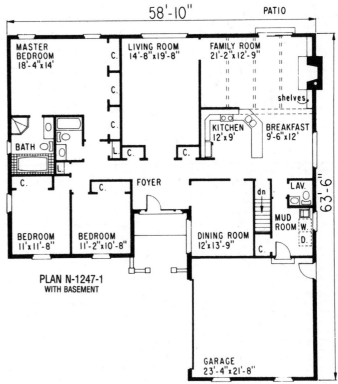

PLAN N-1247-1
WITH BASEMENT

Plan N-1247-1

Master Suite Features Luxurious Bath

This lovely French Provincial design features a master suite with a deluxe compartmentalized bath which includes a vaulted ceiling with sky lights, garden tub, shower, linen closet and a separate dressing room with double vanity and large walk-in closet. Two additional bedrooms with ample closet space share a second compartmentalized bath.

Living and dining rooms are located to the side of the formal foyer. The family room features a raised hearth fireplace and double doors leading onto a screened-in back porch. A U-shaped kitchen with an island counter opens to the breakfast bay allowing more casual living. Fixed stairs in the family room provide access to attic storage above.

Also included in the 2,400 sq. ft. of heated living area is a utility room with half bath.

Total living area: 2,400 sq. ft.
(Not counting basement or garage)

Specify crawlspace, basement or slab foundation when ordering.

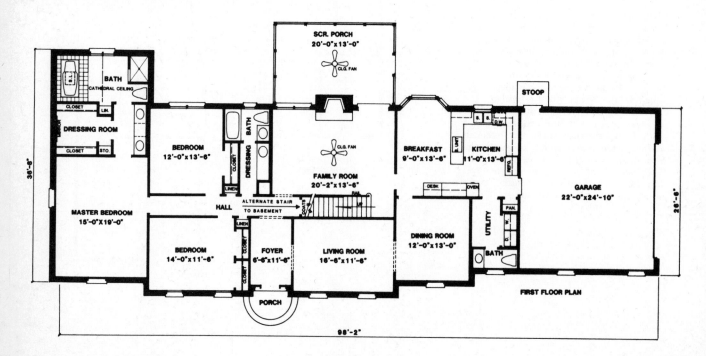

Blueprint Price Code C
Plan C-8363

Full of Surprises

- While dignified and reserved on the outside, this plan presents delightful surprises throughout the interior.
- Interesting angles, vaulted ceilings, surprising spaces and bright windows abound everywhere you look in this home.
- The elegant, vaulted living room is off the expansive foyer, and includes an imposing fireplace and large windows areas.
- The delightful kitchen includes a handy island and large corner windows in front of the sink.
- The nook is brightened not only by large windows, but also by a skylight.
- The vaulted family room includes a corner wood stove area plus easy access to the outdoors.
- A superb master suite includes an exquisite bath with a skylighted dressing area and large walk-in closet.
- Three secondary bedrooms share another full bath, and the large laundry room is conveniently positioned near the bedrooms.

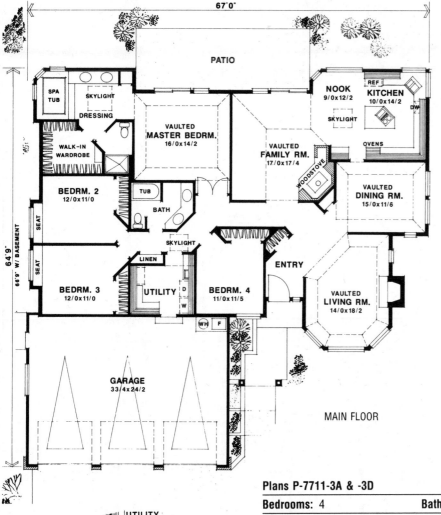

67'0"

PATIO

SPA TUB

SKYLIGHT

DRESSING

WALK-IN WARDROBE

VAULTED MASTER BEDRM.
16/0x14/2

NOOK
9/0x12/2

REF

KITCHEN
10/0x14/2

DW

SKYLIGHT

OVENS

VAULTED FAMILY RM.
17/0x17/4

WOODSTOVE

VAULTED DINING RM.
15/0x11/6

BEDRM. 2
12/0x11/0

TUB

BATH

SEAT

SEAT

SKYLIGHT

LINEN

UTILITY

D

W

BEDRM. 4
11/0x11/5

ENTRY

VAULTED LIVING RM.
14/0x18/2

BEDRM. 3
12/0x11/0

WH F

64'9"   66'9" W/ BASEMENT

GARAGE
33/4x24/2

MAIN FLOOR

UTILITY

W

DN

GARAGE
PLAN P-7711-3D
WITH DAYLIGHT BASEMENT

Plans P-7711-3A & -3D

Bedrooms: 4	Baths: 2

Space:

Main floor (non-basement version):	2,510 sq. ft.
Main floor (basement version):	2,580 sq. ft.
Basement:	2,635 sq. ft.
Garage:	806 sq. ft.

Exterior Wall Framing:	2x6

Foundation options:
Daylight basement (Plan P-7711-3D).
Crawlspace (Plan P-7711-3A).
(Foundation & framing conversion diagram available — see order form.)

Blueprint Price Code:	D

Plans P-7711-3A & -3D

Four-Bedroom Home
Includes Deluxe Master Suite

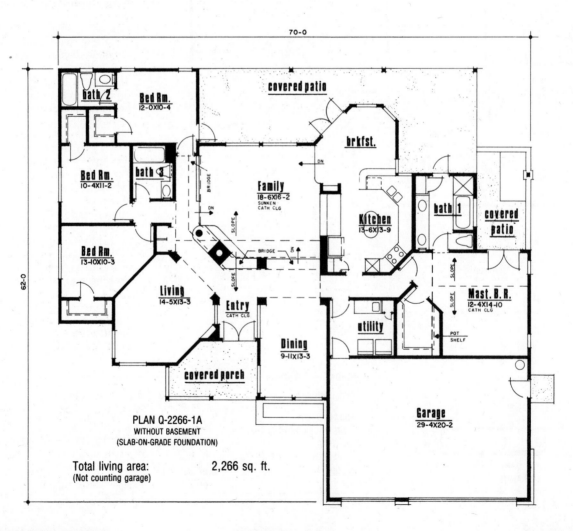

70-0

62-0

bath 2

Bed Rm.
12-0X10-4

covered patio

brkfst.

Bed Rm.
10-4X11-2

bath 3

BRIDGE

Family
18-6X16-2
SUNKEN
CATH CLG

Kitchen
13-6X13-9

bath 1

covered patio

DN

SLOPE

Bed Rm.
13-10X10-3

BRIDGE

DN

SLOPE

SLOPE

Living
14-5X13-3

Entry
CATH CLG

utility

SLOPE

Mast. B.R.
12-4X14-10
CATH CLG

Dining
9-11X13-3

POT
SHELF

covered porch

Garage
29-4X20-2

PLAN Q-2266-1A
WITHOUT BASEMENT
(SLAB-ON-GRADE FOUNDATION)

Total living area: 2,266 sq. ft.
(Not counting garage)

TO ORDER THIS BLUEPRINT,
CALL TOLL-FREE 1-800-547-5570

Blueprint Price Code C

Plan Q-2266-1A

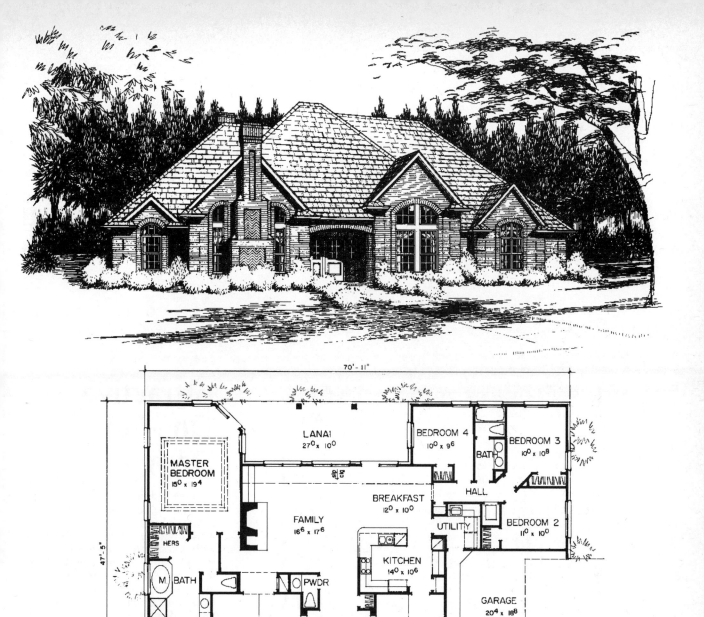

Plan DW-2403

LANAI 27⁰ x 10⁰

MASTER BEDROOM 15⁰ x 19⁴

BEDROOM 4 10⁰ x 9⁶

BEDROOM 3 10⁰ x 10⁸

BATH

HALL

BEDROOM 2 11⁰ x 10⁰

FAMILY 16⁶ x 17⁶

BREAKFAST 12⁰ x 10⁰

UTILITY

HERS

KITCHEN 14⁰ x 10⁶

M. BATH

PWDR

GARAGE 20⁴ x 18⁸

HIS

LIVING 15⁰ x 15⁰

FOYER 10⁶ x 8⁶

DINING 12⁰ x 15⁰

PORCH

70'-11"

47'-5"

Drama Inside and Out

- Dramatic arched top windows, a brick chimney and rear lanai accent the exterior of this stylish transitional one-story.
- Vaulted living and dining areas flank the spacious foyer.
- Off the open kitchen and breakfast area is the central family room with 10' sloped ceiling, fireplace and built-in entertainment center.
- The secluded master suite offers a coffered ceiling, angled wall with access to the lanai, and private bath with separate closets, vanities and tub and shower.
- Three additional bedrooms share a second full bath at the opposite end of the home.

Plan DW-2403	
Bedrooms: 4	**Baths:** 2 ½
Space:	
Main floor	2,403 sq. ft.
Total Living Area	**2,403 sq. ft.**
Basement	2,403 sq. ft.
Garage	380 sq. ft.
Exterior Wall Framing	2x4
Foundation options:	
Standard Basement	
Crawlspace	
Slab	
(Foundation & framing conversion diagram	
available—see order form.)	
Blueprint Price Code	C

Plan DW-2403

Attractive One-Story Design

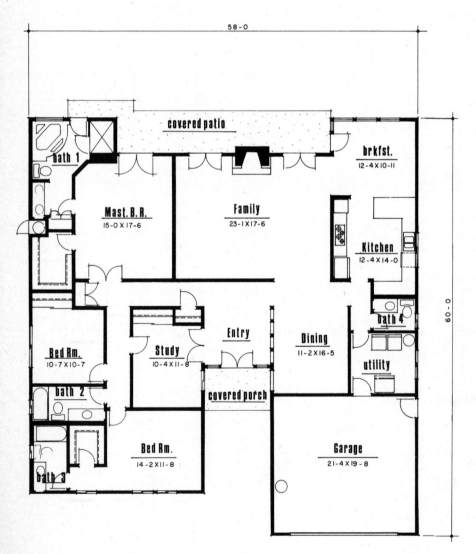

- Three bedrooms are more-or-less isolated in a quiet zone at the left, and each has a private bath.
- Master suite features deluxe bath with access to a covered patio.
- Main part of the home is designed in a Great Room concept, with the family room, dining room, breakfast nook and kitchen all flowing together.
- A study off the entry way can serve as a home office or sitting room off the bedroom hallway.
- A convenient utility room and powder room are located in the passage way from the garage to the kitchen.

Plan Q-2476-1A

Bedrooms: 3	Baths: 3½
Space:	
Total living area:	2,476 sq. ft.
Garage:	420 sq. ft.
Exterior Wall Framing:	2x4
Foundation options:	
Slab only. (Foundation & framing conversion diagram available — see order form.)	
Blueprint Price Code:	C

Plan Q-2476-1A

Spacious and Inviting

The four-column front porch, picture window, siding, brick, stone and cupola combine for a pleasing exterior for this three-bedroom home.

Extra features include a fireplace, screen porch, deluxe master bath and a large separate breakfast room.

Total living area: 2,306 sq. ft.
(Not counting basement or garage)

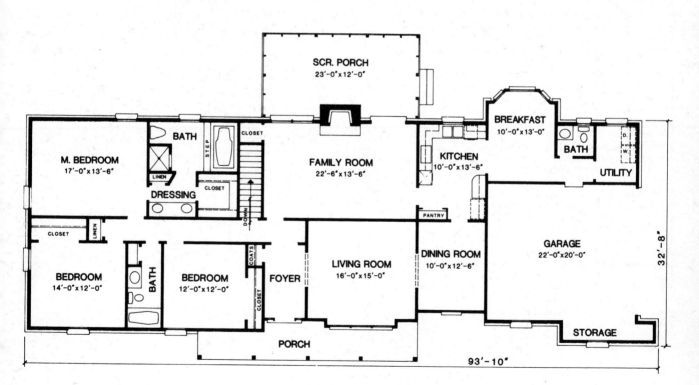

Specify basement, crawlspace or slab foundation.

The Envy of Your Neighborhood

This elegantly styled home will be the envy of your neighborhood, no matter where you plan to settle.

The well-lit entry smoothly ushers you into the uniquely shaped living room, whose graceful step-down curve defines the border between living area and entry. With its large picture window and stately brick fireplace, this room makes a positive statement about the personality of this lavish three-bedroom home. Note how the ample-sized dining room opens off both the living room and the entry, and is graced by a large illuminating window at its far end.

The country kitchen, located at the rear of the home beyond a pleasant archway, is a spacious area that can perform several functions at the same time, while keeping the separate identities of the individual spaces intact. The highlights of this grand room include a convenient cooking island, double ovens, and a built-in pantry.

Located through another inviting archway situated off the main entry is a smaller entry hall that leads through a pair of doors to the elegant master suite.

The master bath is a well-designed combination of functional spaces, which include a walk-in wardrobe, shower, and a spacious bathing area with twin vanities. The posh spa tub has its own private view into a discreetly enclosed courtyard.

Total living area: 2,417 sq. ft.
(Not counting garage)

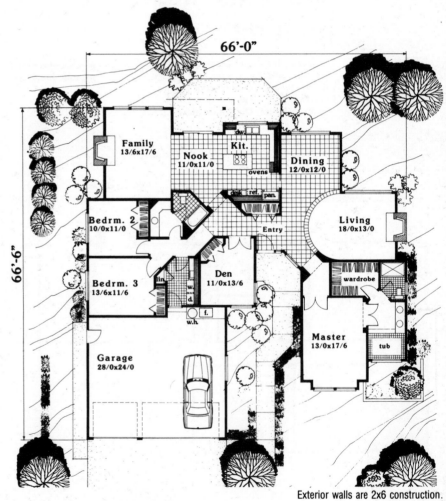

PLAN R-1069
WITHOUT BASEMENT
(CRAWLSPACE FOUNDATION)

Exterior walls are 2x6 construction.

Blueprint Price Code C
Plan R-1069

Floor Plan Fits Large Family

- This sprawling Southwestern attracts the large or growing family — with accommodations for four bedrooms, formal dining room and attached living room, and relaxing family room.
- The kitchen is designed for efficiency, with direct entrances from the family room, dining room, and breakfast area with bar.
- Master bedroom has private bath with walk-in closet and access to a covered patio, which borders the rear of the home.

Plan Q-3296-1A

Bedrooms: 4	Baths: 3
Space:	
Total living area:	3,296 sq. ft.
Garage:	731 sq. ft.
Exterior Wall Framing:	2x4

Foundation options:
Slab.
(Foundation & framing conversion diagram available — see order form.)

Blueprint Price Code:	E

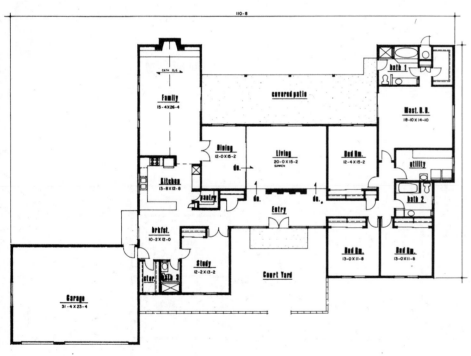

Plan Q-3296-1A

Secluded Master Suite

- A tiled roof lies above an array of arched openings and windows in this elegant Southwestern design.
- Inside, attractions include a generous sunken living room with fireplace and cathedral ceilings, a secluded master suite with double doors at its main entrance and its private patio entrance, and an attached bath with large hot tub.
- Kitchen and dining room also have access to the outdoors, a feature found in nearly each room.
- A walk-through utility room is convenient to both the kitchen and the accessory bedrooms.
- A study faces the front porch with plenty of light for reading.

Plan Q-2864-1A

Bedrooms: 3	Baths: 2

Space:

Total living area:	2,864 sq. ft.
Garage:	548 sq. ft.

Exterior Wall Framing:	2x4

Foundation options:
Slab.
(Foundation & framing conversion diagram available — see order form.)

Blueprint Price Code:	D

Plan Q-2864-1A

Space to Spare

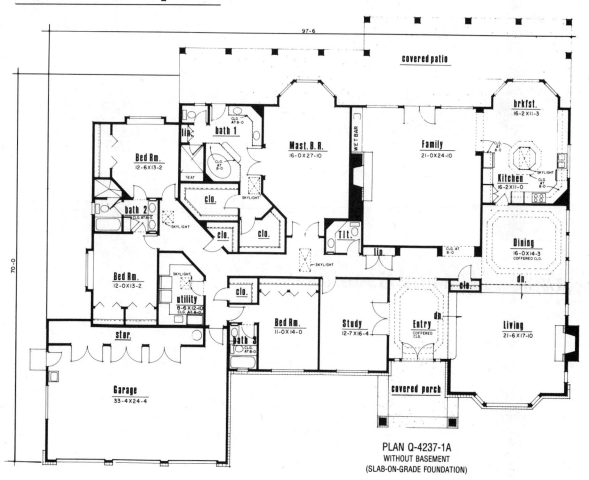

covered patio

97-6

bath 1
CLG
AT 8-0

lin.

Bed Rm.
12-6X13-2

CLG.
AT
8-0

SEAT

clo.

bath 2
CLG. AT 8-0

SKYLIGHT

clo.

clo.

Mast. B.R.
16-0X27-10

WET BAR

SKYLIGHT

Family
21-0X24-10

brkfst.
16-2X11-3

CLG
AT
8-0

SKYLIGHT

Kitchen
16-2X11-0

CLG
AT
8-0

Tlt.

SKYLIGHT

lin.

CLG AT
8-0

Dining
16-0X14-3
COFFERED CLG.

dn.

Bed Rm.
12-0X13-2

SKYLIGHT

utility
8-6X12-10
CLG. AT 8-0

clo.

clo.

Bed Rm.
11-0X14-0

Study
12-7X16-4

clo.

Entry
COFFERED
CLG.

dn.

dn.

Living
21-6X17-10

stor.

bath 3
CLG.
AT 8-0

covered porch

Garage
33-4X24-4

70-0

PLAN Q-4237-1A
WITHOUT BASEMENT
(SLAB-ON-GRADE FOUNDATION)

Total living area: 4,237 sq. ft.
(Not counting garage)

Blueprint Price Code G

Plan Q-4237-1A

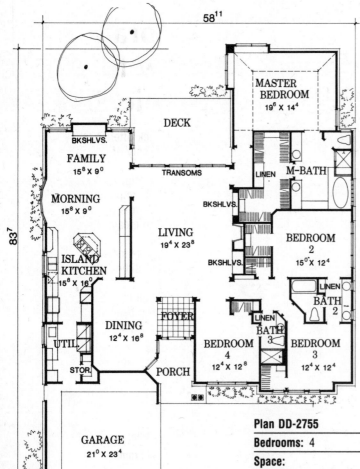

58¹¹ → 58^{11}

83^7

MASTER BEDROOM
19^8 X 14^4

DECK

FAMILY
15^8 X 9^0

BKSHLVS.

TRANSOMS

LINEN M-BATH

MORNING
15^8 X 9^0

BKSHLVS.

LIVING
19^4 X 23^8

BEDROOM 2
15^0 X 12^4

ISLAND KITCHEN
15^8 X 16^0

BKSHLVS.

LINEN

BATH 2

DINING
12^4 X 16^8

FOYER

LINEN

BATH 3

BEDROOM 4
12^4 X 12^8

BEDROOM 3
12^4 X 12^4

UTIL

STOR.

PORCH

GARAGE
21^0 X 23^4

Central Living Room Overlooks Deck

- This stylish, updated home offers an open floor plan that revolves around a spacious living room; an attached deck is visible through a spectacular rear window wall. A fireplace flanked by bookshelves and a high ceiling add more drama to this attention center.
- An island kitchen, morning room with bay window and family room combine for convenient family dining or entertaining.
- A formal dining room on the other side is also handy for meal serving.
- The sleeping wing includes three bedrooms, two baths and an elegant master suite; a beautiful cornered bay window and gambrel ceiling in the bedroom and dual vanities and closets and a 6' tub in the private bath are highlights.

Plan DD-2755

Bedrooms: 4	Baths: 3

Space:	
Main floor:	2,868 sq. ft.
Total living area:	2,868 sq. ft.
Basement:	(approx.) 2,800 sq. ft.
Garage:	496 sq. ft.

Exterior Wall Framing:	2x4

Foundation options:
Basement.
Crawlspace.
Slab.
(Foundation & framing conversion diagram available — see order form.)

Blueprint Price Code: D

Plan DD-2755

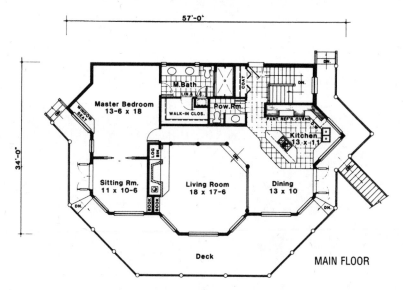

MAIN FLOOR

57'-0"

34'-0"

- Master Bedroom 13-6 x 18
- M.Bath
- WALK-IN CLOS.
- Pow.Rm.
- PANY. REF'R OVEN'S
- Kitchen 13 x 11
- WINDOW SEAT
- Sitting Rm. 11 x 10-6
- LOG BIN
- BOOK
- Living Room 18 x 17-6
- Dining 13 x 10
- Deck

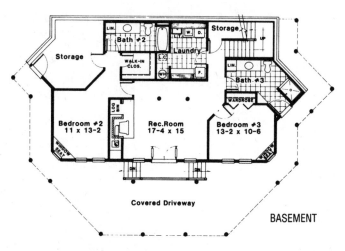

BASEMENT

- Bath #2
- LIN.
- Storage
- Laundry
- W D
- Storage
- WALK-IN CLOS.
- LC
- LIN.
- Bath #3
- WARDROBE
- Bedroom #2 11 x 13-2
- LOG BIN
- Rec.Room 17-4 x 15
- Bedroom #3 13-2 x 10-6
- WINDOW SEAT
- Covered Driveway

Panoramic View for Scenic Site

- Large deck offers a panoramic view and plenty of space for outdoor living.
- Sunken living room features big windows and impressive fireplace.
- Living room is set off by railings, not walls, to create visual impact of big space.
- Master suite includes private bath, large closet, sitting area and access to deck.
- Lower level includes rec room with fireplace, two bedrooms, two baths and large utility area.

Plan NW-779

Bedrooms: 3	Baths: 3½

Space:

Main floor:	1,450 sq. ft.
Lower floor:	1,242 sq. ft.

Total living area:	2,692 sq. ft.

Exterior Wall Framing:	2x6

Foundation options:
Daylight basement only.
(Foundation & framing conversion diagram available — see order form.)

Blueprint Price Code:	D

Plan NW-779

Spectacular Sweeping Views

- The elegant brick facade of this exciting home conceals a highly contemporary interior.
- The foyer opens to a huge Grand Room that further opens to a delightful rear porch, also accessed through the morning room, pool bath and master suite.
- Completely surrounded in windows and high fixed glass is a spacious gathering room, also featuring a three-sided fireplace and built-in entertainment center.
- The spectacular master suite is secluded to the rear of the home, but wrapped in windows and offering its own fantastic bath with luxury tub and bidet.
- Two additional sleeping suites found at the other end of the home share a bath with private vanities.

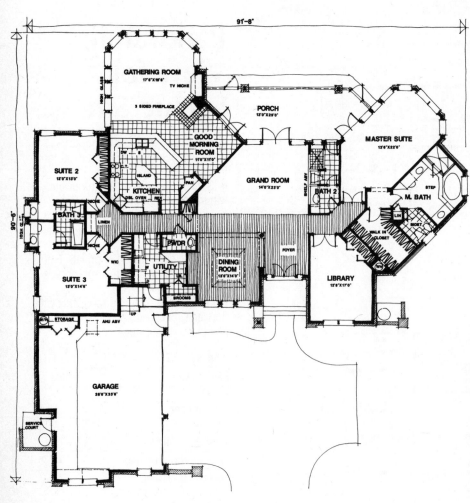

Plan EOF-8	
Bedrooms: 3-4	**Baths:** 3 ½
Space:	
Main floor	3,392 sq. ft.
Total Living Area	**3,392 sq. ft.**
Garage	871 sq. ft.
Exterior Wall Framing	2x6
Foundation options:	
Slab	
(Foundation & framing conversion diagram available—see order form.)	
Blueprint Price Code	E

Plan EOF-8

103'-0"

59'-0"

Sitting

Master
15/0x18/6

Mstr.Bath

wardrobe

Br.3
11/0x13/0

Dining
12/0x15/6

Nook
10/0x10/0

Family
18/0x16/6

Kitchen
21/6x15/6

Br.2
14/6x13/0

bar

Util.
7/0x11/0

w. d.

pant

frzr.

down

Bath

Entry

Living
20/6x17/0

Den/Br.4
12/0x16/0

Garage
31/0x23/6

seat

Luxurious Master Bedroom Suite

This is a one-level dream home with a three-car garage and 3,455 sq. ft. The gourmet kitchen comes equipped with an island, breakfast nook, and a separate pantry. The family room has a beautiful fireplace and even a bar!

Then, for the ultimate in comfort, check out the master suite. While strolling through, one will find a cozy sitting area. The spacious bathroom comes with all of the extras, including a spa and a very large walk-in wardrobe.

PLAN R-1071
WITHOUT BASEMENT
(CRAWLSPACE FOUNDATION)

Total living area: 3,455 sq. ft.
(Not counting garage)

Blueprint Price Code E

Plan R-1071

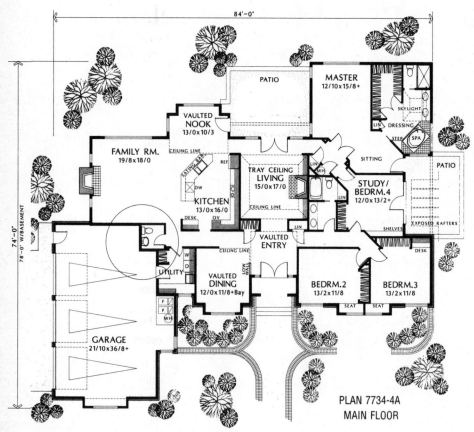

84'-0"

78'-0" W/BASEMENT
74'-0"

PATIO

MASTER
12/10x15/8+

SKYLIGHT

LIN DRESSING

STEP SPA

VAULTED
NOOK
13/0x10/3

FAMILY RM.
19/8x18/0

CEILING LINE

SITTING

PATIO

TRAY CEILING
LIVING
15/0x17/0

STUDY/
BEDRM.4
12/0x13/2+

EATING BAR

REF

DW

KITCHEN
13/0x16/0

DESK OV

CEILING LINE

EXPOSED RAFTERS

SHELVES

VAULTED
ENTRY

DESK

UTILITY

VAULTED
DINING
12/0x11/8+Bay

BEDRM.2
13/2x11/8

BEDRM.3
13/2x11/8

GARAGE
21/10x36/8+

SEAT SEAT

PLAN 7734-4A
MAIN FLOOR

FAMILY

DN

GARAGE

PLAN 7734-4D
W/DAYLIGHT BASEMENT

Impressive Design Offers Daylight Basement Option

- This stunning design not only presents an impressive facade, but also includes an equally impressive interior.
- Delightful master suite includes a spacious bath and large closets.
- First-rate kitchen/nook/family room combination provides room for a busy family.
- The living room offers a fireplace and a trayed ceiling.
- Dining room also features a vaulted ceiling and adjoins the high-ceilinged entry area.
- Optional fourth bedroom could easily be made into a pleasant study or home office.
- Daylight basement version doubles the size of the home.

Plans P-7734-4A & P-7734-4D

Bedrooms: 3-4	Baths: 2½
Space:	
Main floor:	2,950 sq. ft.
Basement:	2,950 sq. ft.
Garage:	800 sq. ft.
Exterior Wall Framing:	2x4

Foundation options:
Daylight basement, Plan P-7734-4D
Crawlspace, Plan P-7734-4A
(Foundation & framing conversion diagram available — see order form.)

Blueprint Price Code: D

Plans P-7734-4A & 4D

Satisfaction On A Single Level

- Affordable amenities charm this sprawling Mediterranean, with such favorites as a sunken living room with vaulted ceilings, party sink, and a skylight above an interior planter.
- The roomy kitchen is nestled between a formal dining area and an informal family room. It offers a generous work area, pantry, and breakfast bar.
- Sleeping accommodations are provided on the opposite wing of the home, with a master bedroom and private patio, three additional bedrooms, and three baths.

Plan Q-2883-1

Bedrooms: 4	Baths: 3½
Space:	
Total living area:	2,883 sq. ft.
Garage:	458 sq. ft.
Exterior Wall Framing:	2x4
Foundation options:	
Slab. (Foundation & framing conversion diagram available — see order form.)	
Blueprint Price Code:	D

Plan Q-2883-1

Spectacular Sun-Drenched Home

- Sweeping hip rooflines, stucco siding with interesting quoins and banding, and interesting arched transom windows give this exciting sunbelt design a special flair.
- From an important 1½ story covered entry leading into the foyer, guests are greeted with a stunning view. A bay-window-wall opens the living room, straight ahead, to the covered patio, rear yard, and possible pool. To the left is an open-feeling formal dining room with columns and spectacular receding tray ceiling.
- The island kitchen overlooks the large family room with corner fireplace and breakfast bay.
- The master wing, well separated from the secondary bedrooms, features a coffered ceiling, sitting area with patio access, massive walk-in closet, and sun-drenched garden bath.

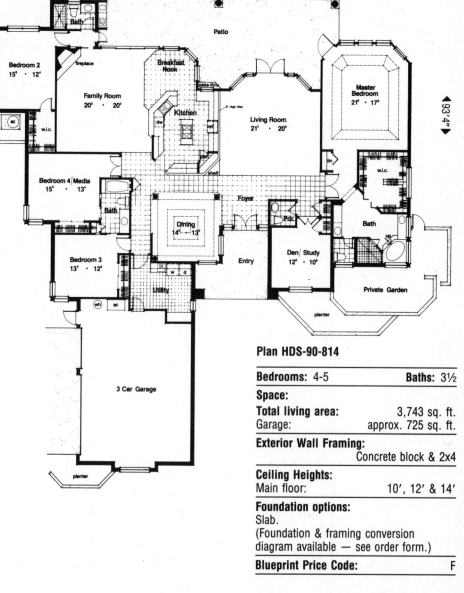

Plan HDS-90-814

Bedrooms: 4-5	Baths: 3½
Space:	
Total living area:	3,743 sq. ft.
Garage:	approx. 725 sq. ft.
Exterior Wall Framing:	
	Concrete block & 2x4
Ceiling Heights:	
Main floor:	10', 12' & 14'
Foundation options:	
Slab.	
(Foundation & framing conversion diagram available — see order form.)	
Blueprint Price Code:	F

Plan HDS-90-814

Sprawling, Substantial Ranch

- Here's another design that proves it pays to keep it simple.
- Clean lines and a straightforward floor plan make for solid, economical construction and easy-living comfort.
- A welcoming porch with columns and planters opens to a functional, attractive entryway, leading ahead to a magnificent family room or to a formal living/dining area at the right.
- The huge family room features a vaulted, beamed ceiling, impressive fireplace and hearth with a built-in wood box, plus built-in bookshelves and desk.
- The large, beautiful kitchen is between the formal dining room and informal eating area, and next to a convenient and spacious utility area, half-bath and garage entry.
- The majestic master suite includes a sumptuous private bath and huge walk-in closet.
- Three secondary bedrooms likewise have large closets, and share a second full bath.

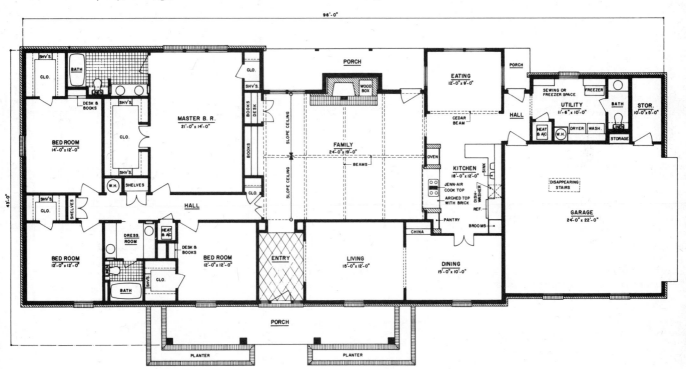

Plan E-2700

Bedrooms: 4	Baths: 2½

Space:

Total living area:	2,719 sq. ft.
Garage:	533 sq. ft.
Storage:	50 sq. ft.
Porches:	350 sq. ft.

Exterior Wall Framing: 2x6

Foundation options:
Crawlspace.
Slab.
(Foundation & framing conversion diagram available — see order form.)

Blueprint Price Code: D

Home Court Advantage

- A dramatic front courtyard takes center stage in this U-shaped ranch design. Plenty of windows and covered walkways take full advantage of the view into the courtyard.
- Double doors at the front entry open into a sunken living room with vaulted ceiling, corner fireplace and French doors to a rear patio.
- The formal dining room also has a vaulted ceiling and enjoys the living room fireplace.
- The kitchen/breakfast room has a half-wall opening into the family room, allowing conversation and a view of the second fireplace and rear covered patio.
- The lavish master suite is well separated from the three secondary bedrooms for privacy.

Plan Q-2762-1A

Bedrooms: 4	Baths: 3

Space:	
Total living area:	2,762 sq. ft.
Garage:	556 sq. ft.

Exterior Wall Framing:	2x4

Foundation options:
Slab.
(Foundation & framing conversion diagram available — see order form.)

Blueprint Price Code:	D

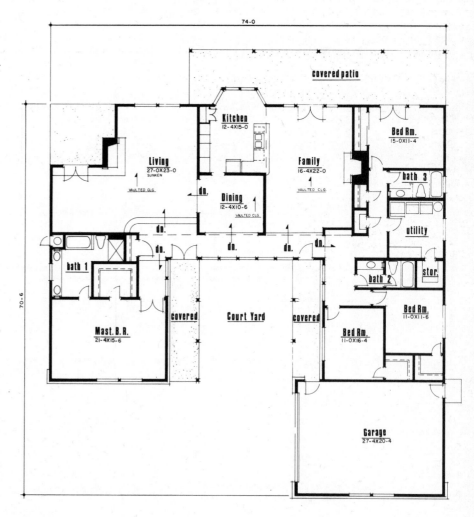

Plan Q-2762-1A

Solid Quality in a One-Story Design

- This roomy one-story presents four bedrooms, plus plenty of other space for living and entertaining.
- Large family room features exposed beams in a vaulted ceiling.
- Roomy kitchen adjoins a sunny raised eating area, and the utility room is close by.
- Spacious master bedroom includes a deluxe bath and large walk-in closet.
- Living and dining rooms join together to provide space for larger groups.

Plan E-2602	
Bedrooms: 4	**Baths:** 2½
Space:	
Total living area:	2,597 sq. ft.
Garage:	462 sq. ft.
Porches, storage:	394 sq. ft.
Exterior Wall Framing:	2x4

Foundation options:
Crawlspace.
Slab.
(Foundation & framing conversion diagram available — see order form.)

Blueprint Price Code:	D

Floor Plan

SHV'S
CLO.
SUNKEN TUB
UP
BATH
LINEN
SITTING AREA
PORCH
EATING
RAISED 6"
12' X 9'
WASH. DRYER
W.H.
STORAGE

DRESS
TURNED WOOD POST
HALL UTILITY
8' X 6'

KNEE SPACE
BOOKS
TURNED WOOD POST

BED ROOM
14' X 12'
MASTER BED RM.
21' X 14'
FAMILY ROOM
24' X 18'
VAULT
SINK
D.W.
SURF UNIT & HOOD
CLO.
SHV'S SHELVES
HEARTH
RAISED HEARTH
REF.
KIT
13' X 12'
OVEN
BRM'S
OVEN

W.H.
SHV'S CLO.
HALL
VAULT
SHV'S
BEAMS
PANTRY
GARAGE
22' X 21'

BED ROOM
12' X 12'
HEAT & AC
DRESS
BED ROOM
12' X 11'
DESK BOOKS
ENTRY
LIVING
14' X 12'
R/A

BATH
CLO.
CLO.
DINING
15' X 10'

PORCH

42'

94'

Angles Add Spark to Floor Plan

- Here's a one-story plan that provides plenty of space for active family living as well as business or personal entertaining.
- A majestic entry leads into a splendid sunken living room with fireplace, vaulted ceiling and built-in planter.
- A uniquely angled dining area is bathed in light from multiple windows and overlooks the living room.

- A stunning multi-sided kitchen includes a convenient island and adjoins a large pantry, breakfast nook and utility area.
- An incredible master suite boasts a magnificent bath, two huge walk-in closets and a striking bow window.
- A second bedroom also includes a large closet, and shares a walk-through bath with the parlor which could easily be a third bedroom, guest room or office.

Plan Q-3009-1A

Bedrooms: 2-3	**Baths:** 2½

Space:

Total living area:	3,009 sq. ft.
Garage:	632 sq. ft.

Exterior Wall Framing:	2x4

Foundation options:
Slab only.
(Foundation & framing conversion diagram available — see order form.)

Blueprint Price Code:	E

Plan Q-3009-1A

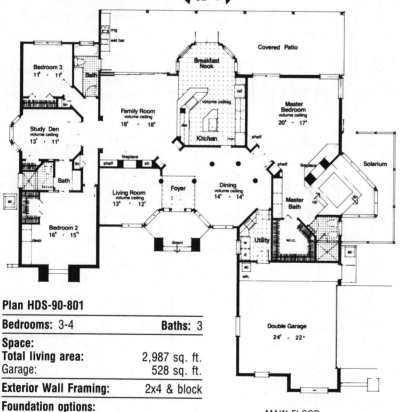

◀ 82'-4" ▶

◀ 80'-4" ▶

mg
wet bar
Covered Patio
Bedroom 3
11⁴ · 11⁵
Bath
Breakfast Nook
Family Room
18⁴ · 18⁵
volume ceiling
ref
Master Bedroom
volume ceiling
20⁰ · 17²
Study Den
volume ceiling
13⁴ · 11⁵
Kitchen
open
shelf
Bath
fireplace
shelf
sh
shelf
fireplace
Solarium
Living Room
volume ceiling
13⁴ · 12²
Foyer
Dining
volume ceiling
14⁴ · 14²
Master Bath
up
Bedroom 2
16⁴ · 15¹⁰
down
Utility
w.i.c.
w.i.c.
desk
ac
ac
wh.

Double Garage
24⁰ · 22⁰

MAIN FLOOR

Plan HDS-90-801

Bedrooms: 3-4	Baths: 3

Space:

Total living area:	2,987 sq. ft.
Garage:	528 sq. ft.

Exterior Wall Framing: 2x4 & block

Foundation options:
Slab only.
(Foundation & framing conversion diagram available — see order form.)

Blueprint Price Code: D

Gracious Mediterranean Style

- This design speaks of elegance and luxury both inside and out.
- A cloud shade and arched windows add elegance to the entrance.
- The foyer opens up to the breathtaking openness of high vaulted ceilings and a gorgeous octagonal dining room.
- The generously sized family room expands visually as the eye follows the high interior vaults.
- The kitchen also features a vaulted ceiling, and adjoins a nook which lends an open-air appearance to the area.
- The spectacular suite boasts a raised-hearth fireplace that's open to both the bath and bedroom sides.
- Bedroom 2 is spacious, and shares a connecting bath with the den, which could serve as a guest bedroom.
- Bedroom 3 adjoins another bath, and includes a large closet.
- A large covered patio across the back of the home includes a built-in wet bar and outdoor grill.

Plan HDS-90-801

Merging Kitchen, Nook, Family Room

- A covered entry, arched windows and stucco siding create a look and feel of grandeur.
- The sunken living room features a coved ceiling, fireplace and high arched windows.
- Opposite, the open dining room has vaulted ceilings and unique columns that allow a wider surrounding view.
- Double recessed doors lead to the luxurious master suite, offering his 'n her walk-in closets, large custom bath and an adjoining den and/or library.
- A jacuzzi tub, separate shower and two large vanities make up the attached master bath.
- The gourmet kitchen features two walk-in pantries, an island cooktop/eating bar, plus attached nook and family room.

Plan S-122089

Bedrooms: 3-4	**Baths: 2½**
Space:	
Total living area:	2,591 sq. ft.
Garage:	556 sq. ft.
Exterior Wall Framing:	2x6
Ceiling Heights:	
Upper floor:	9'
Main floor:	9'
Foundation options:	
Standard basement.	
Crawlspace.	
(Foundation & framing conversion diagram available — see order form.)	
Blueprint Price Code:	D

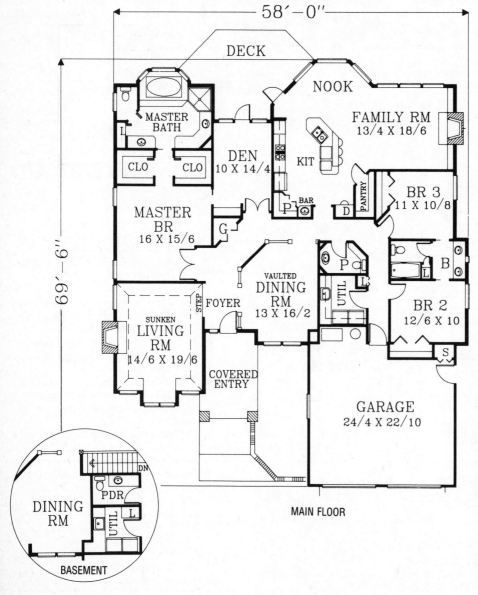

MAIN FLOOR

BASEMENT

TO ORDER THIS BLUEPRINT,
CALL TOLL-FREE 1-800-547-5570

Plan S-122089

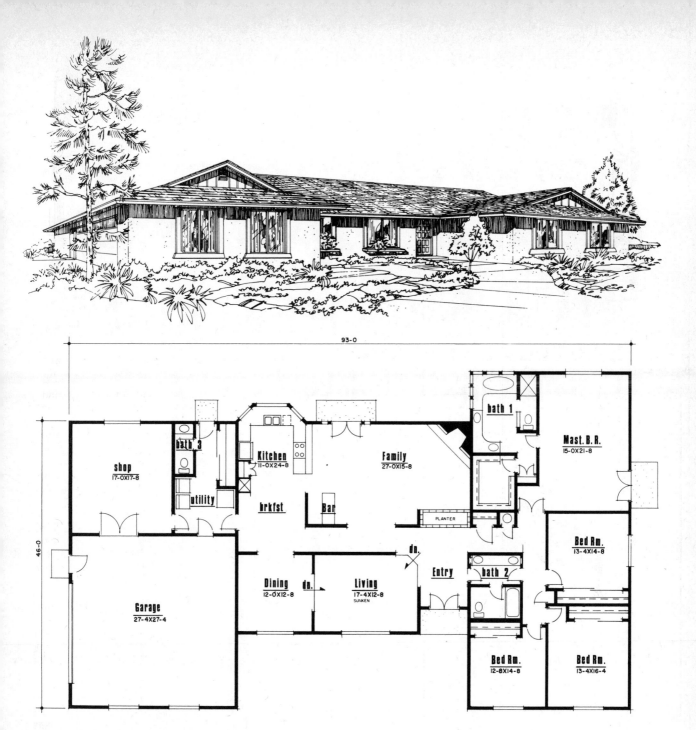

93-0

46-0

shop
17-0X17-8

bath 3

Kitchen
11-0X24-8

utility

brkfst

Bar

Family
27-0X15-8

PLANTER

bath 1

Mast. B. R.
15-0X21-8

Bed Rm.
13-4X14-8

Garage
27-4X27-4

Dining
12-0X12-8

dn.

Living
17-4X12-8
SUNKEN

dn.

Entry

bath 2

Bed Rm.
12-8X14-8

Bed Rm.
13-4X16-4

Multi-Purpose
Room Highlight

- Call it a shop, a hobby room, a home office — whatever you call it, the multi-purpose room in this plan is a delightful bonus. It is well separated from the main living areas for privacy and quiet, with the utility room as a buffer.
- A double-doored entry opens to a view into the sunken living room to the left, with the formal dining room beyond.
- Straight ahead of the entry, over a half-wall planter, lies the family room with corner fireplace, enjoyed from the kitchen as well.
- The four bedrooms of the sleeping wing are highlighted by a lavish master suite with double doors, private patio access, walk-in closet and garden bath.

Plan Q-2937-1A	
Bedrooms: 4	Baths: 2½
Space:	
Main floor:	2,937 sq. ft.
Garage:	747 sq. ft.
Exterior Wall Framing:	2x4

Foundation options:
Slab.
(Foundation & framing conversion diagram available — see order form.)

Blueprint Price Code: D

Plan Q-2937-1A

Spacious Living Room Features High Ceiling, Large Fireplace

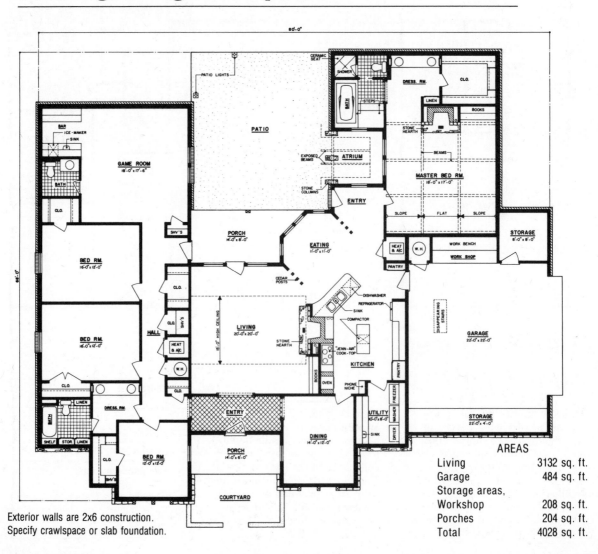

Exterior walls are 2x6 construction.
Specify crawlspace or slab foundation.

AREAS

Living	3132 sq. ft.
Garage	484 sq. ft.
Storage areas,	
Workshop	208 sq. ft.
Porches	204 sq. ft.
Total	4028 sq. ft.

Blueprint Price Code E
Plan E-3100

52'

Octagonal Dining Area, Deluxe Master Bedroom Suite

BATH

MASTER SUITE
18' x 16'

SLOPE CEILING
SKYLIGHT
SKKLIGHT

CLO.

PLAN E-1912
(WITHOUT BASEMENT)

CLO. CLO.

PORCH
14' x 10'
SKYLIGHT

BED RM.
14' x 12'

76'

KITCHEN
SLOPE CEILING
REF.
SKYLIGHT

DINING
14' x 14'

SLOPE CEILING

OVEN D.W.
COOK TOP
BAR
PANT.

BATH
VANITY
LIN

LIVING
20' x 18'

HALL
STOR

SLOPE CEILING

STORAGE
10' x 6'
W.H.

UTIL
8' x 6'
DRY WASH

STOR

CLO.

HEAT & A/C

CLO.

GARAGE
22' x 22'

ATTIC STAIRS

PORCH
10' x 5'

BED RM.
14' x 12'

SEAT

Exterior walls are 2x6 construction.
Specify crawlspace or slab foundation.

AREAS

Living	1946 sq. ft.
Porches	282 sq. ft.
Garage & Storage	562 sq. ft.
Total	2790 sq. ft.

Distinctive One-Level Four-Bedroom

Finished in vertical and angled wood siding, this distinctive one-story four-bedroom passive solar design is a great energy saver, which can be oriented to suit a variety of sites and topography. Sunlight penetrates deep into the rear zone of the house. Solar energy is absorbed and settled in the ceramic-tiled thermal floor for nighttime radiation; heat generated in the sun room is shared with the adjoining areas.

To guard against heat waste, walls and ceilings are well-insulated; entrance vestibule functions as a protective air lock; double-layer glazing is specified; high-efficiency fireplace complements the informal family room.

For summer cooling, the design incorporates a row of clerestory windows that open to create an air current, while roof overhangs shade the interior.

Inside, the bright, cheerful plan focuses on a sun room that glows with natural light. U-shaped kitchen serves the formal dining room and the cozy breakfast niche. Tucked in a quiet wing are four bedrooms. Master suite features a dressing area, fenced private terrace and a personal bath that includes a whirlpool tub. Living area, excluding the sun room, is 1,948 sq. ft.; optional basement is 1,264 sq. ft.; garage, mud room, etc. 530 sq. ft.

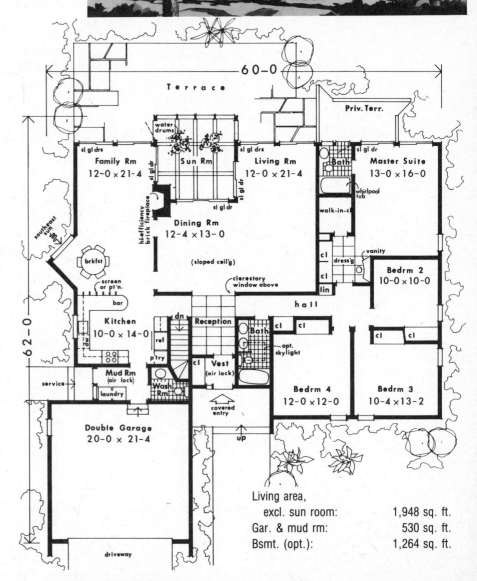

Living area,
excl. sun room: 1,948 sq. ft.
Gar. & mud rm: 530 sq. ft.
Bsmt. (opt.): 1,264 sq. ft.

Blueprint Price Code B
Plan K-502-J

Soaring Spaces under Vaulted Ceilings

- A dignified exterior and a gracious, spacious interior combine to make this an outstanding plan for today's families.
- The living, dining, family rooms and breakfast nook all feature soaring vaulted ceilings.
- An interior atrium provides an extra touch of elegance, with its sunny space for growing plants and sunbathing.
- The master suite is first class all the way, with a spacious sleeping area, opulent bath, large skylight and enormous walk-in closet.
- A gorgeous kitchen includes a large work/cooktop island, corner sink with large corner windows and plenty of counter space.

Plans P-7697-4A & -4D

Bedrooms: 3	Baths: 2

Space:

Main floor (crawlspace version):	2,003 sq. ft.
Main floor (basement version):	2,030 sq. ft.
Basement:	2,015 sq. ft.
Garage:	647 sq. ft.

Exterior Wall Framing:	2x4

Foundation options:
Daylight basement (Plan P-7697-4D).
Crawlspace (Plan P-7697-4A).
(Foundation & framing conversion diagram available — see order form.)

Blueprint Price Code:	C

Floor Plan

63'0"

PATIO

COVERED PATIO

SUNKEN TUB · DRESSING · SKYLIGHT

VAULTED NOOK · D.W.

WALK IN W'ROBE · SKYLHT · SHWR

MASTER 12/0x15/0

VAULTED FAMILY RM. 21/6x16/10

KITCHEN 10/0x14/8 · REF

WOODSTOVE

DESK

ATRIUM

VAULTED DINING RM. 12/0x10/0

BEDRM. 2 10/8x11/0 · LIN · LIN

STEP

SEAT · SEAT

BATH

UTILITY · W · D

VAULTED ENTRY

STEP

BEDRM. 3 11/8x10/0

TUB · F · WH

VAULTED SUNKEN LIVING RM. 13/4x17/0

GARAGE 31/4 x 20/8

61'0"

RAILING · DN

BATH · W · D

VAULTED ENTRY

PLAN P-7697-4D
WITH DAYLIGHT BASEMENT

Plans P-7697-4A & -4D

**TO ORDER THIS BLUEPRINT,
CALL TOLL-FREE 1-800-547-5570**
(prices and details on pp. 12-15.)

Ideal for Formal Entertaining

This lovely 1,940 sq. ft. French Provincial design features a formal foyer flanked by the living room on one side and the dining room on the other. A family room with a raised-hearth fireplace and double doors to the patio, and the L-shaped island kitchen with breakfast bay and open counter to the family room, allow for more casual living.

Adjacent to the breakfast bay is a utility room with outside entrance.

The master suite includes one double closet and a compartmentalized bath with walk-in closet, step-up garden tub, double vanity and linen closet. Two front bedrooms and a second full bath with linen closet complete the design. A recessed entry and circular porch add to the formal exterior.

Total living area: 1,940 sq. ft.
(Not counting basement or garage)

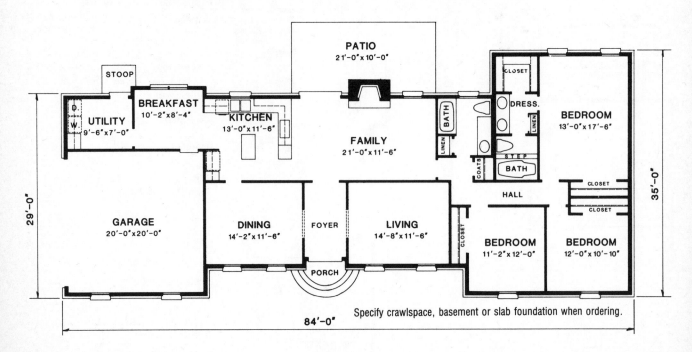

Specify crawlspace, basement or slab foundation when ordering.

Blueprint Price Code B
Plan C-8103

Southern Country

- This home is distinctly Southern Country in style, from its wide front porch to its multi-paned and shuttered windows.
- The living room boasts a 12′ cathedral ceiling, a fireplace and French doors to the rear patio.
- The dining room is open, but defined by three massive columns with overhead beams.
- The delightful kitchen/nook area is spacious and well-planned for both efficiency and pleasant kitchen working conditions.
- A handy utility room and half-bath are on either side of a short hallway leading to the carport.
- The master suite offers his and hers walk-in closets and an incredible bath which incorporates a plant shelf above the garden tub.

Plan J-86140	
Bedrooms: 3	**Baths: 2½**
Total living area:	2,177 sq. ft.
Basement:	2,177 sq. ft.
Carport:	440 sq. ft.
Storage:	120 sq. ft.
Porch:	233 sq. ft.
Exterior Wall Framing:	2x4
Ceiling Heights:	9′

Foundation options:
Standard basement.
Crawlspace.
Slab.
(Foundation & framing conversion diagram available — see order form.)

Blueprint Price Code:	C

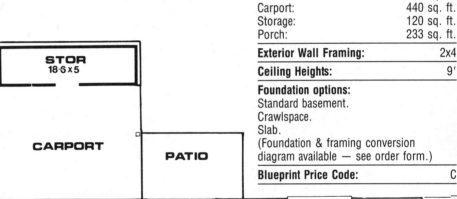

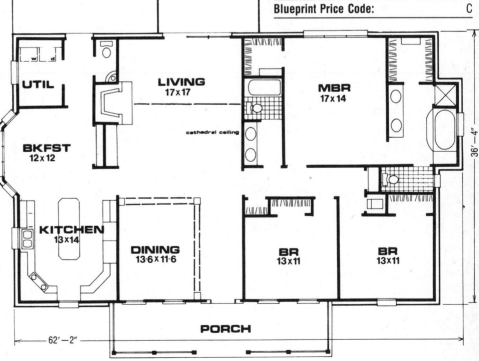

Plan J-86140

"Adult Retreat" in Master Bedroom Suite

- Exciting living room is virtually open on three sides.
- Wet bar lies between living area and large kitchen, which offers an eating bar and island cooktop.

- Elegant master suite features sitting area and attached bath with romantic angled tub covered with skylight and flanked by his 'n hers vanities.

Plan E-2106

Bedrooms: 3	Baths: 2

Space:	
Total living area:	2,177 sq. ft.
Basement:	approx. 2,177 sq. ft.
Garage and storage:	570 sq. ft.
Porches:	211 sq. ft.

Exterior Wall Framing:	2x4

Foundation options:
Standard basement.
Crawlspace.
Slab.
(Foundation & framing conversion diagram available — see order form.)

Blueprint Price Code:	C

**NOTE:
The above photographed home may have been modified by the homeowner. Please refer to floor plan and/or drawn elevation shown for actual blueprint details.

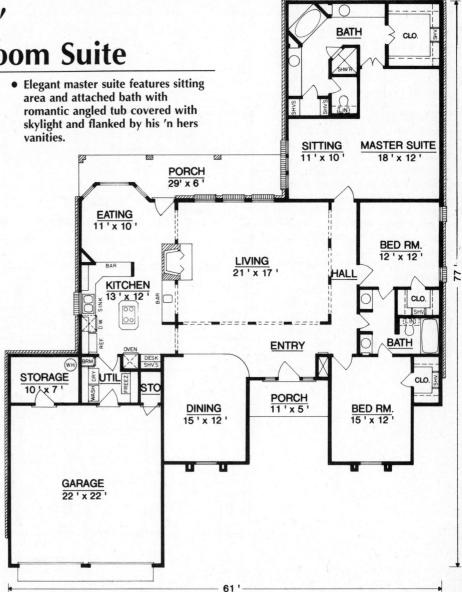

Plan E-2106

TO ORDER THIS BLUEPRINT,
CALL TOLL-FREE 1-800-547-5570

(prices and details on pp. 12-15.)

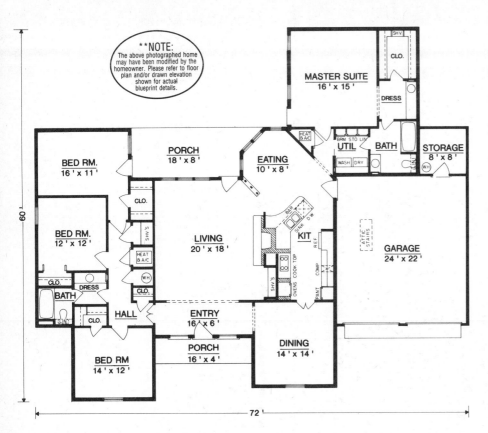

NOTE:
The above photographed home may have been modified by the homeowner. Please refer to floor plan and/or drawn elevation shown for actual blueprint details.

MASTER SUITE
16' x 15'

SHV
CLO.

DRESS

HEAT B A/C

BRM STO LIN

BATH

STORAGE
8' x 8'

UTIL

WASH DRY

LIN
WH

BED RM.
16' x 11'

PORCH
18' x 8'

EATING
10' x 8'

CLO.

SHV'S

LIVING
20' x 18'

KIT

SINK DW

REF

ATTIC STAIRS

GARAGE
24' x 22'

BED RM.
12' x 12'

HEAT B A/C

WH

CLO.

SHV'S

OVENS COOK TOP

COMP

PANT

BATH

DRESS

CLO.

CLO.

HALL

ENTRY
16' x 6'

BED RM
14' x 12'

PORCH
16' x 4'

DINING
14' x 14'

60'

72'

Luxury Living on One Level

- Exterior presents a classic air of quality and distinction in design.
- Spacious one-story interior provides space for family life and entertaining.
- The large central living room boasts a 13' ceiling and large hearth.
- A roomy formal dining room adjoins the foyer.
- The gorgeous kitchen/nook combination provides a sunny eating area along with an efficient and attractive kitchen with eating bar and abundant counter space.
- The master suite is isolated from the other bedrooms for more privacy, and includes a luxurious bath and dressing area.
- Three additional bedrooms make up the left side of the plan, and share a second bath.
- The garage is off the kitchen for maximum convenience in carrying in groceries; also note the storage space off the garage.

Plan E-2208

Bedrooms: 4	Baths: 2
Total living area:	2,252 sq. ft.
Garage:	528 sq. ft.
Storage:	64 sq. ft.
Exterior Wall Framing:	2x6

Typical Ceiling Heights:
8' unless otherwise noted.

Foundation options:
Standard basement.
Crawlspace.
Slab.
(Foundation & framing conversion diagram available — see order form.)

Blueprint Price Code: C

Plan E-2208

Isolated Master Bedroom Suite

Exterior walls are 2x6 construction.
Specify basement, crawlspace or slab foundation.

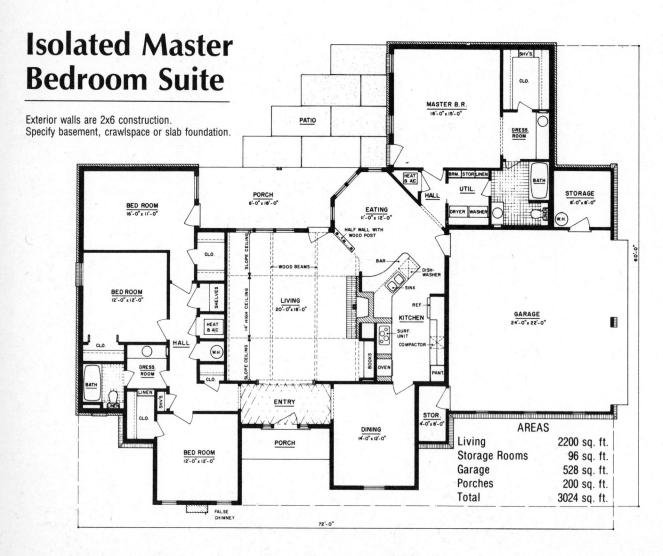

AREAS	
Living	2200 sq. ft.
Storage Rooms	96 sq. ft.
Garage	528 sq. ft.
Porches	200 sq. ft.
Total	3024 sq. ft.

Blueprint Price Code C
Plan E-2206

High Luxury in One-Story Plan

- 12' ceilings are featured in the entryway and living room.
- 400 sq. ft. living room boasts a massive fireplace and access to the rear porch.
- Corridor-style kitchen has angled eating bar and convenient nearby laundry facilities.
- Master suite incorporates unusual bath arrangement consisting of an angled whirlpool tub and separate shower.
- Secondary bedrooms are zoned for privacy and climate control.

Plan E-2302

Bedrooms: 4	Baths: 2

Space:	
Total living area:	2,396 sq. ft.
Garage and storage:	590 sq. ft.
Porches:	216 sq. ft.

Exterior Wall Framing:	2x6

Foundation options:
Standard basement.
Crawlspace.
Slab.
(Foundation & framing conversion diagram available — see order form.)

Blueprint Price Code:	C

Plan E-2302

Photo by Mark Englund/HomeStyles

NOTE:
The above photographed home may have been modified by the homeowner. Please refer to floor plan and/or drawn elevation shown for actual blueprint details.

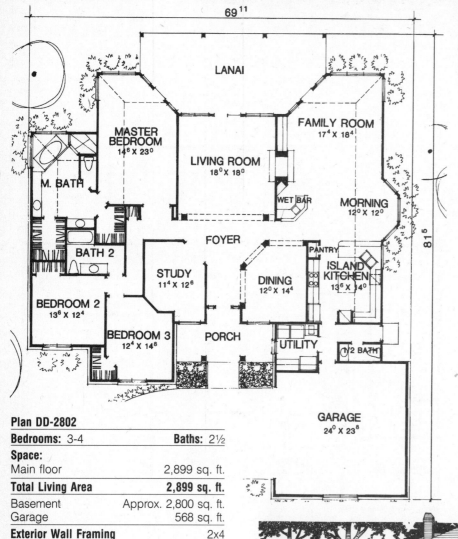

Unique Inside and Out

- This plan gives new dimension to one-story living. The exterior features graceful arched windows and a sweeping roofline The interior is marked by unusual angles and curves.
- The living areas are clustered around a large "lanai," or covered porch. French doors in the master bedroom and the family room angle toward the porch.
- Extras include the two-way fireplace, warming both the family room and the living room. The home's expansiveness is enhanced by ceilings that slope up to 10 feet. Columns frame both the living room and the formal dining room, echoing the columns of the porches.
- The island kitchen and the morning room are open to the family room, which features a wet bar. The living room is highlighted by French doors and arched transom windows.
- The formal dining room and the study are stationed near the front of the home, away from the major activity areas.
- The master bedroom includes an irresistible bath with a spa tub, dual vanities, two walk-in closets and a separate shower.
- Two more good-sized bedrooms share another full bath.
- A large utility room and a half-bath are conveniently located between the kitchen and the garage.

Plan DD-2802

Bedrooms: 3-4	**Baths:** 2½

Space:

Main floor	2,899 sq. ft.
Total Living Area	**2,899 sq. ft.**
Basement	Approx. 2,800 sq. ft.
Garage	568 sq. ft.
Exterior Wall Framing	**2x4**

Foundation options:
Partial basement
Crawlspace
Slab
(Foundation & framing conversion diagram available—see order form.)

Blueprint Price Code	**D**

Plan DD-2802

Southern Colonial with Authentic Style

- Porch columns, brick siding, and shuttered windows all contribute to this classic facade.
- This spacious home features large but detailed rooms, including a formal dining room and grand-sized

family room and living room, each with fireplaces.
- King-sized closets, large baths, and generous bedrooms make up the sleeping quarters, well separated from the main living areas.

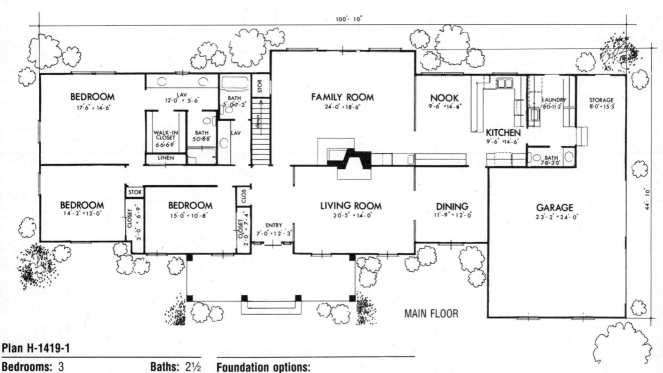

MAIN FLOOR

Plan H-1419-1

Bedrooms: 3	Baths: 2½
Total living area:	2,558 sq. ft.
Basement:	approx. 2,558 sq. ft.
Garage:	556 sq. ft.
Exterior Wall Framing:	2x6

Foundation options:
Standard basement only.
(Foundation & framing conversion diagram available — see order form.)

Blueprint Price Code: D

Plan H-1419-1

"Down-Home" Country Flavor

AREAS

Living	2522 sq. ft.
Garage	484 sq. ft.
Porches	444 sq. ft.
Storage Rooms	90 sq. ft.
Total	3540 sq. ft.

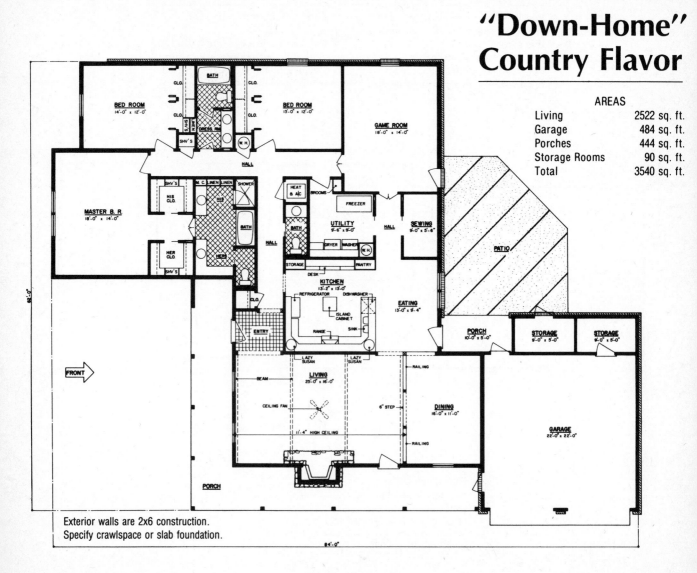

Exterior walls are 2x6 construction.
Specify crawlspace or slab foundation.

Blueprint Price Code D
Plan E-2502

Simple Exterior, Luxurious Interior

- Modest and unassuming on the exterior, this design provides an elegant and spacious interior.
- Highlight of the home is undoubtedly the vast Great Room/Dining area, with its vaulted ceiling, massive hearth and big bay windows.
- An exceptionally fine master suite is also included, with a large sleeping area, luxurious bath and big walk-in closet.
- A beautiful kitchen is joined by a bright bay-windowed breakfast nook; also note the large pantry.
- The lower level encompasses two more bedrooms and a generously sized game room and bar.

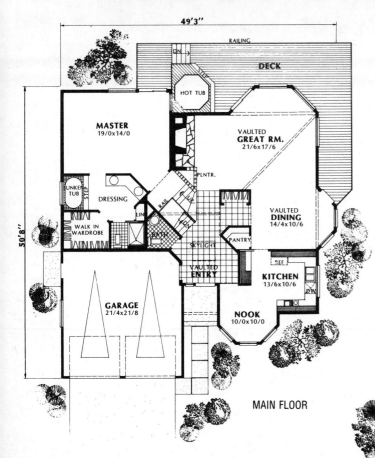

MAIN FLOOR

BASEMENT

Plan P-6595-3D

Bedrooms: 3	Baths: 2½

Space:

Main floor:	1,530 sq. ft.
Lower level:	1,145 sq. ft.
Total living area:	**2,675 sq. ft.**
Garage:	462 sq. ft.

Exterior Wall Framing:	2x6

Foundation options:
Daylight basement only.
(Foundation & framing conversion diagram available — see order form.)

Blueprint Price Code:	D

Plan P-6595-3D

Dramatic Contemporary Takes Advantage of Slope

- Popular plan puts problem building site to work by taking advantage of the slope to create a dramatic and pleasant home.
- Spacious vaulted living/dining area is bathed in natural light from cathedral windows facing the front and clerestory windows at the peak.
- Big kitchen includes pantry and abundant counter space.
- Three main-level bedrooms are isolated for more peace and quiet.
- Lower level includes large recreation room, a fourth bedroom, third bath, laundry area and extra space for a multitude of other uses.

Photo by Kevin Robinson

NOTE:
The above photographed home may have been modified by the homeowner. Please refer to floor plan and/or drawn elevation shown for actual blueprint details.

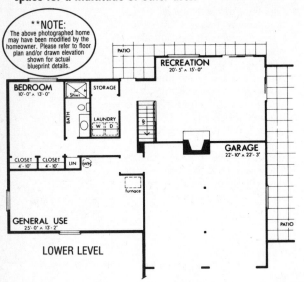

LOWER LEVEL

BEDROOM 10'-0" x 13'-0"
STORAGE
BATH
Shwr
LAUNDRY
W D
RECREATION 20'-5" x 15'-0"
PATIO
GARAGE 22'-10" x 22'-3"
CLOSET 4'-10"
CLOSET 4'-10"
LIN
WH
furnace
GENERAL USE 25'-0" x 13'-2"
PATIO

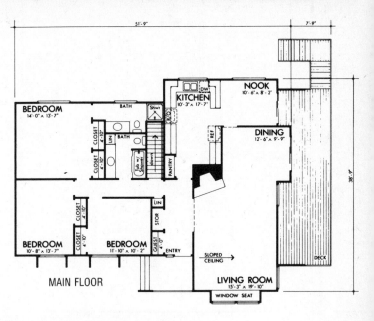

MAIN FLOOR

51'-9"
7'-9"
38'-9"
BEDROOM 14'-0" x 13'-7"
KITCHEN 10'-3" x 17'-7"
DW
NOOK 10'-6" x 8'-2"
REF
DINING 12'-6" x 9'-9"
BATH
Shwr
CLOSET 4'-10"
CLOSET 4'-10"
BATH
LIN
Tub w/ Shower
PANTRY
CLOSET 4'-10"
BEDROOM 10'-8" x 13'-7"
CLOSET 4'-10"
BEDROOM 11'-0" x 10'-2"
GUEST
STOR
LIN
ENTRY
SLOPED CEILING
LIVING ROOM 15'-3" x 19'-10"
WINDOW SEAT
DECK

Plan H-2045-5	
Bedrooms: 4	**Baths:** 3

Space:	
Main floor:	1,602 sq. ft.
Lower floor:	1,133 sq. ft.
Total living area:	2,735 sq. ft.
Garage:	508 sq. ft.

Exterior Wall Framing:	2x4

Foundation options:
Daylight basement only.
(Foundation & framing conversion diagram available — see order form.)

Blueprint Price Code:	D

Plan H-2045-5

REAR VIEW

Spacious Western Ranch

- A three-bedroom sleeping wing is separated from the balance of the home, with the master suite featuring a raised tub below skylights and a walk-in dressing room.
- Sunken living room is enhanced by a vaulted ceiling and fireplace with raised hearth.
- Family room is entered from the central hall through double doors; a wet bar and a second fireplace grace this gathering spot.
- Kitchen has functional L-shaped arrangement, attached nook, and pantry.

Plan H-3701-1A

Bedrooms: 4	Baths: 3½
Total living area:	3,735 sq. ft.
Garage:	830 sq. ft.
Exterior Wall Framing:	2x4

Foundation options:
Crawlspace only.
(Foundation & framing conversion diagram available — see order form.)

Blueprint Price Code:	F

DECK

110'-0"

BEDROOM 16'-6" x 20'-0"

wdw. seat

BATH 12'-7" x 12'-2" skylights

raised tub

WC

Shower

linen

dresser

raised hearth

WALK-IN DRESSING ROOM 11'-3" x 7'-6"

furnace

SUNKEN LIVING ROOM 30'-0" x 20'-0"

vaulted ceiling

folding screen

DINING 15'-9" x 14'-0"

steps down

clerestory window

WET BAR

KITCHEN 15'-4" x 11'-6"

ref.

PANTRY

CLOSET

LINEN

BEDROOM 12'-0" x 14'-6"

STOR

BATH

LAV

wdw. seat

BEDROOM 12'-0" x 14'-6"

wdw. seat

POWDER ROOM

CLOSET

CLOSET

ENTRY 15'-3" x 15'-3"

steps down

FAMILY ROOM 15'-0" x 24'-0"

NOOK 11'-6" x 10'-0"

DECK

Shower

BATH

BEDROOM 19'-0" x 13'-0"

wdw. seat

LAUNDRY skylight

D W

furnace

CLOSET

STORAGE

THREE CAR GARAGE 31'-10" x 23'-8"

64'-0"

Plan H-3701-1A

Photo by Mark Englund/HomeStyles

Plan E-2004

Bedrooms: 3		**Baths:** 2

Space:

Total living area:	2,023 sq. ft.
Garage:	484 sq. ft.
Storage & Porches:	423 sq. ft.

Exterior Wall Framing:	2x6

Foundation options:
Crawlspace.
Slab.
(Foundation & framing conversion diagram available — see order form.)

Blueprint Price Code: C

Exciting Floor Plan In Traditional French Garden Home

- Creative, angular design permits an open floor plan.
- Living and dining rooms open to a huge covered porch.
- Kitchen, living and dining rooms feature impressive 12' ceilings accented by extensive use of glass.
- Informal eating nook faces a delightful courtyard.
- Luxurious master bath offers a whirlpool tub, shower, and walk-in closet.
- Secondary bedrooms also offer walk-in closets.

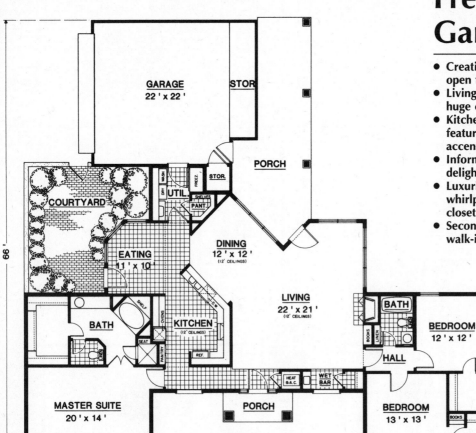

**NOTE:
The above photographed home may have been modified by the homeowner. Please refer to floor plan and/or drawn elevation shown for actual blueprint details.

Plan E-2004